Da Capo Press Music Reprint Series
GENERAL EDITOR
FREDERICK FREEDMAN
VASSAR COLLEGE

THE RISE OF ENGLISH OPERA

The Opera Rehearsal by Marco Ricci

This sketch in oils (18 in. by 22 in.) was painted about 1708 and shows a group of instrumentalists and singers rehearsing an opera—probably *Pyrrhus and Demetrius* by Alessandro Scarlatti, the first performance of which in England was given at the Queen's Theatre in the Haymarket (December 14, 1708). Reading from centre to right, Nicolo Haym, the composer, is seated at the harpsichord; the *castrato* Nicolini, then newly arrived in England, is standing by him; Margherita de l'Epine, the Italian soprano who had come to England in 1692, holds a fan; Mrs. Tofts, the English singer, is touching the harpsichord; 'the Baroness' (so-called), mother of Margherita, is holding a muff; Dr. Pepusch, Margherita's husband, is facing her; and J. J. Heidegger, the Swiss impressario, is seated with a score. Among the instrumentalists, Festini is playing the first violin and Corporali the violoncello.

THE RISE OF
ENGLISH OPERA

BY ERIC WALTER WHITE

INTRODUCTION BY BENJAMIN BRITTEN
NEW FOREWORD BY THE AUTHOR

DA CAPO PRESS · NEW YORK · 1972

Library of Congress Cataloging in Publication Data

White, Eric Walter, 1905-
  The rise of English opera.

  (Da Capo Press music reprint series)
  Reprinted from the 1st ed., New York, 1951.
  Bibliography: p.
  1. Opera, English—History and criticism.
  2. Operas—Bibliography. I. Title.
ML1731.W6   1972   782.1'0942   78-87683
ISBN 0-306-71709-3

This Da Capo Press edition of *The Rise of English Opera*
is an unabridged republication of the first edition
published in New York and London in 1951. It is reprinted
by special arrangement with The Philosophical Library, Inc.

Published by Da Capo Press, Inc.
A Subsidiary of Plenum Publishing Corporation
227 West 17th Street, New York, New York 10011

FOREWORD TO THE REPRINT EDITION

This book arose out of a conviction that visitors to Great Britain during the Festival of Britain, 1951, would be interested to read an illustrated study of the new English operas that had appeared since the end of the Second World War— a comparatively modest project, but one that grew in size and scope as soon as I realized that such a study would have to be set in the context of the history of English opera. At that point I discovered that serious histories of opera in general paid scant attention to English opera in particular, and that the authors of studies of British music usually betrayed signs of nervous insecurity when they found music being written for the theater instead of the church or concert hall. This meant that I had perforce to embark on a research campaign on my own, and with comparatively little time in which to carry it out.

The final result was an improvement on my original plan, because at least it presented the important postwar renaissance of English opera in its proper perspective; but the book inevitably bears marks of the haste with which it was written. To give only one example, it would be difficult to claim complete accuracy for the short list of English operas and semi-operas in Appendix A. Nevertheless, the greater part of the book is reasonably reliable, except for the entries for the final year (*viz.* 1951). These were based on advance information which was correct at the time of going to press; but in the event, dates and places of opera productions were changed, and in one case a title was altered at the last moment. As this reprint is a facsimile of the first edition, correcting these and other mistakes has not been possible; but those readers who wish at least to have a cor-

rect list of the English operas produced in 1951 are referred
to my article, "A Decade of English Opera, 1951–1960,"
printed in *Theatre Notebook* XV, 4, 1961.

E.W.W.

THE RISE OF ENGLISH OPERA

THE RISE
OF ENGLISH
OPERA

ERIC WALTER WHITE

WITH AN INTRODUCTION BY
BENJAMIN BRITTEN

1951
LONDON : JOHN LEHMANN

FIRST PUBLISHED IN 1951 BY
JOHN LEHMANN LTD
6 HENRIETTA STREET LONDON W.C.2
MADE AND PRINTED IN GREAT BRITAIN BY
PURNELL AND SONS LTD
PAULTON (SOMERSET) AND LONDON
SET IN 12PT. BEMBO, 1½PT. LEADED

to

PETER BROOK

with admiration and

in friendship

THIS book sets out to give an account of English opera over a period of three centuries or more; and English opera is here defined as a stage action with vocal and instrumental music written by a British composer to an English libretto.

The title is a challenge. It would be idle to pretend that the course of English opera has always been one of smooth and steady development—the story unfolded in this book shows otherwise—but the progress made in recent years is so encouraging as to justify the suggestion of a general upward trend. Whatever faults, disappointments and disasters there may have been in the past, the auguries are more favourable now than at any other period.

There is a large audience in this country for opera in general, and its numbers appear to be growing. An increasing proportion are devotees of opera in English, and from these are drawn the supporters of English opera. Contemporary British composers appear to be anxious to work in this art-form, which in its present guise is a comparative newcomer in the twenty-five-centuries-old stream of European culture. Its potentialities have certainly not been exhausted by the experiments of the last 350 years; and the international success of Benjamin Britten's recent operas has shown that this country can rightly claim to be in the forefront of twentieth-century operatic progress. Added to this is the fact that for the first time in our history there is the possibility of reasonable security and permanence for a limited number of our opera houses and opera companies. The attitude of the State has changed from complete indifference to active interest and support.

This book does not pretend to be a comprehensive history of English opera. Such a work, when it comes to be written, will cover several volumes, the first of which appeared nearly a quarter of a century ago—I refer to Edward J. Dent's *Foundations of English Opera*. As a survey, however, this book sketches the main incidents of the life-story of English opera from *The Siege of Rhodes* (1656) to *Billy Budd* (1951). It is concerned with organisation and management, with composers and librettists rather than singers and conductors, and seeks to illustrate the workings of the operatic principle rather than to summarise librettos or analyse musical scores. Comment and criticism have, as far as possible, been drawn from contemporary or near-contemporary sources.

A considerable amount of material has been relegated to the appendices.

Appendix A is a list of nearly six hundred English operas and semi-operas from the seventeenth century to the present day. Any such list is bound to be selective and to reflect the compiler's personal bias. In my case, although I have been anxious to keep the emphasis on thorough-composed opera rather than light opera, or ballad opera, or comic opera, or romantic opera, or whatever other title English semi-opera may have assumed at different periods, I have no wish to decry semi-opera, which has undoubtedly played a most important part in the history of English opera. This means that, while a measure of completeness has been aimed at in the list of operas, the semi-operas have been arbitrarily selected. Other rules of thumb that have been followed in making this list are set out in the introduction to the Appendix.

Appendix B takes nine important foreign opera composers and shows when and where their operas were first given in this country.

Appendix C records the pioneer work of the three main existing companies—the Carl Rosa, Sadler's Wells and Covent Garden—in presenting foreign operas in English.

The purpose of Appendix D is to give samples of London's operatic fare in five arbitrarily chosen years each roughly half a century apart. The different works (which include a number of musicals) reflect the audiences' changing tastes. An interesting sidelight is thrown on those London theatres where opera has been presented at various times.

Appendix E is a note on the special contribution made by amateurs and students during the present century.

Appendix F is a select bibliography. Taken together with the bibliography of English opera to 1911 given in Cecil Forsyth's *Music and Nationalism*, it could form the nucleus of a comprehensive bibliography on this subject.

These Appendices are useful mainly as basic records of English opera, opera in English and opera in Great Britain. In compiling them, I have been indebted to the late Dr. Alfred Loewenberg, whose monumental *Annals of Opera* has been my continual source of reference. It is with sincere gratitude that I acknowledge his kindness, shortly before his death, in reading some of my material in draft and allowing me to make use of his researches. But the fact that more than half the operas listed in Appendix A are not included in his *Annals* should be sufficient to show that I have not followed him blindly, but have gone to numerous other sources in an attempt to make my lists as comprehensive as possible.

In a work of this kind there must naturally be many particular acknowledgments of indebtedness. But, in addition, there are some persons whose names would not normally appear, but who in earlier years helped to direct my interest and affection to the theatre in general and opera in particular, and whom I should like to take this opportunity of thanking.

First, my mother, whose impromptu and immensely spirited rendering of the role of Carmen in our drawing-room gave me as a boy an impression of that opera that no subsequent stage performance has ever completely effaced.

Next, Douglas Cleverdon, who in the summer of 1925 introduced me to Diaghilev's Russian Ballet (*Le Train Bleu* at the Coliseum with the monumental Picasso act-drop) and opened my eyes to the wonders of design and colour on the stage.

Then Edmund A. Davies, who has experienced and can communicate all the enjoyments of the true amateur of opera, and who helped me to share the delights of the Glastonbury Festival and other kindred performances in the West Country.

Finally, Lotte Reiniger, who in September 1928 introduced me to *Die Dreigroschenoper* by Brecht and Weill at the Theater am Schiffbauerdamm, Berlin, and three years later accompanied me to the Städtische Oper to see Carl Ebert's unforgettable production of Verdi's *Macbeth*.

When I came to write this book, information was readily given by many people whom I had occasion to consult, including:

Professor Edgar L. Bainton	Mr. R. J. Forbes
Mr. Rutland Boughton	Mr. Arthur Hammond
Dr. Ernest Bullock	Mrs. N. Phillips
Mr. John Christie	Mr. Norman Tucker
Professor Walter J. Dilling	Mr. David Webster
Dr. Christopher Edmunds	Mr. Michael Wood

Useful and sometimes valuable material was placed at my disposition by:

Miss Bridget D'Oyly Carte	Mr. John Piper
Mr. Edward J. Chadfield	Dr. Martin Shaw
Mr. Peter Gellhorn	Mr. Richard Southern
Mr. J. L. Hodgkinson	Dr. W. K. Stanton
Mr. George Howard	Mr. Michael Tippett

My debt to Professor Edward J. Dent is particularly great. He has helped me unstintedly by wise advice, stimulating commentary and careful correction.

A number of persons carried out special searches: Mr. Ifan Kyrle Fletcher for suitable illustrative material; Herr Hans Rutz for particulars of the Viennese productions of certain operas by Storace and Hatton; the Earl of Mount Edgcumbe for the manuscript score of his great-grandfather's opera *Zenobia*; and the Manager of Barclay's Bank, Pall Mall (the successors of Messrs. Ransom & Co.), to see if any trace remained in their records of the manuscript of the uncompleted opera by Rossini that was supposed to have been deposited there in 1824. Dr. R. S. Thatcher, on behalf of the Royal Academy of Music, generously allowed me to photograph the manuscript score of Purcell's *The Fairy*

Queen that is in the Academy's library. Mr. Gordon Craig, with the utmost goodwill, delved into his notebooks and memory to satisfy my curiosity about his production of *Dido and Aeneas* half a century ago.

Mr. Benjamin Britten has done me the signal honour of finding time in the midst of the composition of *Billy Budd* to write a special introduction. This is more than a mere act of kindness on his part. It is yet another sign of his dedication to the cause of English opera and his belief in its ultimate triumph.

All these I thank for their help and kindness.

To Miss Elizabeth Austen, who has been responsible for collecting and checking most of the material for the Appendices, I owe a special debt of gratitude. Without her researches this part of the book would have been greatly impoverished.

No one is more conscious than myself of the faults and imperfections of this work; but if it draws attention to the neglected story of English opera and helps indirectly to revive the native tradition and stimulate interest in new English operas, it will have served its purpose.

E. W. W.

London, November, 1950.

INTRODUCTION

I WELCOME this finely detailed study of English Opera. English opera always seems to me, perhaps too hopefully, the Cinderella of the arts. This book makes it quite clear why the poor girl is having to wait so long for her handsome Prince. The three things English opera needs, as does any opera, are business organisation (including cash), public goodwill, and composers to write new operas. Never yet in this country have these three things coincided. Mr. White describes the launching of many admirable enterprises, good teams of singers engaged (there always seems to be good material available if not the good artistic direction to develop it)—and then the public response fails. We read of good composers with exciting ideas for operas —and the backers are not impressed. And we read of flourishing seasons failing, because there are no new operas. It makes gloomy if fascinating reading!

But why should anyone mind?—who cares if there is English opera? We are told so often that Italian and German, even Russian and French, opera is superior to ours (true, in spite of *Dido and Aeneas*), and people have been known to say that the English language is ugly when sung (quite untrue, although it is more difficult to manage than, say, Italian). All the same, if we continue to perform opera, and to perform it in a language that most of the audience does not understand, one of the essentials of opera is lost. It is not enough to know *roughly* what is happening at a particular moment; if one thinks with what infinite precision a Mozart or a Verdi points the smallest word or tiniest shade of emotion, that will be clear. For this reason I am an unrepentant supporter of the regular seasons of opera in England being sung in English. But, however brilliant the translators' work may be, obviously it is not ideal; the composers' prosody must necessarily suffer, and the character of the opera change.

So ideally then we must have English operas, settings of English libretti by English composers. Although this book certainly records hundreds of such operas, it seems either that the composers were not very gifted, or that the more gifted were not wisely encouraged. Precious few of their operas are still in the repertoire. All the same, one wonders whether there may not be one or two satisfactory ones among them all. After all, the operatic repertoire of today is terribly narrow; only prejudice or undue box-office caution can be keeping out the masterpieces we already know exist. Let us hope, then, that people will be encouraged by Mr. White's industry and persuasive power to explore some of these forgotten works, and that their efforts will not be wasted.

One final point, a selfish one, because I am going to speak for the composer. Writing operas is a very tricky business; only a great gift coupled with hard-won experience can produce enduring masterpieces. Today few composers can acquire the experience, even granted they have the gift. Therefore, let the managements and the public (not to mention the Press) be a little lenient about their early efforts. We have no small opera houses in the provinces in England where their immature works can be tried out—they must face the full glare of metropolitan publicity. Perhaps, in the feeble, gawky show we are watching, are hidden the seeds of some valuable operatic talent. Do not let us entirely crush them with damning criticism, and let us resist the opportunity for brilliant wit at their expense. After all, Mozart had to start with *Apollo and Hyacinth*, and Verdi composed operas almost annually for fifty years before they achieved the dazzling perfection of *Otello* and *Falstaff*.

BENJAMIN BRITTEN

ACKNOWLEDGEMENTS

Thanks for permission to quote from copyright material are due to:

Sir Thomas Beecham, Bart., and Hutchinson & Co. Ltd.: *A Mingled Chime*.

Rutland Boughton and Wm. Reeves (Bookseller) Ltd.: *Music Drama of the Future*.

Benjamin Britten, Eric Crozier (editor) and The Bodley Head: *Peter Grimes* (Sadler's Wells Opera Books).

Benjamin Britten, Eric Crozier (editor), Ronald Duncan and The Bodley Head: *The Rape of Lucretia: a symposium*.

Joan Cross, Eric Crozier (editor) and The Bodley Head: *Opera in English* (Sadler's Wells Opera Books).

Edward J. Dent and the Cambridge University Press: *Foundations of English Opera*.

Edward J. Dent and Messrs. Duckworth: *Handel* (Great Lives Series).

Edward J. Dent and T. V. Boardman & Co.: *A Theatre for Everybody*.

Edward J. Dent and John Lehmann Ltd.: *Purcell's 'The Fairy Queen'*.

The Executor of the late Cecil Forsyth and Macmillan & Co. Ltd.: *Music and Nationalism*.

The Executor of the late Herman Klein and Routledge & Kegan Paul Ltd.: *The Golden Age of Opera*.

Professor Allardyce Nicoll and the Cambridge University Press: *A History of English Drama* (1660–1900).

J. B. Priestley and Novello & Co. Ltd.: *The Olympians*.

The late G. Bernard Shaw: *London Music in 1888–89, Music in London 1890–94* and *The Perfect Wagnerite*.

The Executor of the late Dame Ethel Smyth and Longmans Green & Co. Ltd.: *What Happened Next*.

The Executor of the late Charles V. Stanford and Constable & Co. Ltd.: *Studies and Memories*.

The loan of a block from *Theatre Notebook* is gratefully acknowledged.

Thanks for permission to reproduce some of the illustrations are due to:

The Tate Gallery (Plate 8)

The National Portrait Gallery (Plates 5, 7, 11, 14, 15, 21 and 25)

The National Gallery of Scotland (Plate 1)

The Royal Academy of Music (Plate 6)

The Chatsworth Estates Company (Plates 2, 3 and 4)

The Art Institute of Chicago; The Charles Deering Collection (Plate 13)

Mr. Ralph Bankes (Plate 3)

Miss Bridget D'Oyly Carte (drawing, p. 113)

Mr. E. Gordon Craig (woodcut, p. 147)

Mr. Kenneth Green (Plate 30)

Mr. George Howard (frontispiece)

Mr. John Piper (Plate 30)

Mr. Steven Spurrier, A.R.A., R.B.A. (Plate 23)

Mr. Michael Tippett and Messrs. Schott (Plate 27)

Most of the remaining illustrations have been drawn from material in the author's private collection.

CONTENTS

B

ILLUSTRATIONS

PLATES

LINE BLOCKS IN TEXT

PART ONE

Sketch of the
History of English Opera

CHAPTER I

Early Representations
(Seventeenth Century)

The Florentine Camerata—Opera in Venice, Rome and Naples—
Influence of Seneca on English Drama—Jigs—Court Masques—
Sir William Davenant—Order for the Suppression of Stage Plays—
The Siege of Rhodes—Restoration Theatres—Operatic Adaptations
of Shakespeare—The Rise of French Opera—Shadwell's Psyche—
Dryden's The State of Innocence—*Albion and Albanius—*
*Masques for Amateurs—*Dido and Aeneas—*Purcell's Semi-operas*
—Collier's Attack on King Arthur

OPERA is a fruit of the Italian Renaissance. By the sixteenth century science and art had combined in that country to produce some of the most humane masterpieces of architecture, sculpture and painting. Music, too, flourished, mainly in a polyphonic form—in the church, the court and the chamber; but in the theatre it played as yet only an incidental part.

In Florence, at the end of the century, a group of enthusiastic intellectuals—musicians, poets, scientists—was in the habit of meeting at the palazzo belonging to Giovanni Bardi, Conte di Vernio, in the Via de' Benci. There they discussed the reform of the drama in the light of what they considered to be the example of Greek classical tragedy and the part music had played in it. Two things seemed clear to them. In the first place, they thought that, as the words of the action were as important as the accompanying music, polyphony must give way to monody. Secondly, they held that a new style of recitative must be evolved to reproduce the special species of musical declamation and accentuation that had been the distinguishing feature of the presentation of Greek tragedy. As Jacopo Peri wrote in his Preface to *Euridice*: 'In dramatic poetry, where it was necessary to imitate in singing the spoken language (for one never speaks in singing), I think that the ancient Greeks and Romans (who, according to general

23

opinion, sang whole tragedies) used a musical tone (*un armonia*) which far surpassed ordinary speech and yet never developed into a sung melody, but remained an intermediary between the two.'

In 1597 the theories of this Camerata were put into practice when *Dafne* was performed at the Palazzo Corsi during the Carnival. Here, for the first time, dramatic action was entirely set to music in what was called the new *Stile Rappresentativo*. The libretto was by Ottavio Rinuccini, and the music by Peri, with Giulio Caccini and Jacopo Corsi as his collaborators. Although the score has been lost, it is clear from this work's immediate successor, *Euridice* (produced at the Palazzo Pitti on October 6, 1600, with words by Rinuccini and music by Peri) that the composers of the Camerata learned, as Caccini says,[1] 'to cultivate the art so highly praised by Plato and other philosophers, who affirmed that music is the orderly union of words, rhythm and tone, if one desires that it should penetrate the hearer's intelligence and produce the wonderful effect admired by great writers, and which was impossible to obtain by counterpoint and modern methods'. Though by modern standards the results may seem frigid and artificial, there is no doubt that the reaction of the Florentine audience to this innovation was most enthusiastic.

The Camerata's experiment was soon repeated elsewhere in Italy—particularly in Venice where centuries of trading down the Adriatic coast had kept the inhabitants in close touch with the Greeks. Here the Florentine theories took on new life, and through the genius of Claudio Monteverdi Italian music drama reached a pitch of lyrical perfection that has rarely been surpassed since. Operatic subject matter was extended to include historical as well as classical subjects; the orchestra standardised and subdivided into its family groups with *concertante* as well as *ripieno* players; and for the first time operas were performed to a paying audience in public theatres rather than private houses or the courts of noblemen or princes.

In Rome the enthusiasm for opera spread to the Church. Performances were given in convents and monasteries, and eminent

---

[1] Preface to *Le Nuove Musiche* by Giulio Caccini.

cardinals even wrote librettos and designed scenic apparatus and costumes; but the religious symbolism that was sometimes adopted to cloak the profanity and licence of the stage action in no wise brought these works nearer to the religious significance of their Greek prototypes.

Naples was the last of the great Italian cities to succumb; but when finally it opened its theatres to opera it impressed so individual a stamp on this new art form as profoundly to modify the original Florentine conception. Instead of taking drama and raising its expression to a much higher power through the medium of music, the Neapolitan composers looked on the words and action merely as a pretext for a series of *pezzi staccati* with closed form—airs, duets, trios, ensembles, choruses, etc.—interspersed with stretches of comparatively unimportant recitative; and so strong was the influence of their comic operas on general operatic development that it was not until the time of Christopher Gluck that the Florentine ideal re-emerged in all its original force.

In sixteenth-century England interest in classical drama was directed to Latin rather than Greek sources. The plays of Seneca, with their reliance on the strength of rhetorical declamation, had a dominating effect on English tragedy during its formative period. 'It seems strange at first sight that this unacted dramatist of the time of Nero should become the major influence in English tragedy in the sixteenth century. But he was, in the first place, far more easily accessible than any Greek dramatist, for few of the Elizabethan dramatists could have read a play in Greek.'[1] Though Seneca had studied Greek drama—particularly the plays of Euripides—and tried to reproduce in his tragedies such typical Greek features as the unities of time, place and action, the chorus, and the messenger, he did not succeed in capturing (even if he had wanted to) the Greek religious spirit. In his plays the chorus was no longer an active protagonist, but its appearances were relegated to the end of the acts; and thereby he showed that he either misunderstood, or deliberately wished to forgo, the essential role played by song and dance in Greek drama.

[1] B. Ifor Evans, *A Short History of English Drama*. London (Penguin), 1948.

THE RISE OF ENGLISH OPERA

Gorboduc, written by Thomas Norton and Thomas Sackville and performed before Queen Elizabeth at Whitehall in 1562, marks the beginning of the period of Seneca's influence. Twenty years later all his ten tragedies had been translated into English and published; and when Italy was starting to experiment with opera, the full extent of his influence in England could be seen in many of the plays of Kyd, Marlowe, Shakespeare and Ben Jonson.

About the time *Dafne* was being produced in Florence, Shakespeare was busy with his lyrical tragedy of *Romeo and Juliet* and his lyrical comedy of *A Midsummer Night's Dream.* Both plays tremble on the brink of music; and, indeed, at later dates each has served as basis for operatic compositions. How is it that with a playwright so sensitive to music as Shakespeare, and with so brilliant a galaxy of composers as flourished in England then, opera was not born in London at the same time as in Florence?

The answer must be that drama in this country developed on lines that precluded the participation of music in it on concurrent terms. The form of the plays, based on Latin rather than Greek models, was inimical to music, except as an incidental embellishment that had little or nothing to do with the fundamental dramatic purpose. In default of music, however, it was necessary to find some way of raising declamation to tragic heights; and here the Elizabethan playwrights were remarkably successful. Blank verse was the solution. The mighty line that Marlowe forged became mightier yet in Shakespeare's hands—subtler, deeper, capable of wider inflexions—especially when used in combination with rhymed verse and prose. If the form of tragedies like *Romeo and Juliet* and *Hamlet* is analysed from the point of view of prose, blank verse and rhyming verse, soliloquy and dialogue, it will be found that in some ways they are as carefully constructed as a music drama or an opera with *pezzi staccati,* and as carefully orchestrated.[1]

---

[1] Compare Bernard Shaw's admission in 'The Play of Ideas' (*The New Statesman and Nation,* May 6, 1950) that 'opera taught me to shape my plays into recitatives, arias, duets, trios, ensemble finales and bravura pieces to display the technical accomplishments of the executants'.

There is, however, one aspect of Elizabethan and early Jacobean theatre that deserves special mention here, and that is the after-piece or jig. This kind of entertainment was often tagged on at the end of a stage play, and traces of this custom are to be found in Shakespeare's *Henry IV* (Part Two) and *Twelfth Night*. By origin the jig was probably a simple combination of ballad and dance accompanied by pipe and tabor; but gradually the number of characters was increased, and the entertainment grew into a more complex form. The subject matter of these jigs was often coarse and sometimes libellous, and they became the cause of such scandal that in 1612 the Middlesex Justices made an order for their suppression. But it is clear from the examples that have been preserved, some of which are mentioned in Appendix A, that, consisting for the most part of song-dialogues set to specified popular tunes, they anticipated, on a modest scale, the ballad operas that became so enormously popular a century later. As Baskervill writes in *The Elizabethan Jig*: 'The farce jig was itself a distinct form of comic opera, and it survived until after the more definite movement towards opera began with Davenant. In the long run it may have been responsible in no small measure for the complete triumph of English comic opera in the form of ballad opera. Among the later jigs *The Black Man*, for example, shows a variety of effects in its interspersed prose, its street cries that were probably chanted, and its shifting verse forms for dialogue, including lyric measures.'

The most important form in which music and spectacle developed in this country during the seventeenth century was the court masque. For some centuries dances in masquerade had been one of the favourite amusements of the court at West-minster and on royal progresses; and in the reigns of James I and Charles I these entertainments reached a hitherto unknown degree of splendour. It was Ben Jonson who first revealed the full literary possibilities of this form, and Inigo Jones who developed the spectacular side—designing of costumes, scene-painting and stage-carpentry—to such a pitch that it sometimes became difficult to know which was the more important partner in this work of collaboration: the poet or the artist. As well as speech and spectacle, however, the masques included songs and dances; and many musicians composed special scores for them. In Ben Jonson's *Lovers Made Men* (1617), the directions go so far as to explain that 'the whole masque was sung after the Italian manner, *stylo recitativo*, by Master Nicholas Lanier; who ordered and made both the scene and the music'. William and Henry Lawes both wrote music for several masques, of which the most important was undoubtedly Milton's *Comus* (Henry Lawes); and other composers whose names are recorded in this connection include Thomas Campion, John Coprario, Alfonso Ferrabosco, Simon Ives and Louis Richard.

Of all the various elements that went to make up a masque, the essential and invariable feature was the presence of a group of dancers. These masquers were usually distinguished amateurs —sometimes the King and Queen themselves—who took no part in the speaking or singing, but merely had to make a striking impression in their magnificent costumes and to dance. As a foil to their performance, the later masques contained an anti-masque, generally of grotesque nature, acted by professional dancers; and the popularity of the anti-masques was such that they soon assumed a very important part in this scheme of entertainment and may in some measure be said to have been forerunners of the modern ballet.

In 1637 Sir William Davenant, then aged thirty-one, was appointed Poet Laureate in succession to Ben Jonson, two years after he had written his first masque, *The Temple of Love*. This was followed by other essays in the same form; but that he cherished wider ambitions than merely to continue as a purveyor of fashionable court entertainment could be seen from the fact that in 1639 he obtained from Charles I a theatre patent which authorised him 'from time to time to act plays in such house to be by him erected, and exercise musick, musical presentments, scenes, dancing, or any other the like, at the same or other houses at times, or after plays are ended'. Had he been able to put this plan into operation, his theatre would have marked an important step towards the popularisation of the masque and other similar entertainments, the presentation of which had so far been confined mainly to the court and nobility, and might even have led to the immediate development of native opera; but for some reason or other he did not, or could not, proceed with the scheme, and two years after the performance of his last masque, *Salmacida Spolia*, the theatres were closed by an order of the Lords and Commons dated Die Veneris, September 2, 1642, which ran as follows:

'Whereas the distressed Estate of Ireland, steeped in her own Blood, and the distracted Estate of England, threatned with a Cloud of Blood, by a Civill Warre, call for all possible meanes to appease and avert the Wrath of God appearing in these Judgements; amongst which, Fasting and Prayer having bin often tryed to be very effectuall, have bin lately, and are still ejoyned; and whereas publike Sports doe not well agree with publike Calamities, nor publike Stage-playes with the Seasons of Humiliation, this being an Exercise of sad and pious solemnity, and the other being Spectacles of pleasure, too commonly expressing lacivious Mirth and Levitie: It is therefore thought fit, and Ordeined by the Lords and Commons in this Parliament Assembled, that while these sad Causes and set times of Humiliation doe continue, publike Stage-Playes shall cease, and bee forborne. Instead of which, are recommended to the people of this Land, the profitable and seasonable Considerations of Repentance, Reconciliation, and peace with God, which probably may produce outward peace and prosperity, and bring againe Times of Joy and Gladnesse to these Nations.'

The Civil War and Commonwealth effectively brought to an end the great period of Elizabethan and Jacobean drama and also of the court masque. But Davenant, despite numerous set-backs to his plans and even a term of imprisonment on account of his royalist activities during the Civil War, was still resolute in his ambition to succeed as a dramatist. A first tentative step towards the eventual reopening of the theatres was taken in 1656 when, after various entertainments had been given in private houses, he organised a kind of public lecture-recital in costume, described as 'The First Dayes Entertainment at Rutland-House by Declamations and Musick: after the manner of the Ancients'. The

Prologue alludes, in apologetic terms, not only to the fact that the room where these declamations took place was low, narrow and inconvenient—

> '*Think this your passage, and the narrow way*
> *To our Elisian field, the OPERA:*
> *Tow'rds which some say we have gone far about,*
> *Because it seems so long since we set out.*'

but also to the author's unsuccessful attempt to build an opera-house seventeen years previously.

There were ten performances of this recital; and then the following autumn (1656) *The Siege of Rhodes* was produced— also 'at the back part of Rutland-House in the upper end of Aldersgate Street'. Although the title-page to the libretto explained that the subject had been 'made a Representation by the art of Prospective in Scenes, and the Story sung in Recitative Musick', and the five entries (or acts) were set by Henry Lawes (first and fifth), Captain Cooke (second and third), and Matthew Locke (fourth), while instrumental music was provided by Charles Coleman and George Hudson, it does not appear likely that the work was originally planned as an opera at all. Davenant's prime object was clearly to get the theatres reopened and his plays performed; and Edward J. Dent suggests that he 'originally wrote the work as a drama in rhymed heroic couplets, and that it was only when he found it impossible to produce it as a play that he decided to turn it into an opera by cutting it down, altering the lengths of the lines here and there, inserting songs and choruses, and finally getting the whole set to music'.[1] This is to some extent borne out both by a passage in the Preface where Davenant, while apologising for certain shortcomings in his libretto, explains that he had found himself 'constrain'd to prevent the length of *recitative* musick', which presumably means that he had had to compress his text to allow for the slower delivery of the singers, and also by the fact that when the theatres were reopened after the Restoration *The Siege of Rhodes* was revived with considerable success at the Lincoln's Inn Theatre before the

[1] Edward J. Dent, *Foundations of English Opera*.

King and the Duke of York,[1] but apparently shorn of much of its recitative and music, which was then no longer needed as a guarantee of respectability. For this revival a second part was added (in five acts) with only one cue for music—namely, a symphony expressing a battle in the last act.

Writing about twelve years later in his 'Essay of Heroic Plays' prefixed to *The Conquest of Granada*, John Dryden clearly looked on *The Siege of Rhodes* as an experiment in the heroic play convention which had been temporarily forced into an operatic mould by the accident of the time in which it was written. But by 1692 the anonymous author of the text of *The Fairy Queen* could maintain in his Preface: 'That Sir William Davenant's *Siege of Rhodes* was the first Opera we ever had in England, no Man can deny; and is indeed a perfect Opera: there being this difference only between an Opera and a Tragedy; that the one is a Story sung with proper Action, the other spoken.'

The Siege of Rhodes was also remarkable for the fact that it was the first public stage production in England, as distinct from the Court and private masques, to employ scenery. Davenant in his address to the reader, which appeared only in the first edition of the play, made the following apology: 'It has been often wisht that our Scenes (we have oblig'd ourselves to the variety of five changes, according to the Ancient Dramatic distinctions made for time), had not been confined to eleven foot in height, and about fifteen in depth, including the places of passage reserv'd for the Musick. This is so narrow an allowance for the fleet of Solyman the Magnificent, his army, the Island of Rhodes, and the varieties attending the Siege of the City, that I fear you will think we invite you to such a contracted trifle as that of the Caesars carved upon a nut.' The original designs by John Webb are extant.

Davenant followed *The Siege of Rhodes* with *The Cruelty of the Spaniards in Peru* (1658) and *The History of Sir Francis Drake*

---

[1] 'The first time the King was in a Publick Theatre.' J. Downes, *Roscius Anglicanus*. This occasion, on which Downes himself acted the part of the eunuch Haly and suffered so badly from stage-fright that he was hissed off the stage, is also recorded by Samuel Pepys under the date July 2, 1661.

(1659), both produced at the Cockpit in Drury Lane. They were described as plays 'expresst by Instrumentall and Vocall Musick, and by the Art of Perspective in Scenes'; and after the Restoration they became Acts IV and III respectively of a strange mixed programme by Davenant known as *The Playhouse to be Let*. The music to all these three representations has been lost.[1] But whether they are ultimately to be judged as heroic plays or operas proper, there is no doubt that Davenant himself thoroughly understood the principles of the *stilo recitativo*, as may be seen from the following extract from *The Playhouse to be Let*:

> '*Recitative Musick is not compos'd*
> *Of matter so familiar, as may serve*
> *For every low occasion of discourse.*
> *In Tragedy, the language of the Stage*
> *Is rais'd above the common dialect;*
> *Our passions rising with the height of Verse;*
> *And Vocal Musick adds new wings to all*
> *The flights of Poetry.*'

At the time of the Restoration the dislocation caused by the Civil War and the Commonwealth made it difficult to resume the theatrical tradition at the point where it had been broken off twenty years before. In the first place new theatre buildings were needed, and their style had to be modified to suit the change in public taste. In contrast to the Elizabethan playhouse with its apron-stage, inner-stage, balconies and open auditorium, the Restoration theatre (largely under the guidance of Davenant) went indoors into a building like a tennis court,[2] where representations with scenery and machines could be given under cover, somewhat on the lines of the court masques, and where the growing importance of the stage picture led speedily to the evolution of the proscenium as a device for framing it in the audience's eyes. On January 15, 1663, Davenant surrendered the patent he had held from Charles I dated March 26, 1639, and

[1] With the exception of a 'Symeron's dance' by Locke from *The History of Sir Francis Drake*.

[2] According to J. Downes (*op. cit.*), a New House for the actors was built in Gibbon's tennis court in Clare Market in 1660; and in 1695 the New Theatre in Lincoln's Inn Fields was fitted up from a tennis court.

NICHOLAS LANIER

Chalk sketch by Sir Anthony Van Dyck. Lanier was the first
composer in England to write in the new Italian style of recitative
(in Ben Jonson's masque, *Lovers Made Men*, 1617).

above: SIR WILLIAM DAVENANT: engraving after the picture by John Greenhill.

below: *The Temple of Love:* design by Inigo Jones for Davenant's masque, 1635.

above: THOMAS BETTERTON as Solyman in *The Siege of Rhodes*:
crayon sketch by John Greenhill, dated 1663.

below: The Siege of Rhodes: John Webb's design for the
proscenium and permanent wings used at the opera's first
production at Rutland House, 1656.

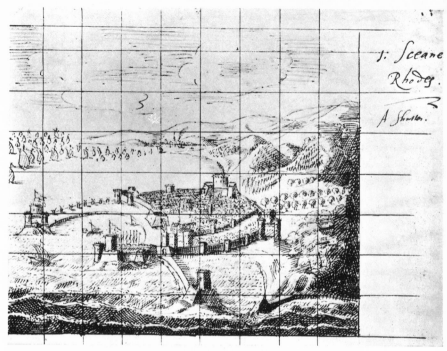

The Siege of Rhodes

J. Webb's designs for (*above*) the shutter used in the first scene (or entry), showing a prospect of the city of Rhodes and the Turkish fleet approaching; and (*below*) 'Releive', or recessed scene, in the third entry, showing a Royal Pavilion with Solyman's Imperial Throne.

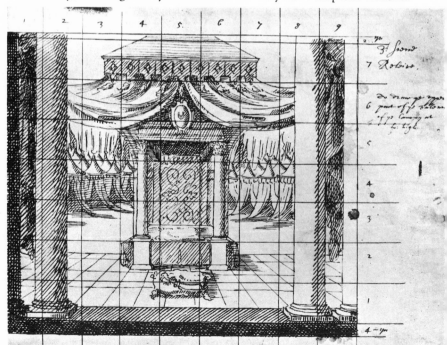

obtained from Charles II a new patent, whereby he and his heirs and assigns had the right 'to exercise and act tragedies, comedies, plays, operas and other performances of the stage' at the theatre in Lincoln's Inn Fields where his company was already installed, or in a new theatre to be built for the purpose. A few months earlier Charles II had granted a similar patent to Thomas Killigrew (dated April 25, 1662); and this was directly connected with the building of the Theatre Royal, Drury Lane, which opened on May 7, 1663, with Beaumont and Fletcher's *The Humorous Lieutenant*. Meanwhile Davenant engaged Sir Christopher Wren as his architect and set about building a theatre in Dorset Garden. On Davenant's death, in 1668, the patent and management devolved on his widow and son, and the building was eventually opened on November 9, 1671, with a revival of Dryden's *Sir Martin Mar-all*. This theatre, known first as the Duke's Theatre and later as the Queen's Theatre, specialised in the more spectacular types of representation, and most of the dramatic operas of the last quarter of the century were performed there. Towards the end of the century, however, it became deserted—there is record of a penny lottery being drawn there in 1698—and ultimately the building was demolished in June, 1709, just four years after the opening of the new Queen's Theatre in the Haymarket, built under the direction of Sir John Vanburgh and William Congreve.

The other great theatrical change brought about by the Restoration was that women began to appear on the stage. Mrs. Coleman, who sang the part of Ianthe in *The Siege of Rhodes* (1656), was the first actress of whom there is record in this country; and, although Downes lists half a dozen men who still acted women's parts in the Duke's Servants playing at the Cock Pit, Drury Lane, in 1659,[1] the Killigrew and Davenant patents of 1662 and 1663 expressly state that in these two companies the women's parts shall be performed by women, and by 1667 the

[1] Of Mr. Kynaston, Downes writes, 'he being then very Young made a Compleat Female Stage Beauty, performing his Parts so well . . . that it has since been Disputable among the Judicious, whether any Woman that succeeded him so Sensibly touch'd the Audience as he'.

c

pendulum had swung so far that in the Prologue to his version
of *The Tempest*, Dryden was constrained to write:

> 'But if for Shakespear *we your grace implore*,
> *We for our Theatre shall want it more;*
> *Who by our dearth of Youths are forc'd t'employ*
> *One of our Women to present a Boy.*
> *And that's a transformation you will say*
> *Exceeding all the Magick in the Play.*'

This innovation was bound ultimately to revolutionise the stage.

A result of these developments was that playwrights like
Davenant, Dryden and Shadwell deemed it advisable to make
drastic adaptations of Shakespeare's plays to suit the new theatres
and the new audience. *Macbeth* and *The Tempest* seemed particularly suited to decorative and musical elaboration; and special
versions of these two that were almost operatic in treatment were
given in the Duke's Theatre in Dorset Garden. Downes describes
Davenant's alteration of *Macbeth* as being 'drest in all it's Finery,
as new Cloath's, new Scenes, Machines, as flyings for the Witches;
with all the Singing and Dancing in it: The first Compos'd by
Mr. *Lock*, the other by Mr. *Channell* and Mr. *Joseph Preist*; it
being all Excellently perform'd, being in the nature of an Opera,
it Recompenc'd double the Expence'.[1] Shadwell's alteration of
The Tempest appears to have been even more successful. Downes
describes it as 'having all New in it; as Scenes, Machines; particularly, one Scene Painted with *Myriads* of *Ariel* Spirits; and another
flying away, with a Table Furnisht out with Fruits, Sweet meats and
all sorts of Viands; just when Duke *Trinculo* and his Companions'
were going to Dinner; all was things perform'd in it so Admirably
well, that not any succeeding Opera got more Money'.[2]

As during his years of exile Charles II had become extremely
familiar with French music and French representations, it was
natural that after the Restoration he should favour French
musicians at his court. It should also be borne in mind that a
good royalist like Davenant must also have learned a great deal
about French theatre on his various visits to France, and that

[1] J. Downes, *op cit.* [2] *Ibid.*

professional theatre people in England went frequently to Paris and were familiar with the details of French entertainments from backstage.

The predominant feature of French theatre in the middle years of the century was the dazzling rise of Corneille and Molière; and both playwrights became intimately connected with the fortunes of French opera. One of the earliest experiments in this direction was *Andromède*, a *tragédie à machines*, with text by Corneille and music by Dassoucy, written in 1647, but not produced until February 1650. In this representation, music did not really play so important a part as the stage machinery. As Corneille explained in the Preface to his libretto: 'I have taken care not to have anything sung that is necessary for the understanding of the piece, because owing to the fact that words that are sung can usually be heard only with difficulty by the audience on account of the confusion caused by the diversity of voices chanting them together, the meaning of the work would be too obscured if such passages were intended to communicate something of importance to the listener.'

This particular difficulty was partly overcome a few years later in the case of the new type of *comédie-ballet*, where the songs and dances were confined to short interludes or codas that followed each act of the play. The first of these productions, *Le Mariage Forcé*, appeared in 1664 with the comedy written by Molière and the music for the ballet by Lulli the Italian, who had just become a naturalised Frenchman. This type of entertainment well suited the taste of the court of Louis XIV for magnificence; and in 1671, when Molière was at the height of his career as a manager of spectacle, *Psyché* was produced as a *tragédie-ballet*. On this occasion the stage of the Palais Royal was rebuilt at a cost of 1,989 *livres* to accommodate the machines and orchestra; and the text of the play was written by Corneille and Molière in collaboration, with music by Lulli and lyrics by Quinault. The production was an expensive one, costing 4,359 *livres*; but its success was so great that it was performed eighty-two times during the remaining two years of Molière's life, earning a total of 77,119 *livres*.

In 1675 Shadwell is found using this *tragédie-ballet* of Molière and Corneille as a pretext for an English *Psyche*, which was produced at Dorset Garden with music by Locke and Draghi. In his Preface he explains that his 'Design was to entertain the Town with variety of Musick, curious Dancing, splendid Scenes and Machines', and goes on to discount the value of his own contribution insofar as his play was written in verse. But his attitude, though clearly intended .to disarm criticism, is altogether too modest, for in several respects he has improved on the original of Corneille and Molière—particularly in the way he has shown himself sensitive to the cues for music implicit in the action and quick to follow them up, so that the music is by no means confined to the end of the acts, but pervades the whole play.

He took special care to make his words 'proper for Musick', and in the Preface he says: 'I chalked out the way to the Composer (in all but the Song of *Furies and Devils*, in the Fifth Act) having design'd which Line I wou'd have sung by One, which by Two, which by Three, which by four Voices, etc. and what manner of Humour I would have in the Vocal Musick.' Locke, too, wrote a Preface—somewhat petulant in tone—when the score of the vocal music of *Psyche* was published, and there he referred to his compositions as being in their nature 'soft, easy and agreeable' to the design of the poet. In them, he said, 'you have from Ballad to single Air, Counterpoint, Recitative, Fuge, Canon, and Chromatick Musick; which variety (without vanity be it said) was never in Court or Theatre till now presented in this nation'. The instrumental music before and between the acts was composed by Draghi.

Splendid though this representation of *Psyche* must have appeared to English eyes, no more than £800 was spent on its production, or about one-fifth of the cost of its French model. According to Downes, 'it had a Continuance of Performance about 8 Days together it prov'd very Beneficial to the Company; yet the *Tempest* got them more Money'.[1] Charles II and his Court were present at the first performance on February 27, 1675, when,

[1] J. Downes, *op. cit.*

according to the records in the Lord Chamberlain's department of the Public Record Office, a sum of £30 was paid to the players. A further £20 was paid when the King and court attended for the second time three days later (March 2). But these were modest payments in view of the expenses involved; and the lack of a real court subsidy seems to have been a serious deterrent in presenting public performances of this kind of spectacle. In his Epilogue to *Psyche* Shadwell says:

> 'But oh a long farewell to all this sort
> Of Plays, which this vast Town can not support.
> If you could be content th'expence to bear,
> We would improve and treat you better ev'ry year.'

The disposition of the court of Charles II to turn to France for guidance in musical matters was confirmed by the appointment of Louis Grabu, a pupil of Robert Cambert, as Master of the King's Musick in 1666. Eight years later he was responsible for the production of his master's opera (or 'vocal representation'), *Ariane*, in French at the short-lived Royal Academy of Music at the Theatre Royal, Drury Lane, and in 1685 he wrote the music for Dryden's *Albion and Albanius*.

Dryden had already published *The State of Innocence, and Fall of Man* (1677), which he formally designated an 'opera written in heroick verse'. The action was based closely on John Milton's *Paradise Lost*; and it was said that the poet, when asked by Dryden for permission to adapt his epic for the stage, replied, 'Aye, you may *tag* my verses if you will'. In some ways this piece resembled a court masque; and the stage directions contain cues for instrumental symphonies, songs, choruses and dances. As can be seen from the opening direction to Act I, the production was conceived on spectacular lines.

'The first Scene represents a Chaos, or a confus'd Mass of Matter; the Stage is almost wholly dark. A symphony of Warlike Musick is heard for some time; then from the Heavens, (which are opened) fall the rebellious Angels wheeling in the Air, and seeming transfix'd with Thunderbolts. The bottom of the Stage being opened, receives the

Angels, who fall out of sight. Tunes of Victory are play'd, and an Hymn sung; Angels discover'd above, brandishing their Swords. The Musick ceasing, and the Heavens being clos'd, the Scene shifts, and on a sudden represents Hell. Part of the Scene is a Lake of Brimstone or rowling Fire; the Earth of a burnt colour. The fall'n Angels appear on the Lake, lying prostrate; a Tune of Horrour and Lamentation is heard.'

There is no record that music was ever composed to this piece; and Dryden himself says it was never acted on the stage.

Albion and Albanius was originally intended to be merely the introduction to a play with music, like the popular Restoration version of *The Tempest*; but in the composition it was expanded into a three-act dynastic opera in honour of the House of Stuart with Albion typifying Charles II and Albanius his brother the Duke of Albany and York. In the Prologue Dryden went out of his way to praise his French models at the court of Louis XIV.

'. . . *Know*
> *The Wise* Italians *first invented Show;*
> *Thence, into* France *the Noble Pageant past;*
> *'Tis* England's *Credit to be cozen'd last. . . .*
> *In* France, *the oldest Man is always young,*
> *See* Operaes *daily, learns the Tunes so long,*
> *Till Foot, Hand, Head, keep time with ev'ry Song.*
> *Each sings his part, ecchoing from Pit and Box,*
> *With his hoarse Voice, half Harmony, half Pox.*
> *Le plus grand* Roy du Monde, *is always ringing;*
> *They show themselves good Subjects by their singing.'*

The machinery needed for this representation was so complicated that Thomas Betterton, the actor, had to go over to France specially to study the latest scenic devices there. But, although the action devised by Dryden was extremely undistinguished, the failure of the opera was due mainly to Grabu's inadequate music. It must also be admitted that the opera had the misfortune to be 'perform'd on a very Unlucky Day, being the Day the *Duke* of *Monmouth*, Landed in the *West*: The Nation being in a great Consternation, it was perform'd but Six times, which not

ALBION

AND

ALBANIUS:

AN

OPERA.

Perform'd at the QUEENS Theatre
in *Dorset*-Garden.

Written by Mr. Dryden.

Discite Justitiam moniti, & non temnere Divos. Virg.

LONDON,

Printed for *Jacob Tonson*, at the *Judge's Head*
in *Chancery-Lane*, near *Fleet-Street*. 1691.

Title-page of an early quarto edition of the libretto of
Albion and Albanius.

Answering half the Charge they were at, Involv'd the Company very much in Debt'.[1]

Dryden should have known better than to invite as his collaborator a foreign musician who was so barbarously insensitive to the prosody of the English language as Grabu, particularly since in his long and carefully argued Preface to *Albion and Albanius* he was at pains to point out the importance of any librettist showing a proper understanding of this question. "Tis no easie Matter in our Language,' he says, 'to make Words so smooth, and Numbers so harmonious, that they shall almost set themselves, and yet there are Rules for this in Nature: and as great a certainty of Quantity in our Syllables, as either in the *Greek* or *Latin*. . . . The chief Secret is in the choice of Words; and by this Choice I do not here mean Elegancy of Expression; but Propriety of Sound, to be varied according to the Nature of the Subject.' But it is only fair to add that in the same Preface he qualifies his praise of Grabu by saying, 'When any of our Countreymen excell him, I shall be glad, for the sake of old *England*, to be shewn my Errour', and that five years later in the Preface to *Amphitryon* (1690) he made handsome amends by praising 'the excellent composition of Mr. Purcell; in whose Person we have at length found an English Man, equal with the best abroad. At least my opinion of him has been such since his happy and judicious performances in the late opera' (*viz. The Prophetess*). The following year he confided to Purcell the music to *King Arthur*, which he had written as long ago as 1684 as the sequel to *Albion and Albanius*, and, despite the fact that in many places his new collaborator insisted on drastic revisions in the text, paid him the following handsome compliment: 'There is nothing better, than what I intended, but the Musick; which has since arriv'd to a greater Perfection in *England*, than ever formerly; especially passing through the Artful Hands of Mr. *Purcel*, who has Compos'd it with so great a Genius, that he has nothing to fear but an ignorant, ill-judging Audience.'

Although court masques in the strict sense became obsolete

[1] J. Downes, *op. cit.*

after the interregnum of the Commonwealth, the term masque
continued to be used somewhat loosely and was applied at various
times to many different types of dramatic entertainment in which
music played an important part, ranging from private entertainments by amateurs to performances by professionals in the new
public theatres in Lincoln's Inn Fields, Dorset Garden and Drury
Lane. There was good precedent for this, since John Milton's
Comus, as presented at Ludlow Castle so early as 1634 with music
by Henry Lawes, had completely disregarded the accepted conventions of the court masque.

James Shirley forms an interesting link between the earlier
court masque and its later development for amateurs. *The Triumph
of Peace*, which he wrote in 1634 for the Inns of Court, was one
of the most sumptuous and expensive masques ever produced
—it cost over £21,000—but when the Civil War and Commonwealth forced him to abandon his career as a playwright he became a schoolmaster, and *The Triumph of Beauty* (printed in 1646)
was 'personated by some young gentlemen, for whom it was intended, at a private recreation'. His masterpiece, *Cupid and Death*,
was first produced as a private entertainment in honour of the
Portuguese ambassador on March 26, 1653, and the music to it by
Locke and Christopher Gibbons—particularly the declamatory style
of the recitatives—proved most suitable for amateur production.

It must not be thought that it was only the 'young gentlemen
of quality' who enjoyed this form of recreation as part of their
education. The admission of women to the stage after the Restoration made it proper for young ladies at boarding-school, who in
any case enjoyed music in addition to such subjects as modelling
and embroidery in their curriculum, to take part in similar masques
as well; and the schools at Chelsea seem to have been particularly
active in this respect. Mary Ashwell, the servant of Mrs. Pepys,
was apparently at a Chelsea seminary about 1656 when various
masques were acted, parts of which she repeated from memory
to entertain her master and mistress on a Sunday walk in the
cowslip fields south of the river some seven years later.[1] In 1676

[1] *The Diary of Samuel Pepys*, 26 April, 1663.

Thomas Duffett wrote *Beauties Triumph* for presentation by the 'scholars of Mr. Jeffery Banister and Mr. James Hart, at their *New Boarding School* for Young ladies and gentlewomen kept in that House which was formerly *Sir Arthur Gorges* at Chelsey'. And about 1689 or 1690 Purcell obliged Josias Priest, a dancing master, by composing a short musical entertainment for the young ladies in his school—also at Chelsea. Such were the performers for whom *Dido and Aeneas,* the first true English opera, was created.

Until that moment the composer had been secondary to the playwright in the varied and perplexing story of seventeenth-century operatic representations in England. Ben Jonson, Davenant, Shadwell and Dryden had been the dominant figures, rather than Lanier, the brothers Lawes, Locke or Grabu. But with the long-awaited advent of a musician of genius the balance was altered once and for all. Thenceforth the future of opera in this country (as elsewhere) was to lie in the hands of the composer, and the playwright was to change into the librettist.

Some idea of how chequered and fitful was to be the course of English opera can be gained from studying the fate of *Dido and Aeneas.*

No one is likely to claim *Dido* as a faultless masterpiece. It has not even got the dubious merit of being completely original, for in scale and style it follows Locke's setting of the masque of *Orpheus and Euridice* in Settle's *Empress of Morocco* (1673) and the charming *Venus and Adonis* by John Blow (librettist unknown) which was privately performed at court about ten years later by Mrs. Mary (Moll) Davies, one of Charles II's mistresses, and her daughter, Lady Mary Tudor, then aged nine. The libretto by Nahum Tate, the Poet Laureate, has been adversely criticised; but in justice it must be admitted that it contains some single lines of beauty like *Peace and I are strangers grown* and *Great minds against themselves conspire*, together with occasional picturesque, somewhat baroque metaphors, such as Dido's comment when Aeneas first breaks the news that he must leave her—

> '*Thus on the fatal banks of Nile*
> *Weeps the deceitful crocodile*'—

and it certainly gave Purcell an adequate framework for his score. Nevertheless, most people would be prepared to endorse J. A. Westrup's verdict:[1] 'What makes *Dido* immortal is that it triumphs over its weaknesses. It will always hold our admiration and affection for its penetrating revelation of the profoundest secrets of human passion. . . . Purcell's recitative is a brilliant application of the declamatory style to the peculiar accents of English verse.'

There are, of course, special production difficulties arising from the conditions for which it was written. The main vocal parts are all for women. The only male soloist (Aeneas) has no air to sing, but is confined to recitative. Although the action runs to three acts, the time taken in performance is little more than an hour. But these difficulties are by no means insuperable. Nevertheless, after the original performance by the young schoolgirls of Chelsea there is no record of any further stage production of *Dido*—with the exception of its inclusion (probably in a mutilated form) as an interlude in C. Gildon's version of *Measure for Measure* at the Lincoln's Inn Fields Theatre in 1700 and 1704— until it was performed in 1895 at the Lyceum Theatre by students from the Royal College of Music under the direction of Sir Charles Villiers Stanford to commemorate the bicentenary of Purcell's death. Furthermore, the autograph manuscript disappeared at an early date, and the earliest manuscript now known (and possibly the most authoritative) was apparently lost until the middle of the nineteenth century. (Similar difficulties occurred in the case of *King Arthur* and *The Fairy Queen*. The score of *King Arthur* was lost shortly after its first performance, and never recovered. That of *The Fairy Queen* was thought to have been lost shortly after Purcell's death, but was accidentally discovered two centuries later, by which time it had reached the safe keeping of the Royal Academy of Music.) As the value of *Dido and Aeneas*, like that of any true opera, can be rightly appreciated only in actual stage performance, it proved more or less impossible to assess its real significance in the history of English opera until the present century.

[1] J. A. Westrup, *Purcell.*

Not only that, but the subsequent course of Purcell's operatic compositions tends to show that even he did not realise the comparative importance of *Dido,* for he followed it with *The Prophetess, King Arthur* and *The Fairy Queen,* in which he reverted to the type of dramatic opera where drama, dancing,[1] stage machinery, and vocal and instrumental music are used in apposition to each other, but not conjunction. From Downes's comments it would appear that, although each of these three semi-operas pleased the Court and City, only *King Arthur* made money, while the expenses in producing *The Fairy Queen* were so great 'the Company got very little by it'. According to Colley Cibber, however, both *The Prophetess* and *King Arthur* were produced so lavishly that, so far as *The Prophetess* is concerned, the receipts did not cover the costs; and this is certainly borne out by the following passage in Dryden's Prologue:

> '*What* Nostradame, *with all his Art, can guess*
> *The Fate of our approaching* Prophetess?
> *A Play, which, like a Prospective set right,*
> *Presents our vast Expences close to Sight;*
> *But turn the Tube, and there we sadly view*
> *Our distant Gains, and those uncertain too;*
> *A sweeping Tax, which on our selves we raise,*
> *And all, like you, in hopes of better Days.*
> *When will our Losses warn us to be Wise?*
> *Our Wealth decreases, and our Charges rise.*
> *Money, the sweet Allurer of our Hopes,*
> *Ebbs out in Oceans, and comes in by Drops.*'

Nevertheless, there might still have been a chance for Purcell to establish a live and indigenous operatic tradition in England, had it not been for his tragically early death at the age of thirty-six. Dryden in his commemorative elegy wrote:

> '*So ceas'd the rival Crew, when Purcell came,*
> *They Sung no more, or only Sung his Fame.*
> *Struck dumb, they all admir'd the godlike man:*

[1] The dances for each of these three semi-operas were made by Joseph Priest.

> *The godlike man,*
> *Alas, too soon retir'd,*
> *As He too late began.'*

Too soon . . . too late. . . . Dryden, alas! was right; and not even
the eloquent force of his tribute could arrest the decline in his
great collaborator's influence and fame.

Three years after Purcell's death Jeremy Collier included *King
Arthur* in his general attack on stage poets and the playhouses
of his day. The virulence of the divine is perhaps partly to be
accounted for by the fact that just before Venus's patriotic ditty,
'Fairest Isle, all Isles Excelling', three peasants have a harvest-catch,
in which they inveigh merrily against the custom of tithes.

> '*We ha' cheated the Parson, we'll cheat him agen;*
> *For why shou'd a Blockhead ha' One in Ten?*
> *For Prating so long like a Book-learn'd Sot,*
> *Till Pudding and Dumplin burn to Pot.'*

This levity is severely rebuked; but graver charges are reserved
for other parts of Dryden's libretto. 'Now here is a strange Jumble
and Hotch-potch of Matters, if you mind it. Here we have *Genii,*
and *Angels, Cupids, Syrens,* and *Devils; Venus* and St. *George,*
Pan and the *Parson,* the Hell of Heathenism, and the Hell of
Revelation; A fit of Smut, and then a Jest about Original Sin.
And why are Truth and Fiction, Heathenism and Christianity,
the most Serious and the most Trifling Things blended together,
and thrown into one Form of Diversion? Why is all this done
unless it be to ridicule the whole, and make one as incredible,
as the other?'[1] The conclusion he reaches is that 'the Representation it self is scandalously irreligious'.

Although no attack is made on Purcell personally, Collier is
only too suspicious of the role played by music in the theatre.
'Now granting the *Play-House-Musick* not vicious in the Composition, yet the design of it is to refresh the *Idea's* of the *Action,*
to keep *Time* with the *Poem,* and be true to the *Subject.* For this
Reason among others the *Tunes* are generally Airy and Gailliar-
dizing: They are contriv'd on purpose to excite a sportive

[1] Jeremy Collier, *A Short View of the Immorality and Profaneness of the English Stage.*

Humour, and spread a Gaiety upon the Spirits. To banish all Gravity and Scruple, and lay Thinking and Reflection asleep. This sort of Musick warms the Passions, and unlocks the Fancy, and makes it open to Pleasure like a Flower to the Sun. It helps a Luscious Sentence to slide, drowns the Discords of *Atheism,* and keeps off the Aversions of Conscience. It throws a Man off his Guard, makes way for an ill Impression, and is most Commodiously planted to do Mischief. A Lewd *Play* with good Musick is like a Loadstone *Arm'd*, it draws much stronger than before. . . . Musick is almost as dangerous as Gunpowder; And it may be requires looking after no less than the *Press,* or the *Mint.* Tis possible a Publick Regulation might not be amiss. . . . If [the English] have any advantage in their *Instrumental* Musick, they lose it in their *Vocal.* Their *Songs* are often rampantly Lewd, and Irreligious to a flaming Excess.'[1]

The influence of Collier should not be overrated. It may be no more than a coincidence, and yet it is significant, that the publication of *A Short View* more or less coincided with a decline in the production of English operas generally, and also with the advent of Italian operas where, even if the matter was still tainted with the profanity and lewdness Collier so vehemently deplored, the words were at least unintelligible to the major part of the audience and so might be said to cause proportionately less offence.

As for Purcell, by 1789, nearly a hundred years after his death, Dr. Charles Burney, who rightly considered him to be 'as much the pride of an Englishman in Music, as Shakespeare in productions for the stage, Milton in epic poetry, Lock in metaphysics, or Sir Isaac Newton in philosophy and mathematics',[2] had to admit that his reputation had so far diminished that soon it would be 'as difficult to find his songs, or, at least to *hear* them, as those of his predecessors, Orpheus and Amphion';[3] and, in spite of occasional revivals in the eighteenth and nineteenth centuries, his operas have had to wait till the present century for their full rehabilitation.

---

[1] Jeremy Collier, *op. cit.*
[2] Dr. Charles Burney, *A General History of Music from the Earliest Ages to the Present Period,* Vol. III.
[3] *Ibid.*

CHAPTER II

The Handelian Catastrophe
(Eighteenth Century)

Italian Opera in English—Italian Opera in Italian—Italian Opera Combated—Italian Castrati—Handel in Hamburg—Handel in Italy—Handel Visits London—The Royal Academy of Music—Handel as Operatic Manager—Catastrophe—Lampe—Smith—Dr. Arne—Artaxerxes—Need for Operatic Reform

---

I N THE *beginning of the Eighteenth Century the Italian Tongue was so well understood in English in England that Operas were acted on the publick Stage in that Language.* This is the sort of erroneous reflection that Joseph Addison imagined[1] the music historian of 1950, or thereabouts, might easily be led to make if he were ignorant of the real circumstances that led to the predominance of Italian opera in London at that time. That Addison felt particularly bitter about this vogue is understandable when it is remembered that in 1707 his own opera *Rosamond*, which was intended to be an English dynastic opera 'after the Italian manner' for the Duchess of Marlborough, proved a dismal failure, and its music by Thomas Clayton was slated by critics as being abominably incompetent.

During the previous century travellers and connoisseurs had freely acknowledged the supremacy of Italian opera. Dryden, after a momentary aberration in the Preface to *Albion and Albanius* when he speculated that it might have been the Spanish Moors with their *zambras* rather than the Italians who were the true inventors of this form of representation, never deviated from the orthodox view and was particularly frank about his admiration for Italian as a language. 'All, who are conversant in the *Italian*,' he wrote, 'cannot but observe, that it is the softest, the sweetest, the most harmonious, not only of any modern Tongue, but even

[1] *The Spectator*, March 21, 1711.

47

beyond any of the Learned. It seems indeed to have been invented for the sake of Poetry and Musick.'[1] Indeed, the Italian style of recitative had been known and admired in London at least since Lanier's experiment in Ben Jonson's masque, *Lovers Made Men,* in 1617; and it was to prove particularly suited to the taste of eighteenth-century audiences.

Arsinoe, Queen of Cyprus, was the precursor of the Italian invasion. Translated by Pierre Motteux from the original of Tomaso Stanzani (1677), with a hotch-potch of musical numbers composed by Thomas Clayton, Nicolino Haym and Charles Dieupart, it was produced at Drury Lane in 1705 as 'an Opera after the Italian manner; all sung'. Four years later this *pasticcio* received the following slashing criticism: 'There is nothing in it but a few Sketches of antiquated Italian Airs, so mangled and sophisticated, that instead of *Arsinoe,* it ought to be called the Hospital of the old Decrepit Italian operas.'[2] Nevertheless, the Italian vogue continued; and in 1706 appeared *Camilla,* an opera with music by Marcantonio Bononcini and words by Silvio Stampiglia that had originally been published in Naples in 1696 and was now adapted for the English stage by Northman and Motteux, with its score edited by Haym. The success of these and other translations was such that certain people (Addison included) tried to plan their own operas closely after Italian models; but either these home-made products were unsuccessful or, as in the case of *Alarbas,* a dramatic opera written by a gentleman of quality (1709), they did not reach production, since (as the anonymous author complained in his preface) 'the nature of the play will not admit of its representation in either house, the Opera-Theatre being wholly taken up with Italian airs, and the other totally excluding the musical part'.

'The next Step to our Refinement,' says Addison, 'was the introducing of Italian Actors into our Opera; who sung their Parts in their own Language at the same time that our Country-men performed theirs in our native Tongue.' And some of these

---

[1] Preface to *Albion and Albanius.*
[2] *A Critical Discourse on Opera's and Musick in England,* 1709.

HENRY PURCELL

Oil painting by John Closterman
(29 in. by 24¼ in.).

The Fairy Queen: page from the MS. score showing Juno's air 'Thrice Happy Lovers' in Purcell's autograph.

JOHN GAY, unfinished oil sketch
(13 in. by 10 in.) by Sir Godfrey
Kneller. (Identity uncertain.)

The Beggar's Opera: engraving showing Casey as Captain Macheath (*circa* 1750). '*How happy could I be with either, were t'other dear charmer away?*'

The Beggar's Opera
Satirical engraving by W. Hogarth

The Beggar's Opera
Oil painting by W. Hogarth (22 in. by 28½ in.), of the
original production (1728).

Italians were indeed magnificent singers—for example, the *castrato* Nicola Grimaldi, known as Nicolini, who first appeared in London in Haym's adaptation of Alessandro Scarlatti's *Pyrrhus and Demetrius* (1708).[1] As can be imagined, the admixture of the two languages proved but a halfway stage towards the performance of operas wholly in Italian. *Almahide*, with music by Giovanni Bononcini, is considered to have been the first opera to be heard in London completely in its Italian form, though there appear to be some grounds for thinking that Jakob Greber's *The Loves of Ergasto* was sung in Italian at the opening of the Queen's Theatre in the Haymarket in 1705. *Almahide* was played at the Haymarket in January 1710; and just over a year later the same theatre saw the first performance of *Rinaldo*, the first of Handel's Italian operas to be written and produced in England.

The strength of the vogue for Italian opera in London during the first few decades of the eighteenth century can be reliably gauged from the vehemence with which it was attacked. Writing in 1708, Downes complained that had the new Queen's Theatre in the Haymarket been opened three years previously 'with a good new *English* opera, or a new Play' instead of an Italian opera 'they would have preserv'd the Favour of Court and City, and gain'd Reputation and Profit to themselves'. Richard Steele and Addison satirised its foibles unmercifully in *The Tatler* and *The Spectator*. William Rufus Chetwood, referring to *Camilla*, called it 'an odd Medley . . . Valentini courting amorously in [*Italian*], a *Dutch* woman, that committed Murder on our good old *English*, with as little Understanding as a *Parrot*'.[2] Alexander Pope was severer. In *The Dunciad* (1728) he personified Italian opera as 'a harlot form' and jibed at its 'affected airs, its effeminate sounds, and the practice of patching up these operas with favourite songs, incoherently put together'. Dr. Samuel Johnson, writing in his *Lives of the Poets* (1781) of John Hughes, author of the libretto of *Calypso and Telemachus* (1712), said that the texts of some of Hughes's 'cantatas' were intended to 'oppose or

---

[1] Cf. frontispiece.
[2] W. R. Chetwood, *A General History of the Stage*. Dublin.

exclude the Italian opera, an exotick and irrational entertainment, which has been always combated, and always has prevailed'.[1] Contrary to what has been widely and erroneously stated in recent years, this celebrated dictum does not appear in Johnson's Dictionary. The definition of opera there given is based on Dryden's description of it in the *Albion and Albanius* Preface as 'a poetical tale, or fiction, represented by vocal and instrumental music'.

Dean Swift, with his almost morbid sensitivity to physical details, went even further than these writers when he stigmatised as 'unnatural' the taste for Italian music, 'which is wholly unsuitable to our northern climate, and the genius of the people, whereby we are over-run with Italian effeminacy and Italian nonsense', and went on to report an extraordinary conversation he had had with an old gentleman who had told him that 'many years ago, when the practice of unnatural vice grew frequent in London, and many were prosecuted for it, he was sure it would be the forerunner of Italian operas and singers'.[2]

In this indictment of Italian music, he was presumably confusing unnatural vice with the unnatural practice of castration, which had been widely accepted in Italy since the seventeenth century as a means of building up a unique race of *evirati* or male *castrati* singers. The operation, provided it is carried out before puberty, has an effect on the larynx which goes beyond the mere prolongation or preservation of a boy's treble voice. It appears that 'the rest of the body, apart from the larynx, shows a greater development in eunuchs than in normal men. The capacity of the lungs and the force of expiration are equal to, if not greater than, that of a mature man, so that the power of the voice of the *castrato* is very great.'[3]

Today it is easy to sneer at this artificial convention and criticise the taste of an audience that could submit to such incongruities

---

[1] It should be noted that Dr. Johnson's stricture refers only to *Italian* opera in England, and not to opera in general. The phrase 'an exotick and irrational entertainment' has been removed from its context and widely misquoted in recent years.
[2] *The Intelligencer*, No. 3.
[3] V. E. Negus, F.R.C.S., in Grove's *Dictionary of Music and Musicians*, 4th edition.

of casting and monotony of vocal register as occur in operas specially devised for the *castrato* voice; but it is clear that once the taste for its peculiar timbre was acquired, the Hanoverian audience found its distinctive quality just as acceptable as Elizabethan and Jacobean audiences had found the early stage custom of entrusting women's parts to young boys with unbroken voices. That Handel accepted the current practice of his time, not only writing important parts for the male *castrato* voice, but also going out of his way to secure some of the most celebrated *castrati* singers for his companies—particularly Nicolini and Senesino—shows that he was a sound business man as well as being a great composer. It was due more to bad luck than bad judgment on his side that the convention round which his operas were so carefully constructed fell out of favour shortly after his death, and any possibility of its revival disappeared early in the nineteenth century when Napoleon made the practice of castration an indictable offence.

The last public appearance of an Italian *castrato* on the London stage would appear to have been that of Velluti in 1825. In his *Musical Reminiscences* the Earl of Mount Edgcumbe describes how at that time, as no such singer had appeared in London for over a quarter of a century, 'a generation had sprung up who had never heard a voice of the sort, and were strongly prejudiced against it'. The opera chosen for his first performance at the King's Theatre was Meyerbeer's *Il Crociato in Egitto*. 'At the moment when he was expected to appear, the most profound silence reigned in one of the most crowded audiences I ever saw, broken on his advancing by loud applauses of encouragement. The first note he uttered gave a shock of surprise, almost of disgust, to inexperienced ears, but his performance was listened to with attention and great applause throughout, with but few *audible* expressions of disapprobation speedily suppressed.' John Ebers has left an account of the same occasion, in which, referring to the first notes Velluti uttered, he says: 'There was something of a preternatural harshness about them, which jarred even more strongly on the imagination than on the ear. But, as he proceeded, the sweetness and flexibility of those of his tones which yet remained unimpaired by time, were fully perceived and felt.'[1]

One of the results of the disappearance of the *castrato*, however, is that today it is almost impossible successfully to mount Handel's operas. Either women must sing the main male parts, which renders their stage presentation ridiculous (though this defect can be partly overcome in broadcast performances), or there must be so drastic a rearrangement of registers and keys as to wreck the original scheme of tonality and the vocal tessitura of their scores. Despite certain tentative revivals in England and Germany, mainly during the third and fourth decades of the present century, his operas remain like a series of splendid old mansions, now deserted by their former inhabitants, dilapidated and partly ruined, but still haunted by ghost voices of fabulous virtuosity.

Handel's operatic apprenticeship was served with Reinhart Keiser and Johann Mattheson in Hamburg between 1703 and 1706. Hamburg at that time did much to justify its description as the Venice of the North. A powerful Hanseatic port with a strong tradition of enterprise and independence, a taste for the fine arts as well as a flair for commerce, and a strong appetite for sensual and often licentious pleasures, it was the foremost operatic centre in Germany, possessing an opera house in the Goosemarket which had been founded in 1678 by Gerhard Schott, a local councillor, and which, like the half-dozen or more houses then active in Venice, was open to the general public. Four of Handel's operas were written for Hamburg; and of these, the first, *Almira* (1705), appears to have been the most successful. Although he remained there for only three years, he was held in esteem long after his departure; and no fewer than fifteen of his subsequent thirty-seven operas were repeated there—usually with the recitative in a German translation and the airs in Italian—shortly after their first performances in Italy or England. It should be noted that most of these were given during the period (1722–32) when Thomas Lediard, secretary to the British Envoy Extraordinary

[1] John Ebers, *Seven Years of the King's Theatre.*

to the Hans towns, was closely connected with the opera house in the Goosemarket either as director or designer.[1]

Handel left Hamburg in 1706 at the age of twenty-one in order to visit Italy. According to Mattheson,[2] he had the possibility of making a free journey with a Herr von Binitz. A fuller account of the reasons for this Italian visit is given by the Rev. John Mainwaring in his *Life of Handel*[3] published in 1760, the year after his death. It appears that, during his residence in Hamburg, he met Ferdinando, Prince of Tuscany, the brother of Gian Gastone de' Medici and son of the then reigning Grand Duke, who spoke to him in praise of Italian music generally and invited him to visit Florence at an early date. Handel, to whom the Prince had shown a large collection of Italian music, 'plainly confessed that he could see nothing in the Music which answered the high character his Highness had given it. On the contrary, he thought it so very indifferent, that the singers, he said, must be angels to recommend it. . . . However, what his Highness had told him, and what he had before heard of the fame of the Italians, would certainly induce him to undertake the journey he had been pleased to recommend, the moment it should be convenient.' In actual fact, his Italian tour lasted three years (1707–10) and culminated in the successful production of *Agrippina* at the Teatro San Giovanni Crisostomo, Venice, the performance of which (according to Mainwaring) was punctuated with 'shouts and acclamations of *viva il caro Sassone!* and other expressions of approbation too extravagant to be mentioned'.

Although a detailed record of his stay in Italy is hard to reconstruct, it is generally accepted that the Italian years were the most formative period of his life. Dent says:[4] 'Handel came to Italy as

---

[1] For further particulars about Lediard and his connection with the Hamburg opera, see *Theatre Notebook*, Vol. II, No. 3, April–June, 1948.

[2] *Grundlagen einer Ehren-Pforte*, Hamburg, 1740.

[3] It is true that subsequent scholarship has shown Mainwaring to be untrustworthy on certain points of detail—especially dates—but, by and large, this pioneer monograph, which was written under the inspection of John Christopher Smith the younger, Handel's amanuensis, is reliable in its main outlines; and its testimony, where unchallenged by weightier authorities, should command respect. Cf. William C. Smith, *Concerning Handel*.

[4] Edward J. Dent, *Handel* (Great Lives Series).

a German; he left Italy an Italian, as far as his music was concerned, and, despite all other influences, Italian was the foundation of his musical language.' Although no one is likely to dispute the important effect on him of the various musical circles at Florence, Rome, Venice and Naples, with which he came in touch, yet it is doubtful whether any Italian, either then or later, would agree to recognise the music of his maturity as being truly Italian in nationality. In Italy he was hailed as *il caro Sassone*, the admired foreigner: in London, although he became naturalised as a British subject in 1726, he was looked on as no more of a native than the royal members of the House of Hanover and in the year after his death he was referred to by his biographer as 'this illustrious Foreigner', whose example it was hoped would 'rather prove an incentive, than a discouragement to the industry and genius of our own countrymen'.[1] Whereas by birth and upbringing he was a German whose musical style matured only after he had become thoroughly familiar with Italian music, his Italian operas as created in London were not accepted by the Italians as belonging to the true canon of Italian opera, nor did they in any way help to develop the tentative English operatic tradition that had begun to emerge at the end of the previous century. Yet they cannot be ignored in any survey of English opera, for they were written in England for the delectation of the English nobility and formed the most striking feature of London's operatic fare for a third of a century.

The period they cover may be conveniently divided into four main parts: (1) 1711–17, (2) 1720–28, (3) 1729–37, (4) 1738–41.

During the last years of Queen Anne's reign and the first years of George I he wrote four operas for the Queen's (later the King's) Theatre in the Haymarket. *Rinaldo* (1711) was written for Aaron Hill on his first visit to England; *Il Pastor Fido* (1712) and *Teseo* (1713) for Owen MacSwiney on his second. But the instability of the opera in London at that time may be gauged from the fact that after the second performance of *Teseo* MacSwiney

---

[1] Rev. J. Mainwaring, *op. cit.*

absconded, and thereupon the management was taken over by
J. J. Heidegger, the Swiss impresario, for whom Handel composed
Amadigi di Gaula (1715). During the next two years there
were revivals of *Rinaldo* and *Amadigi,* but no new opera from
Handel.

From the end of the 1717 season to the spring of 1720 there
was no opera in London; but during this period plans were made
by the nobility to revive Italian opera by the flotation of a company to be called the Royal Academy of Music[1] with a share
capital of £50,000, towards which George I himself contributed
£1,000. Handel was not appointed one of the directors, but
became a paid servant of the company and as such wrote fourteen operas for it in the nine years during which it functioned at
the King's Theatre (1720–28). Other composers were engaged,
including Giovanni Bononcini from Rome and Attilio Ariosti
from Berlin; but, despite the keen competition, more than half
the total performances given by the Royal Academy of Music
were of operas by Handel, and he showed himself to be pre-
eminently successful in writing for the company's principal
singers, particularly the *castrato* Senesino, and the rival sopranos
Francesca Cuzzoni and Faustina Bordoni.

Although the Academy would seem to have been launched
with sufficient initial capital and its first seasons were financially
successful, its business affairs were not conducted wisely enough
to save it from disaster in the long run. Its collapse at the end of
eight seasons, however, was probably hastened by the extraordinary behaviour of Cuzzoni and Faustina, who on June 6, the
last night of the 1727 season, when the Princess of Wales was
present at a performance of Bononcini's *Astianatte,* allowed themselves to be egged on by their partisans, until in exasperation one
fell upon the other and the two queens of song indulged in a free
fight, on the stage, to the delight of their rival factions in the
theatre, but to the scandal of all decent-minded people.

The crash did not come until the following April (1728), when

[1] Not to be confused with the seventeenth-century Royal Academy of Music that
was set up on the French model at the Theatre Royal, Bridges Street, Covent Garden,
in Charles II's reign and lasted only a few years.

it was probably hastened by the success of *The Beggar's Opera*. Handel, however, was undeterred. With the £10,000 he had saved during his employment by the Academy he decided to embark on operatic management himself in partnership with Heidegger, who had been one of the directors of the Academy and now owned most of its scenery and properties. They accordingly took a five-year lease of the King's Theatre; and during that period Handel wrote seven new operas and several of his old ones were revived. Of the star singers who had been associated with the last years of the Academy, Cuzzoni, Faustina and Senesino had returned to Italy in 1728; but two years later Senesino was back in London, singing old and new Handelian roles at a reduced fee for the season—1,400 instead of 2,000 guineas. Relations between him and Handel, however, soon became so strained that when in 1733 a rival syndicate called the Opera of the Nobility was set up at the Lincoln's Inn Fields Theatre he allowed himself to be lured away. Heidegger, too, left Handel in the course of time; and on the expiry of the King's Theatre lease in the summer of 1734 the composer found the theatre let over his head to his rivals.

Nevertheless, he was still not prepared to acknowledge defeat, but decided to continue the struggle as best he could. After entering into an arrangement with John Rich to use the new theatre in Covent Garden that had been opened two years before, he produced eight new operas there between 1735 and 1737; but neither these nor his oratorios which were occasionally performed there on opera nights could entice the public away from the dazzling virtuoso attractions of Cuzzoni, Montagnana and the two great *castrati*, Senesino and Farinelli, now at the Haymarket.

In the end, the two rival enterprises effectively killed each other; and the reasons for this collapse are clearly and concisely stated by Mainwaring:[1] 'It soon appeared that the relish of the English for Music, was not strong enough to support two Operas at a time. There were but few persons of any other class, besides

[1] Rev. J. Mainwaring, *op. cit.*

that of the Nobility, who had much knowledge of the Italian, any notion of such compositions, or consequently any real pleasure in hearing them. Those among the middling and lower orders, whom affection or curiosity had drawn to the Theatre at his first setting out in conjunction with Rich, fell off by degrees. His expenses in providing Singers, and in other preparations, had been very large; and his profits were in no way proportionate to such charges. At the end of three or four years, instead of having acquired such an addition to his fortune as from his care, industry, and abilities, he had reason to expect, he was obliged to draw out of the funds almost all that he was worth, in order to answer the demands upon him.' The result was that at the age of fifty-two he found himself more or less bankrupt at a time when his health collapsed and he became partly paralysed.

After this catastrophe the fourth and last period of his operatic activity proved to be no more than a brief coda. First he made a determined attempt to recover his health by taking a prolonged cure at Aix-la-Chapelle; and then on his return to London he doggedly set out to retrieve his fortunes. But though he wrote a further five operas, none of them was really successful, and for most of the time he was turning his attention to oratorio. *Deidamia,* the last of his operas, had only three performances at the Lincoln's Inn Fields Theatre in January, 1741. Henceforward he was to devote his remaining years to showing (in his own words) that 'the English Language, which is so expressive of the sublimest Sentiments, is the best adapted of any to the full and solemn Kind of Musick'[1]—that is to say, to oratorio—and his example was powerful enough to direct the energies of many subsequent English composers to sacred musical drama rather than the stage.

Between 1711 and 1741 Handel wrote about thirty-six operas for London, and these had a total of 631 performances during the same period, an average of seventeen performances per opera. His six most successful works were

[1] Letter from G. F. Handel printed in *The Daily Advertiser*, Jan. 17, 1745.

Rinaldo, 1711	53	performances
Ottone, Re di Germania, 1723	43	do.
Giulio Cesare in Egitto, 1724	38	do.
Admeto, Re di Tessaglia, 1727	35	do.
Il Floridante, 1721	31	do.
Rodelinda, 1725	29	do.

and it will be noted that all of them, with the exception of *Rinaldo*, belong to the period of the Royal Academy of Music. The fact that during these thirty years only fifty-seven Italian operas by other composers were produced in London serves to demonstrate Handel's absolute predominance.

'Majesty, grandeur, force, fire and invention'—these, according to Burney,[1] were the qualities in which Handel excelled as a composer of operas. Yet if they are not allied to specifically operatic qualities, such as a feeling for situation, character and action, they will not suffice to keep such works alive. Handel's downfall as an opera composer was spectacular indeed. After so many triumphs in this field the demand for his operas almost completely disappeared during the last years of his life; and when a quarter of a century after his death the first great Handel Festival was held in London (1784) with *Messiah* complete and extracts from the other oratorios performed in Westminster Abbey and a concert of secular works at the Pantheon in Oxford Street, the operatic numbers included in the latter programme seem to have met with a general lack of comprehension and appreciation on the part of an exhausted audience, suffering undoubtedly from musical indigestion as well as the sub-tropical heat of that May evening.[2] It is true that three years later *Giulio Cesare* reappeared on the stage at the King's Theatre for a few performances, but in such a debased version that it was virtually a *pasticcio*, 'for little of the original music was retained, and many of his most favourite songs from other operas were introduced, Verdi prati, Dove sei, Rendi sereno il ciglio, and others'.[3] In fact, his

---

[1] Dr. Charles Burney, *An Account of the Musical Performances etc. in Commemoration of Handel*.

[2] Cf. Dr. Charles Burney, *op. cit.*

[3] The Earl of Mount Edgcumbe, *op. cit.*

operas did not return to the stage in their original form until some were revived, mainly out of musicological interest, in England and Germany during the third and fourth decades of the twentieth century.

There were a few tentative efforts to write English operas after the Italian manner during his lifetime. He himself made a small but important contribution to the native effort when he allowed his masque of *Acis and Galatea*, originally written to words by John Gay in 1719, to be reproduced in 1732[1] as an English pastoral opera sung in costume, but without action, against a background of suitable scenery. The same year J. F. Lampe, a German bassoon player who a little later was to score a considerable success with his burlesque opera, *The Dragon of Wantley*, composed two operas for the Little Theatre in the Haymarket. The first, *Amelia*, was an adaptation by Henry Carey of the Beaumont and Fletcher type of romantic tragi-comedy. The second, *Britannia*, was intended to set forth 'the Glory and Happiness of *Great Britain*'. Here the book was by Lediard, who had just returned to London from the Hamburg Opera House; and according to the advertisement the opera was given 'with the Representation of a Transparent Theatre, curiously illuminated, and adorn'd with a great Number of Emblems, Motto's, Devices, and Inscriptions; and embellished with Machines, in a Manner entirely new'. Another German contribution came from John Christopher Smith, whose father originally came over from Anspach in 1716 to act as Handel's treasurer and secretary. Smith junior began to receive music lessons from Handel in 1725 and at the age of twenty made a setting of Carey's *Teraminta*, which was produced at the Lincoln's Inn Fields Theatre in 1732. Later he became Handel's amanuensis and in 1755 was responsible for an operatic version of *A Midsummer Night's Dream*, called *The Fairies*, which David Garrick produced at Drury Lane.

The one English composer of undoubted originality and talent to appear at this time was Dr. Thomas Augustine Arne. In 1733 at the age of twenty-three he made his first appearance as a stage

[1] For particulars of London's operatic fare during this year see Appendix D.

composer with a new setting of Addison's *Rosamond*. This achieved considerable success and was followed by a number of attempts to modernise the form of the masque. In 1738 he remodelled *Comus*, discarding the original music by Henry Lawes and getting Dr. John Dalton to add various characters and scenes to Milton's original poem. Two years later he dealt with William Congreve's *The Judgment of Paris* in a similar way; and the same year appeared *The Masque of Alfred* with words by James Thomson and David Mallet, which contained a patriotic Ode in Honour of Great Britain, *Rule Britannia!* This was perhaps the moment when Arne might have been expected to strike a blow for native opera and renew the tradition that had been broken by Purcell's death; but that he was in some ways temperamentally unsuited to do so appears from letters he wrote to Garrick about 1770 when a revival of Purcell's *King Arthur* was being discussed. 'The long scene of the sacrifice in Act I may have a solemn and noble effect, provided that the last air and chorus be performed as I have now composed it,' he wrote; 'the introductory air to be sung by Champness, which, being highly spirited, will carry off with an éclat an otherwise dull, tedious, antiquated suite of chorus. . . . The air "Let not a moon-born elf" is after the first two bars of Purcell, very bad. Hear mine. All the other solo songs of Purcell are infamously bad; so very bad that they are the objects of sneer and ridicule to the musicians. I wish you would allow me to doctor this performance. I would certainly make it pleasing to the public.'

Yet it is only fair to add that Charles Dibdin, who was an ardent admirer of Purcell and described his imagination as having 'a majesty and a refulgence, like the sun breaking from a cloud',[1] went out of his way to praise Arne's adaptation of *King Arthur* and to maintain that 'so far from mutilating Purcell, as a modern compiler would have done . . . his whole study was to place his idolized predecessor in that conspicuous situation, the brilliancy of his reputation demanded.[2]

The part played by Arne in the field of comic opera will be

[1] *The Musical Tour of Mr. Dibdin.*   [2] *Ibid.*

touched on in the following chapter; but here should be mentioned his two attempts to write *opera seria* after the Italian manner. For both he turned to Metastasio as his librettist. In 1762 he himself translated *Artaserse* into English and set it in a somewhat extravagant style. *Artaxerxes* was virtually the last of the eighteenth-century English operas after the Italian manner: it proved remarkably successful with the public, and there were occasional revivals of it during the next seventy-five years. Josef Haydn was particularly delighted with it during one of his London visits; and, writes a Mrs. Henslow,[1] 'he told my dear mother (for he was frequently with us at Vauxhall) that he had not an idea we had such an opera in the English language'. Despite its native idiom, however, it was necessary to engage two Italian singers, Tenducci and Perelli, for its first performance at Covent Garden, and this fact roused the wrath of Charles Churchill in the *Rosciad*. His patriotic protest seems all the more barbed when it is remembered that it is directed against the composer of *Rule Britannia!* and the arranger of *God Save our Noble King!*

> '*Let Tommy Arne with usual pomp of style*
> *Whose chief, whose only merit's to compile . . .*
> *Publish proposals, laws for taste prescribe*
> *And chant the praise of an Italian tribe . . .*
> *But never shall a truly British age*
> *Bear a vile race of eunuchs on the stage:*
> *The boasted work's called National in vain*
> *If one Italian voice pollute the strain.*'

Whether or not Arne took Churchill's rebuke to heart, he never followed up *Artaxerxes*; but the next time he wrote an *opera seria* in the Italian manner he left Metastasio's libretto (*Olimpiade*) in the original Italian. This work did not find favour with the public when produced at the Haymarket in 1764, and its music has not survived.

By this time the need for drastic operatic reforms was widely recognised. Lack of co-operation between composer and librettist

---

[1] Letter of Mrs. Henslow quoted in Cradock's *Literary and Miscellaneous Memoirs*, Vol. IV, p. 133.

had led to the undramatic development of opera into a series of *pezzi staccati* strung together by recitative. Recitative itself, whether *secco* or *stromentato*, was apt to sink into a perfunctory routine; and individual numbers were often cast in the form of *da capo* airs, which by the nature of their ternary musical form checked the flow of the drama by material repetitions which might be illogical and unnatural, and sometimes had the effect of a dramatic reversal The position was not improved by the immense power arrogated to themselves by the star singers with their extravagant and self-centred caprices.

Writing in 1762 in his *Saggio sopra l'Opera in Musica*,[1] which he dedicated to William Pitt, Count Francesco Algarotti complained that those responsible for producing operas did not 'pay a proper attention to the several necessary constituents for making an opera perfect'. They were 'remiss in choosing the subject of their dramas, and still more negligent about the words thereof being congenially adapted for the music that is to accompany them. These gentlemen appear to be entirely careless of verisimilitude in the singing and recitative parts—as well as about the connection that ought to subsist between the intervening ballets executed by the dancers, and the main business of the drama. The former should seem to spring genuinely from the latter. They are equally regardless of appropriate decorations in the scenery department; and the faulty structure of their theatres, hitherto, hath quite escaped their notice. What wonder then, if that species of dramatic representation, which, from its nature, ought to prove the most delightful of all scenic entertainments, hath degenerated to such a degree of insipidity and irksomeness to spectators in general!' The remedy he suggested was that 'the poet should resume the reins of power' so as to restore proper order and discipline.

Reform, however, was at hand. The year before Algarotti's *Saggio* was published Gluck's *Orfeo ed Euridice* was produced in Vienna; and in his Preface to *Alceste* (1767) Gluck made it clear

[1] An English translation entitled *An Essay on the Opera* was published in Glasgow by R. Urie in 1768.

that he was now deliberately collaborating with his librettist, R. de' Calzabigi, on the lines that had been independently recommended by Algarotti. 'I endeavoured to reduce music to its proper function,' he wrote, 'that of seconding poetry by enforcing the expression of the sentiment and the interest of the situations, without interrupting the action, or weakening it by superfluous ornament.' And his genius was strong enough to restore to its rightful place in European tradition the true operatic principle as originally enunciated by the Florentine Camerata. England, however, was not touched by this reform, for serious opera in English had completely collapsed and the only signs of real vigour were to be found in various forms of light opera such as ballad opera, comic opera and burlesque.

CHAPTER III

Poor Relations
(Eighteenth Century)

Light Operas—The Beggar's Opera—Ballad Operas—The Gentle Shepherd in Scotland—The Devil to Pay Abroad—Fielding as Librettist—The Dragon of Wantley—Dr. Arne and his Son— Samuel Arnold—Charles Dibdin—Thomas Linley—Anthony Pasquin's Satire on Contemporary Operas—English Operas Abroad— Stephen Storace—Mozart's Operas in England

IT MIGHT have been thought that the downfall of Handel as an operatic composer would bring with it also the collapse of Italian opera in London; but no such thing occurred. Despite all the irrational elements in its structure and production and the need for drastic reform, Italian opera quickly recovered its popularity with the London aristocracy. It continued to be given regularly, mainly at the King's Theatre in the Haymarket; and during the time that elapsed between the death of Handel and the turn of the century Italian operas were played there with music by forty to fifty different composers. Of these, B. Galuppi, G. B. Lampugnani, C. Gluck, D. Terradellas, J. C. Bach, V. Rauzzini, A. Sacchini, M. Cherubini and Martin y Solar, each had one or more of their operas performed in London for the first time on any stage. It should be remembered, too, that Josef Haydn's second London visit (in 1794) was due to a commission to write an opera on the theme of Orpheus for the King's Theatre in the Haymarket; but various delays connected with its production so discouraged him that he returned to Austria with the score unfinished. During the same period the stage activities of English composers were directed to different ends. There is a scene in *The Rehearsal, or, Bays in Petticoats* (1750), a burlesque by Mrs. Clive with incidental music by Dr. William Boyce, where two of the characters discuss the nature of a new piece:

'WITLING: *But pray Madam, you say you are to call your new thing, a Burletto; what is a Burletto?*
MRS. HAZARD: *What is a Burletto? why haven't you seen one at the Haymarket?*
WITLING: *Yes; but I don't know what it is for all that.*
MRS. HAZARD: *Don't you! Why then, let me die if I can tell you, but I believe it's a kind of poor Relation to an Opera.*'

The burletto was not the only poor relation to an opera current in the eighteenth century. There were many other forms of light opera, such as ballad opera, comic opera, musical farce, and musical entertainment, which could perhaps not unjustly be given this description. All these obtained a wide measure of popularity; but they were not operas in the true sense, for in them practically the whole of the action was carried on by spoken dialogue and the music confined almost entirely to the setting of incidental lyrics and various concerted numbers.

The distinction is fundamental. Opera relies on musical principles for its conduct and form; light opera on dramatic principles. It is true that at times the two types will be found to approximate to each other; but however noble and serious light opera may occasionally become, and to whatever levels of light-hearted comedy opera proper may condescend, the truth remains that light opera by its very nature shirks the fundamental esthetic problem that opera tries to solve.

These poor relations have therefore little to add to the story of English opera proper; but their interest resides mainly in the fact that they achieved much wider popularity and currency than the Italian article and persuaded new audiences to accept music as a legitimate partner in stage representation.

The voracious appetite for light music in the eighteenth century undoubtedly owes its inception to the enormous success of *The Beggar's Opera* (1728), whose origin as described by Joseph Spence in his *Observations, Anecdotes, and Characters of Books and Men* is quoted by Dr. Johnson in *Lives of the Poets* (1781). 'Dr. Swift had been observing once to Mr. Gay, what an odd pretty sort of a

E

thing a Newgate Pastoral might make. Gay was inclined to try at such a thing for some time; but afterwards thought it would be better to write a comedy on the same plan. This was what gave rise to the *Beggar's Opera*.' The resulting ballad opera caught the fancy of the public, which found something diverting, if not admirable, in the spectacle of a highwayman hero, though for many years afterwards moralists were apt to censure it on the grounds that its performance encouraged vice and crime, and so late as 1775 Dr. Johnson gave as his considered opinion that 'there is in it such a *labefactation* of all principles, as may be injurious to morality'.[1] Its satire, however, was directed both against the corrupt political administration of Sir Robert Walpole and against the excesses of Italian opera at the Royal Academy of Music, then near the end of its short career; and Gay's own apology that his 'only intention was to lash in general the reigning and fashionable vices, and to recommend and set virtue in as amiable a light' as he could[2] did not prevent his being accused, in general terms, of libel and sedition, so that when he came to ask the Lord Chamberlain for a licence to perform its sequel, *Polly*, he was informed that 'it was not allow'd to be acted, but commanded to be supprest'.[3] This meant that *Polly* had to wait nearly half a century for its first stage performance, which ultimately took place in 1777 at the Little Theatre in the Haymarket.

For both these works Gay used the services of Dr. John Christopher Pepusch, a musician who had come over from Berlin and settled in London towards the end of the seventeenth century. In 1707 Pepusch had been responsible for *Thomyris, Queen of Scythia*, a *pasticcio* sung partly in English and partly in Italian to music by A. Scarlatti, G. Bononcini and others. For *The Beggar's Opera* he took many popular songs, some of which had been used before in Thomas Durfey's comic opera, *Wonders in the Sun, or, The Kingdom of the Birds* (1706), and had appeared in his song collections, *Wit and Mirth, or, Pills to Purge Melancholy*, and also a number of airs that can be attributed to composers such as Purcell,

---

[1] James Boswell, *The Life of Samuel Johnson LL.D.*, 1791.   [3] *Ibid.*
[2] John Gay, Preface to *Polly*, dated March 25, 1729.

Jeremiah Clarke, Henry Carey and Handel himself. He used sixty-nine such airs in all, arranged and orchestrated the score, and added an overture of his own composition. That there should be no misunderstanding about the type of opera this was meant to be, the Beggar was made to say in the Introduction: 'I hope I may be forgiven, that I have not made my Opera throughout unnatural, like those in vogue; for I have no Recitative;' and the quarrel between Polly and Lucy was clearly meant as a satire on the celebrated brawl between Cuzzoni and Faustina in *Astianatte* the previous summer.

The success of *The Beggar's Opera* was phenomenal; and its reception is recorded in the notes to the *Dunciad* as follows: 'This piece was received with greater applause than was ever known. Besides being acted in London sixty-three days without interruption, and renewed the next season with equal applause, it spread into all the great towns of England; was played in many places to the thirtieth and fortieth time; at Bath and Bristol fifty, etc. It made its progress into Wales, Scotland, and Ireland, where it was performed twenty-four days successively. The ladies carried about with them the favourite songs of it in fans, and houses were furnished with it in screens.' It is said that Rich, the proprietor of the theatre in the Lincoln's Inn Fields, netted £4,000 out of it, and Gay nearly £700 for his four benefit nights.

During the next few years ballad operas modelled on *The Beggar's Opera* were poured forth in profusion. Allardyce Nicoll lists nearly 120[1]—most of them in the decade 1728–38. That a collection of popular airs with new lyrics written to fit them could be satisfactorily strung together on the thread of a dramatic action was proved, once and for all, by *The Beggar's Opera*. It is true that, as Allardyce Nicoll says, part of the original worth of a ballad opera must have come 'from the subtle juxtaposition in the mind of the auditor of the *original* tune and words and of the new words written for that music';[2] but even when that particular pleasure has faded, the intrinsic value of the actual words

[1] Cf. *XVIII Century Drama: 1700–1750.* Cambridge University Press, 1925.
[2] *A History of Late Eighteenth Century Drama* (1750–1800). Cambridge University Press, 1927.

and music in *The Beggar's Opera* has remained unaffected by the
passage of time, as can be seen from its continued success in the
twentieth century in the versions of Frederic Austin, Edward J.
Dent and Benjamin Britten. No other work of the same type has
survived in the same way, though two other ballad operas deserve
special mention here: *The Gentle Shepherd* and *The Devil to Pay*.

The first performances of *The Beggar's Opera* in Scotland took
place in Glasgow in August 1728 and Haddington the following
November. Stimulated by the success of this novelty, the pupils
of the Haddington Grammar School looked round for a Scottish
equivalent. *The Gentle Shepherd*, a Scots pastoral comedy which
Allan Ramsay had written in 1725, basing it on two earlier
dialogues between *Patie and Roger* and *Peggy and Jenny*, was
accordingly fitted up with twenty-one ballad airs chosen from
the Scottish songs collected in his *Tea-Table Miscellany* and performed in this new guise—probably by the Haddington pupils
themselves—at the Taylor's Hall, Edinburgh, on February 9,
1729. The work had to wait nearly thirty years for its first professional production at the Canon-gate Theatre, Edinburgh, in
1758; but a one-act reduction by Theophilus Cibber called *Patie
and Peggy, or, The Fair Foundling*, was heard in London as early
as 1730. Its successful revival at the 1949 Edinburgh Festival
showed that the music plays an incidental rather than a dramatic
part in this entertainment; and on that occasion it was presented
by Tyrone Guthrie, the producer, as a concerted poetry recital
where the actors were joined by musicians.

The Devil to Pay, or, The Wives Metamorphos'd, a three-act
ballad opera with text by Charles Coffey, was performed at
Drury Lane, London, in 1731 and proved extremely successful,
not only like *The Beggar's Opera* in England, Ireland, Scotland
and the colonies, but also abroad. A German version, probably
with the original English ballad airs, was given in Berlin in 1743,
and it seems to have exercised a considerable influence on German
comic opera in the eighteenth century. J. C. Standfuss's *Der
Teufel ist Los, oder, Die Verwandelten Weiber*, produced in Leipzig
in 1752, was directly founded on Coffey's text and marked an

important stage in the development of German *Singspiel*. Other operatic versions of *The Devil to Pay* appeared in Germany, France, Italy and Austria in the course of the century; and so late as 1852 a new version of the Coffey text was made by Alfred Bunn for Michael William Balfe, called *The Devil's in It* and later retitled *Letty the Basket Maker* (1871).

It should also be remembered that for a few years one of the most important writers of the century was caught up by the wave of enthusiasm for ballad opera. At the age of twenty-four Henry Fielding produced *The Welsh Opera, or, The Grey Mare the Better Horse* (1731). This was followed, with increasing success, by *The Lottery* (1732) and *The Mock Doctor, or, The Dumb Lady Cur'd* (1732) adapted from Molière. The following year appeared *The Opera of Operas, or, Tom Thumb the Great*, an alteration by Mrs. Haywood and William Hatchett of Fielding's original burlesque, *The Tragedy of Tragedies, or, The Life and Death of Tom Thumb the Great*. This proved so successful that two versions were apparently used, one with music by Dr. Arne, and the other with music by J. F. Lampe.[1] After *An Old Man Taught Wisdom, or, The Virgin Unmask'd* (1735) Fielding wrote no more ballad operas and, in fact, a few years later abandoned the stage for novel writing; but that he remained sensible of the influence originally exercised on him by *The Beggar's Opera* is apparent from the way he deliberately courts comparison with that Newgate comedy in his picaresque satirical novel, *Life of Mr. Jonathan Wild the Great* (1743).

Although the vogue of the ballad opera began to decline about ten years after the production of *The Beggar's Opera*, it certainly gave a great impetus to the native taste for comedy, burlesque and the sort of mixed entertainment that ranges from opera *pasticcio* to pantomime. The general level of English light opera during the last two-thirds of the eighteenth century may not have been high, whether the music was due to an original composer or to an arranger; but a few musicians succeeded in producing attractive and popular pieces on these lines.

[1] Cf. 'Gustavus Waltz; Was he Handel's Cook?' in William C. Smith's *Concerning Handel*.

The Dragon of Wantley, brought out at Covent Garden in 1737, was a satire on Italian *opera seria* in general and Handel's *Giustino* in particular. It was written by Carey, who, in his dedicatory letter addressed to Lampe the composer, said: 'It is a Burlesque Opera: And Burlesque cannot be too low. Lowness (figuratively speaking) is the Sublimity of Burlesque: If so, this opera is, consequently, the tip-top Sublime of its Kind.' Carey's libretto was certainly low; but it was set to a most serious and graceful score by Lampe.

In his middle age Arne tried his hand at light opera and had the good luck to fall in with the dramatist, Isaac Bickerstaffe. The first fruit of their collaboration was *Thomas and Sally, or, The Sailor's Return* (1760), an attractive, light-hearted musical entertainment in two acts with only four characters and recitative instead of spoken dialogue. It was followed by *Love in a Village* (1762), a comic opera in three acts. Bickerstaffe's play was an alteration of Charles Johnson's ballad opera, *The Village Opera* (1729); and for the music Arne collected airs by various composers, adding some original music of his own. Subsequently he wrote other comic operas and musical farces, but none of them had anything like the success of these two pieces.

His son, Michael Arne, also became a stage composer. At the age of twenty-two he collaborated with Jonathan Battishill in writing the music to *The Fairy Tale* (1763), an adaptation of *A Midsummer Night's Dream* made by George Colman the Elder, and followed it up with *Almena* (1764), an 'English opera' (so styled) with libretto by Richard Rolt, and *Cymon* (1767), a dramatic romance by Garrick after Dryden's poem *Cymon and Iphigenia*.

Meanwhile, Bickerstaffe had found other musicians to work with, particularly Samuel Arnold and Charles Dibdin. Just as Goldoni had founded the libretto of *La Buona Figliuola* (set by Piccinni in 1760) on Samuel Richardson's *Pamela, or, Virtue Rewarded*, so Bickerstaffe used the same novel as basis for his libretto for Arnold's *The Maid of the Mill*, which was brought out with considerable success in 1765. This was the same year as François Philidor's *opéra comique* after Fielding's *Tom Jones*, which was produced at the Comédie Italienne, Paris. *The Maid of the Mill* was written on the usual *pasticcio* lines, for it contained numbers by J. C. Bach, Galuppi and N. Jomelli among others; but Arnold's own contributions were of a fairly high standard, and he certainly proved a skilled arranger. Without following up his subsequent career in detail, it should here be mentioned that in 1770 when he was connected with the Marylebone Gardens he appears to have composed the music to Thomas Chatterton's burletta, *The Revenge,* a revised version of an unfinished musical extravaganza originally called *Amphitryon.* Chatterton sold this pot-boiler to Mr. Atterbury, the proprietor of the Gardens, for five guineas, on July 6, just a few weeks before his suicide at the age of seventeen.

The original cast of *The Maid of the Mill* at Covent Garden included Dibdin, then a young singer of twenty, who two years later revealed an instinctive talent for composition when he wrote seven numbers for Bickerstaffe's *Love in the City.* Their collaboration reached its greatest success with *Lionel and Clarissa* (produced in 1768 and revised in 1770 when it was retitled *The School for Fathers*) and *The Padlock* (1768); and a few years later Dibdin could without exaggeration write: 'I certainly have received more public applause than any English composer, except Arne.'[1] Many other stage works followed, for some of which he wrote the words as well as the music. Towards the end of the century, however, his activities took a new direction. His songs, especially the nautical ones, had always been great popular favourites, quite apart from their stage presentation; and in 1787 he began to experiment with miscellaneous performances called Readings and Music, in which he himself appeared as interpreter of his own songs. He wrote an astonishingly vivid and individual account of his musical tour of the provinces in 1787-8, prior to his proposed embarkation for India, and at a later date, in a further attempt to benefit from the popularity of his songs, became his own publisher.

Another popular composer was Thomas Linley of Bath, father-in-law of Richard Brinsley Sheridan and father of a brilliant son,

[1] Charles Dibdin, *op. cit.*

Thomas, who when fourteen years old became friendly with his coeval, Wolfgang Amadeus Mozart, while they were both staying in Florence in 1770, but who tragically met his death by drowning eight years later at the early age of twenty-two. In 1775 Thomas Linley senior supplied the music for his son-in-law's comic opera, *The Duenna*; and, as was the custom of the time, the score was partly a *pasticcio*. Michael Kelly, the singer, relates[1] how Rauzzini's air, '*Fuggiamo di questo loco, in piena libertà*', was used as the setting for Donna Clara's song, 'By him we love offended'; and Linley junior contributed the overture, the songs, 'Could I each fault remember', 'Friendship is the bond of reason' and 'Sharp is the woe', the duet 'Turn thee round, I pray thee', and the trio at the end of the first act. That Sheridan, too, played an important part in the selection and adaptation of the music appears from the following extract from a letter he wrote Linley senior in the autumn of 1775: 'My intention was to have closed the first act with a song, but I find it is not thought so well. Hence I trust you with one of the enclosed papers; and at the same time you must excuse my impertinence in adding an idea of the cast I should wish the music to have; as I think I have heard you say you never heard Leoni,[2] and I cannot briefly explain to you the character and situation of the persons on the stage with him. The first (a dialogue between Quick and Mrs. Mattocks) I would wish to be a pert, sprightly air; for though some of the words mayn't seem suited to it, I should mention that they are neither of them in earnest in what they say. Leoni takes it up seriously, and I want him to show himself advantageously in the six lines beginning "Gentle maid". I should tell you that he sings nothing well, but in a plaintive or pastoral style; and his voice is such as appears to me always to be hurt by much accompaniment. I have observed, too, that he never gets so much applause as when he makes a cadence. Therefore my idea is, that he should make a flourish at

[1] *Reminiscences of Michael Kelly of the King's Theatre and Theatre Royal, Drury Lane*, 2 vols. London, 1826.

[2] Leoni, who was a Jew and accordingly unable to appear on Friday nights, played the part of Don Carlos in *The Duenna*. Quick was Isaac Mendoza, and Mrs. Mattocks Donna Louisa.

THOMAS ARNE (1778)

Mezzotint after the painting by R. Dunkarton

Thomas and Sally (Scene VI): engraving dated 1787.

Midas (Act II):
contemporary engraving.

The Gentle Shepherd (Act V):
engraving dated 1758.

CHARLES DIBDIN (1799)
Oil painting by Thomas Phillips (29 in. by 24½ in.).

The Padlock
Print dated 1769, showing Dibdin playing Mungo in his own opera.

The Maid of the Mill
Scene design made by John Inigo Richards (1768) a foundation member
of the Royal Academy.

The Quaker
Engraving dated 1783.

"shall I grieve thee", and return to "Gentle maid"; and so sing that part of the tune again. After that the two last lines, sung by the three, with the persons only varied, may get them off with as much spirit as possible.'

The Duenna on its production at Covent Garden on November 21, 1775, had a most successful run of seventy-five consecutive performances. The libretto is one of the best of its kind, skilful in construction and brilliant in style; and nearly 170 years later it was set again, but this time as a thorough-composed opera, by the Spanish born Roberto Gerhard.

Towards the end of the century, the general level of light opera was sinking low. It is true that about the 1780's one or two new composers of interest emerged—William Shield and William Jackson, for instance—but there was a strong tendency to debase light opera to the level of farce, and a certain amount of responsibility for this collapse must be laid at the door of J. O'Keefe. Despite William Hazlitt's extraordinary eulogy of this Irish writer in his *Lectures on the English Comic Writers*,[1] where he compares him to Molière, saying that 'in light, careless laughter, and pleasant exaggerating of the humorous, we have had no one equal to him', it must be generally conceded that the greater part of this prolific writer's work is remarkable only for its poverty of invention and mawkish sentimentality, and that none of it rivals so genial and amusing a burletta, for example, as *Midas* by his compatriot, Kane O'Hara, which had been produced in Dublin in 1762. (Michael Kelly, who sang in a revival of *Midas* at Drury Lane on October 25, 1812, considered that O'Hara's work of adaptation was 'not only elegant and tasteful, but evinced a thorough knowledge of stage effect.'[2])

The plight of English opera could not fail to excite comment. Lieutenant-General John Burgoyne in his Preface to *The Lord of the Manor* (1780), the music to which was composed by Jackson, wrote that 'the adopting what is called recitative into a language, to which it is totally incongruous, is the cause of failure in an

[1] Lecture VIII, 'On the Comic Writers of the Last Century'.
[2] Michael Kelly, *op. cit.*

English serious Opera much oftener than the want of musical powers in the performers' and considered that the music in such productions should be subordinate. In this he was acting as advocate of a cause that in view of the absence of a worthy successor to *Artaxerxes* and the general popularity of light opera seemed already to be won. But a few years later John Williams, writing under the pseudonym of Anthony Pasquin, viciously scourged this type of entertainment in his satirical poem, *The Children of Thespis*, saying

> '*an OPERA at best*
> *Is an error-made monster, and national jest;*
> *Manufactur'd the reason of man to affright,*
> *Insulting our wit, while it flatters the sight.*'[1]

Although Pasquin, who was later referred to by Lord Macaulay as 'that filthy and malignant baboon', was clearly an unprincipled and unreliable character, his comments on the people connected with the stage in his day are interesting and not altogether valueless, for they undoubtedly communicate something of that elusive theatrical quality that goes with any successful stage presentation, but is so hard to isolate and define.

In the first place it should be noted that, unlike Dr. Arne, he was an unstinted admirer of Purcell. Writing of Mrs. Crouch, the singer, he says:[2]

> '*When Dryden's gay Venus comes on with a smile,*
> *To chant the best boons of her favorite isle,*
> *The soul of great Purcel bursts forth from the tomb,*
> *And, listening, flutters with joy round the dome.*'

And one of his complaints against the prolific Dibdin is that

> '*He's by Modesty scorn'd, yet he's vulgarly clever,*
> *And makes Vanity even more hideous than ever:*
> *Like the foot of a stocking, his fancy's been torn,*
> '*Tis continually darn'd and continually worn:*
> *With movements from PURCELL and ends of old songs,*
> *To illustrate low trash and inveigle base throngs.*'[3]

---

[1] *The Children of Thespis*, Part III, 1788.   [2] *Op. cit.*, Part I, 1785.   [3] *Ibid.*

Two operas come in for his special strictures: Linley's *Strangers at Home*,

> '*a strange medley indeed!*
> *Where jest, noise and nonsense each other succeed.*'

and Dibdin's *Liberty Hall*.

> *With abortions of Reason he once strove to scrawl,*
> *And baptis'd the vile spectacle—LIBERTY-HALL.*
> *—May shame brand the man who such nonsense protected,*
> *When Genius implor'd him, and Wit lay neglected!*
> *But fiddler with fiddler will huddle together,*
> *Like bugs in a blanket, that sleep in cold weather.*'[1]

It has already been seen that *The Beggar's Opera* was played widely throughout England, Ireland and Scotland immediately after its first production; and the same is true of most other successful eighteenth-century light operas. Dublin in particular, with its theatres in Smock Alley, Aungier Street, Fishamble Street, Crow Street, and Capel Street was an alert and vital capital; and it is not surprising to find so many excellent composers, dramatists and singers have been Irish in origin. But the taste for light opera also crossed the ocean. It spread to America—Baltimore, Charleston, New York and Philadelphia were specially important operatic centres in the United States; and in the West Indies there are records of light operas being given in Jamaica from an early date. Chetwood relates[2] that a 'Company in the Year 1733, came there, and clear'd a large sum of Money where they might have made moderate fortunes, if they had not been busy with the Growth of the Country.[3] They receiv'd 370 Pistoles the first Night to the *Beggar's Opera*, but within the Space of two months they bury'd their 3d *Polly*, and two of their Men'. Despite this Company's inauspicious season, other companies (mostly American) visited the island later on, playing in the theatres at Kingston and Spanish Town and in 'Mr. Lugg's Great Room' at Montego Bay prior to the building of the New Theatre there.

[1] *Op. cit.*, Part I, 1785.   [2] W. R. Chetwood, *op. cit.*
[3] 'The noble Spirit of Rum-Punch, which is generally fatal to new Comers.' *Ibid.*

West Indian themes and settings were very popular in this country, as can be seen from such works as *Polly* and *Inkle and Jarico*. Meanwhile, towards the end of the century, one finds English operatic performances being given as far afield as India; but it is not until the nineteenth century that South Africa and Australia are reached.

With regard to foreign countries, an English company appears to have visited St. Petersburg in the autumn of 1771 and winter of 1772 with *The Padlock, Midas* and *The Maid of the Mill* in its repertory; and in 1795 a Mr. Williamson from Edinburgh opened a short-lived English theatre in Hamburg where various light operas, including *The Shamrock* and *No Song No Supper*, were performed.

The latter work was written by Stephen Storace, son of an Italian double-bass player who had settled in London about the middle of the century. This composer provides an interesting link with Mozart, for in his early twenties he went with his sister Anna to Vienna, where he produced two operas about the time of the first performances of *Der Schauspieldirektor* and *Le Nozze di Figaro*. The first, *Gli Sposi Malcontenti*, which came out in 1785 was followed the next year by *Gli Equivoci*, a *dramma buffo* written by Lorenzo da Ponte after Shakespeare's *Comedy of Errors*. On his return to London in March 1787 he made an English version of Karl Ditters von Dittersdorf's *Doctor und Apotheke* (Drury Lane, 1788) and used parts of the music to *Gli Equivoci* for his English operas, *No Song No Supper* (1790) and *The Pirates* (1792). For *The Siege of Belgrade* (1791), he drew largely on Martin y Solar's music to *Una Cosa Rara* (Vienna, 1786), from the finale to Act I of which it will be remembered Mozart quoted in his *Don Giovanni*; and there is a direct quotation from the Alla Turca movement of Mozart's Piano Sonata in A (K. 331) at the end of the Overture. A scene and a quintet in the third act of *The Pirates* (1792) were taken from Guglielmi's opera *La Bella Pescatrice*; but (in the words of his friend, Kelly) 'whatever Storace selected, his knowledge of stage-effect was so great that the selections were always appropriate, and never-failing.'[1] The principal vocal part in his last

[1] Michael Kelly, *op. cit.*

opera, *Mahmoud* (1796), was written specially to introduce the young tenor, John Braham, to the London stage. His operas were extremely well thought of in England at the time they were produced. The way in which he united English words to the prevailing Italian style of melody was considered to be particularly felicitous; and it was said that he was the first to introduce concerted pieces and finales upon the English stage. When referring to his early death at the age of thirty-three, his great friend, Michael Kelly, drew attention to the 'singular coincidence, that three such great musical geniuses as Purcell, Mozart, and Storace, were nearly of the same age when fate ordained them to their early graves'.[1]

Already at the age of eight Mozart had spent a year in London, where he met J. C. Bach and may possibly have heard at Drury Lane or Covent Garden such new English operas as *Almena*, *The Maid of the Mill*, *Pharnaces*, or Arne's *Olimpiade* (in Italian). Although it took some time for the operas of his maturity to reach England—the first of them to be produced here, *La Clemenza di Tito*, was not given until Mrs. Billington's benefit in 1806[2]— some single numbers appear to have become popular at quite an early date. The duet *Crudel! perchè finora* from *Le Nozze di Figaro* was included in the London production of G. Gazzaniga's *La Vendemmia* in 1789; and Leigh Hunt relates in his *Autobiography* how as a schoolboy of eleven or twelve (*circa* 1796) he bore to Christ Hospital 'the air of *Non più andrai*; and, with the help of instruments made of paper, into which we breathed what imitations we could of hautboys and clarionets, had inducted the boys into the "pride, pomp and circumstance" of that glorious bit of war'. Storace's score of *Gli Equivoci*, written in Vienna just after *Le Nozze di Figaro*, was probably familiar to Mozart, and part of this opera's music was subsequently reproduced in *No Song No Supper* and *The Pirates*.

Writing of Mozart in the *Monthly Magazine* for March 1811, that shrewd critic William Gardiner said:[3] 'His imagination has

[1] Michael Kelly, *op. cit.*
[2] Cf. Appendix B.
[3] Quoted in a footnote to the English translation of Stendhal's *The Life of Haydn in a Series of Letters written at Vienna*, etc. John Murray, 1817.

infused a sublimity into the opera, that now renders it the highest
of all intellectual pleasures. And it is to be lamented that a great
nation, like England, has not talent, or ability, sufficient to represent and perform any of the works of this great master. We are
still doomed to listen to the effeminate strains of Italy, while the
gorgeous and terrific *Don Juan*, and the beautiful *Clemenza de Tito*
lye unopened, and unknown. . . . It is a matter of curious moment,
that we are now in possession of the very works that are to form
the acme of theatrical representation in a succeeding age.' By June
of the following year, however, this reproach had been almost
wholly removed, for there had been performances (in Italian) of
Così Fan Tutte, *Die Zauberflöte*, *La Clemenza di Tito* and *Le Nozze
di Figaro*. In 1817 *Don Giovanni* was added to the repertory;[1] and
by the reign of George IV the Earl of Mount Edgcumbe, a dis-
criminating amateur of Italian opera since 1773 and a pronounced
laudator temporis acti, was prepared not only to praise Mozart's
operas for 'their beauty, their originality, their infinite variety,
and scientific elegance', but also to predict that his name would
'live for ever and his compositions descend as sterling gold to
posterity, and be listened to with delight in all times and in all
places, so long as the natural taste and feeling for music, common
to man in all ages and situations, and the love of its true genuine
beauties, shall continue to exist'.[2]

[1]There is an early reference to it in T. L. Peacock's *Nightmare Abbey* (1818). ' "I am
in the middle of hell" said Scythrop furiously. "Are you?" said she; "then come across
the room and I will sing you the finale of *Don Giovanni*." '

[2] The Earl of Mount Edgcumbe, *op. cit.*

CHAPTER IV

Romantic Operas
(Nineteenth Century)

Rossini's Operas in England—German Opera—The Romantic Movement—Ossian—Ossianic Operas—Sir Walter Scott— Waverley Operas—Byronic Operas—Sir Henry Bishop—Weber's Der Freischütz—Oberon—Bishop's Aladdin—English Romantic Opera—Michael William Balfe—Balfe's National English Opera Scheme—Balfe Abroad—Balfe Returns—The Pyne-Harrison Company—William Vincent Wallace—Collapse of the Pyne-Harrison Company—Appreciation of English Romantic Operas

B Y THE turn of the century the flame of English opera was burning very low. Not only had no serious English opera been written since *Artaxerxes*, but even the astonishing flow of ballad operas, comic operas, and every form of light opera that had poured forth upon the British stage during the latter part of the century began to show signs of being submerged by the so-called burlettas and other musical farces and entertainments that were produced by the non-patent theatres to circumvent the law. The theatre was in the doldrums. There were few English dramatists or composers of initiative or originality; and as far as serious opera was concerned, audiences seemed content with regular annual seasons of foreign operas sung preferably by foreign singers in a foreign tongue.

After the introduction of Mozart's operas the most striking feature of London's operatic life in the early part of the nineteenth century was the meteoric rise to popularity of Gioacchino Rossini. As soon as his *Il Barbiere di Seviglia* was heard in London in 1818, just two years after its original production in Rome, most of his other operas followed suit.[1] He himself visited London in December 1823 and appeared at the pianoforte during the performance of several of his operas at the King's Theatre in the Haymarket. He was indeed supposed to write a new opera before he left; but

[1] Cf. Appendix B.

Ugo, Rè d'Italia,[1] though partly composed, was never finished and when he broke his contract and returned to Paris in the summer of 1824 the incomplete manuscript was left behind, remaining (according to John Ebers, the manager of the King's Theatre) 'in the hands of Messrs. Ransom, the bankers'.[2] When thirty-five years later this firm was asked by H. Sutherland Edwards for information on the subject they declared they had never had a score of Rossini's in their possession;[3] and a careful search of their records carried out by Barclays Bank, Limited, in 1949 revealed that no documents, parcels or other items likely to have been the missing Rossini score had been deposited with them during the years 1824-28.

In 1832, two years after the first performance of *Guillaume Tell* in England, an important development occurred: the first German season in London was given by a visiting company playing Beethoven's *Fidelio* and Weber's *Der Freischütz* at the King's Theatre in the original German. It was followed shortly afterwards by German performances of Mozart's *Don Juan* and *Die Zauberflöte*. The popularity of German opera steadily increased during the reign of Victoria and culminated in 1882 when Richard Wagner's *Der Ring des Nibelungen* was given for the first time in Great Britain at Her Majesty's Theatre, while at Drury Lane Hans Richter conducted the first performances in this country of *Die Meistersinger* and *Tristan und Isolde*.

The interest in German opera and German folklore and mythology was symptomatic of the general shifting of focus from classical tradition to romantic innovation that occurred at the end of the eighteenth and beginning of the nineteenth centuries; and at first it seems strange to find that a word so strongly rooted in Mediterranean culture as 'romantic' should be used to describe a movement that in many of its aspects was in revolt from the hegemony of Southern Europe and tended to glorify the culture of the Goths, Teutons and Celts as opposed to that of the Greeks and Romans.

[1] This unfinished work is sometimes referred to as *La Figlia dell'Aria*.
[2] John Ebers, *op. cit.*
[3] H. Sutherland Edwards, *The Life of Rossini*. London, 1860.

In a quest to return to nature and the ideal natural state the mind of man at the turn of the century was reaching out to explore vast tracts of hitherto unknown or only vaguely apprehended territory. The enthusiasms of the romantics were often fierce and consuming, but they could also be shallow and misleading. Lack of balance, reason and discipline sometimes led to false conclusions or half conclusions; and fallacies abounded—particularly the fallacies of pathos, sensibility, melancholy and horror. It is true that *omne ignotum pro magnifico* might well have been chosen as a catch phrase of the movement; but it should not be forgotten that the strong, desperate, but often indiscriminate enthusiasm for the romantic must have corresponded with the growing sense of frustration in the heart of man.

As is well known, the initial impetus of the romantic movement came largely from Great Britain, and one of its most striking literary manifestations was the poetry of Ossian, as published in three volumes, *Fragments of Ancient Poetry* (1760), *The Poem of Fingal and other Pieces* (1761) and *Temora and the remaining poems of Ossian* (1762) purporting to be translations from the Gaelic or Erse language by James Macpherson. These poems were, in fact, one of the most unscrupulous and successful literary forgeries of all time. Myths that were Irish by origin were appropriated by Macpherson for Scotland; and Scottish pride was so flattered by what appeared to be a national literary discovery of the first magnitude that the Ossianic poems immediately secured a large number of fanatical supporters despite the doubts expressed by many scholars, especially in England and Ireland. Dr. Johnson, in particular, during his tour to the Hebrides in 1773, took a personal interest in the matter, but as not the slightest proof of the authenticity of the poems could be produced he remained a sceptic. In any case, he considered these works had little or no literary merit. When troubled by extravagant statements made by ardent Ossianic supporters he was wont to take evasive action by commenting 'Radaratoo radarate!'[1] and his subsequent quarrel with Macpherson is a matter of literary history.

[1] James Boswell, *The Journal of a Tour to the Hebrides with Samuel Johnson LL.D.* 1785.

F

But however thoroughly Macpherson might be exposed as an unscrupulous charlatan and his Ossianic forgeries shown to be an amalgam of hints culled from genuine Gaelic ballads, recollections of the Bible, *Paradise Lost* and Thomas Gray's *Bard*, mixed with the inventions of a mind nurtured on the picturesque mountain scenery of his native Badenoch, the damage was done. Not only had his poems been widely read throughout Great Britain, but they had been promptly translated into German, Italian, Spanish, French, Dutch, Danish, Swedish, Polish and Russian. Their influence everywhere abroad was great, but perhaps greatest in Germany, where 'the younger school of poets, having thrown off the classical tradition, lacked something to replace the classical models. . . . *Ossian* was studied and absorbed until an Ossianic colour was diffused over all they wrote. The emergence of the Celtic hero-world prompted them to revive that of Germany itself'.[1] Wolfgang von Goethe in his youth warmly admired Ossian and introduced his poems into *Die Leiden des Jungen Werther*. Klopstock and Voss considered him to be the equal of Homer; Friedrich von Schiller in his essay *On the Sublime* declared that a truer inspiration lay in the misty mountains and wild cararacts of Ossian's Scotland than in the fairest of meadows and gardens; and J. G. Sulzer in his *Theorie der Schönen Künste* (1771–4) recommended him as a subject suitable for operatic treatment. But it was not until Napoleon Buonaparte had become Emperor of France that the first Ossianic operas appeared.

Ossian was Napoleon's favourite poet, and he himself suggested to Jean Lesueur the subject of his five-act opera, *Ossian, ou, Les Bardes*, and attended its second performance at the Paris Opéra in 1804. Two years later Etienne Méhul wrote *Uthal* for the Paris Opéra Comique, a one-act opera after Ossian, in which the composer excluded violins from his orchestra in order to create a gloomy and mysterious effect. In 1809 *Colmal*, a three-act opera by Peter von Winter based on Ossian, was produced at Munich. None of these operas reached Great Britain; but *Oithona*, a

[1] J. S. Smart, *James Macpherson: an episode in literature*. David Nutt, London, 1905.

dramatic poem with incidental music by Barthélémon, was performed at the Little Theatre in the Haymarket in 1768, and *Le Songe d'Ossian* was danced as a ballet at the King's Theatre in 1824. In fact, it was not until 1915 that the first English Ossianic opera appeared—*Oithona* by Edgar Bainton, produced at the Glastonbury Festival.

Among the schoolboys in the 1780's who were attracted by Ossian and who could repeat whole cantos of his mock epic by heart was Walter Scott. In later life his taste changed, and he was then wont to admit that Ossian's poems had lost their charms for him; but his own poems and novels succeeded in completing something that Macpherson had merely set in motion. Henceforward, a romance-thirsty world was offered a chance of obtaining a far truer conception of the scenery of Scotland, its history and the characteristics of its people from the honest though sometimes careless writing of Sir Walter Scott than from Macpherson's fustian.

The international world of opera was quick to take advantage of this new material. In 1819, nine years after the publication of *The Lady of the Lake*, a dramatic version of Scott's poem by A. L. Tottola entitled *La Donna del Lago* was set by Rossini and produced in Naples. When in 1823 this opera was given in Italian at the King's Theatre, London, its music, especially the choruses and concerted numbers, was generally acclaimed; but some doubts seem to have been felt about the propriety of the Italian libretto. According to Ebers,[1] 'it gave something like an outline of the incidents of the original; and the names of the characters, and the scene of their action, were somewhat Scotch. But to expect that Signor Tottola, the manufacturer of this drama, should seize anything of the spirit and colouring of the original, the feeling, deeper by its simplicity, with which the character of our Ellen is so ripe, would imply a degree of faith, which a brief experience of the reality would suffice to dissipate.

'And yet no poem, perhaps, in the whole course of our modern literature, is, as a poem of action, more fraught with the requisites

[1] John Ebers, *op. cit.*

of dramatic interest, and situations for dramatic representation, than the Lady of the Lake. The country, the time, the characters, are so essentially those of romance, that it would seem a simple task to transfer to the stage actions and feelings which come before the mind with the vivid reality of an actual performance.

'It appears injudicious to adopt for the scene of a drama, intended to be conveyed in the language of a foreign country, the near neighbourhood of the place where the performance is to be exhibited. The inconsistency between the language and idioms of the writer and those of the scene he intends to adapt his piece to, are by this means brought under more immediate observations, and before judges capable, from personal habit and knowledge, of perceiving and feeling all the solecisms of the dramatist. To an English audience it matters little whether the details of an *Otello* or a *Pietro l'Eremita*[1] be in keeping with their supposed scenes of action or not; but our sympathies are too closely interwoven with the Scottish Lady of the Lake to endure, without jarring, any violation of the costume of the piece.'

From 1816 onwards it is true that the stage in Great Britain put forth many dramatic adaptations of Scott's Waverley Novels;[2] and most of them had incidental music. This was, for instance, the case with Thomas Morton's version of *The Lady of the Lake* entitled *The Knight of Snowdoun* (1811) and Daniel Terry's versions of *Guy Mannering* (written in 1816 in collaboration with Scott himself), *The Heart of Midlothian* (1819) and *The Antiquary* (1820), all of which had music composed by Sir Henry Rowley Bishop. In 1820 one finds Hazlitt complaining that English dramatists were 'periodical pensioners on the bounty of the Scottish press. . . . Mr. Walter Scott no sooner conjured up the Muse of old romance, and brings us acquainted with her in ancient hall, cavern, or mossy dell, than Messrs. Harris and Elliston' (the managers of Covent Garden and Drury Lane) 'with all their tribe, instantly set their tailors to work to take the pattern of the dresses, their artists to paint the wildwood scenery or some

[1] The title in England of Rossini's *Mosè in Egitto*.
[2] Allardyce Nicoll in *A History of Early Nineteenth Century Drama*, 1800–1850 (Cambridge University Press, 1930), lists over a hundred of these.

proud dungeon-keep, their musicians to compose the fragments
of bewildered ditties, and their penmen to connect the author's
scattered narrative and broken dialogue into a sort of theatrical
join-hand'.[1] But the real Waverley operas were written abroad
during the next half-century and, despite Ebers's complaint, many
of them were brought to London and sung there in Italian,
French or German, but rarely English.

After Naples, which had helped to launch Rossini's *La Donna
del Lago*, came the turn of Paris, with productions of Daniel
Auber's *Leicester, ou, Le Château de Kenilworth* (1823), François
Boieldieu's *La Dame Blanche* (1825) founded on *Guy Mannering*
and *The Monastery*, a pasticcio of Rossini's music entitled *Ivanhoe*
(1826), Michele Carafa's *La Prison d'Edimbourg* (1833) founded on
The Heart of Midlothian, and in 1867 Georges Bizet's *La Jolie Fille
de Perth*. Heinrich Marschner composed *Der Templer und die
Jüdin*, founded on *Ivanhoe*, for Leipzig in 1829. In Denmark, Hans
Christian Andersen was the author of *Bruden fra Lammermoor*,
which I. Frederik Bredal set as a 'romantisk Syngestykke' in
1832, fifteen years before Andersen's first visit to England and
Scotland when he wrote 'the magic hand of Walter Scott had
given me the spiritual bread and wine which made me forget the
world around me'. In 1835 another version of the same Waverley
novel was produced at Naples with resounding success, and
Gaetano Donizetti's *Lucia di Lammermoor* rapidly established itself
as one of the most popular operas of the century. In 1848 Henri
Laurant wrote *Quentin Durward* to a libretto by Fitzball; but it
was not until 1865 that a British composer, Balfe, started to work
on a Waverley opera to a text by A. Matthison entitled *The
Knight of the Leopard* (after *The Talisman*). In 1874 this opera was
produced at Drury Lane, four years after Balfe's death; but by
then the taste of the public had departed so far from the common-
sense standpoint of Ebers as quoted above that James Mapleson,
the director of Drury Lane, had to insist on the opera being given
as *Il Talismano* in an Italian translation made by Giuseppe Zaffira.

[1] William Hazlitt; *Criticisms and Dramatic Essays of the English Stage*. London (2nd Ed.),
1851.

After this date the flow of foreign Waverley operas dries up, while an English trickle sets in instead. Sir Arthur Sullivan's *Ivanhoe* (1891) was the first thorough-composed Waverley opera to be sung in English on its first production. Yet the fact that Isidore de Lara's *Amy Robsart* was produced at Covent Garden in 1893 in a French translation of the English libretto (based by A. H. G. Harris and F. E. Weatherley on *Kenilworth*) showed how strongly the foreign language convention still persisted. The following year (1894) the first Scottish Waverley opera, *Jeanie Deans*, with music by Hamish MacCunn and libretto by J. Bennett, appeared in Edinburgh. And so, after three-quarters of a century, part of the romantic impulse originally generated by Sir Walter Scott returned to its native land—but in an exhausted state and a somewhat outmoded operatic guise.

There were Byronic operas, too; and here again the initial impulse came from Italy, although one should not forget that so early as 1818 Michael Kelly had composed music to a drama by William Dimond based on Byron's poem, *The Bride of Abydos*. Donizetti composed a pair of such operas—*Parisina* (1833) and *Marino Faliero* (1835). And so did Verdi—*I Due Foscari* (1844) and *Il Corsaro* (1848). *Lara* served as basis for two operas: one by H. Ruolz (1835) and the other by L. A. Maillart (1864). In addition, Prince Poniatowski's *La Sposa d'Abido* was produced at Venice in 1846, Fibich's *Hedy* (after the episode in *Don Juan*) at Prague (1896) and N. Berg's *Leila* (after *The Giaour*) at Stockholm (1912).

The Ossianic, Waverley and Byronic operas by no means constitute the greater part of the corpus of romantic operas; but their British literary origin fully justifies the special emphasis placed on them in this chapter. It was Great Britain's misfortune from the operatic point of view that at the beginning of the nineteenth century she lacked musicians who could match the genius of her poets and novelists. A similar dearth of talent impoverished the theatre—indeed, it can almost be claimed that the great plays of the first part of the nineteenth century have, whether by accident or design, turned out to be plays for the study, like

Shelley's *The Cenci*[1] (1819), Beddoes's *Death's Jest Book* (first draft 1828) and Browning's *Pippa Passes* (1841), and not for the stage at all. During the period 1804 to 1834, despite the activities of various minor composers like Thomas Attwood, Domenico Corri, Charles Horn, Michael Kelly, Joseph Mazzinghi, George Reeve and George Rodwell, the only figure of any importance in the operatic world was Bishop. At various times he was associated with the musical direction of Covent Garden, Drury Lane, the King's Theatre in the Haymarket, and Vauxhall Gardens; and the greater part of his work consisted in making adaptations for the London stage of foreign operas by Boieldieu, Mozart, Rossini, Weber, Auber and Meyerbeer. He also refurbished a number of English eighteenth-century operas, including *The Lord of the Manor* (1812), *Lionel and Clarissa* (1814), *Artaxerxes* (1814) *Cymon* (1815), Dr. Arne's *Comus* (1815) and *The Beggar's Opera* (1839).

A damning comment on Bishop's work as an adaptor is to be found in the letters of Prince Pückler-Muskau, a German nobleman who paid various visits to England between 1826 and 1829. Writing of a performance of *Figaro* at Drury Lane, he said: 'You will hardly believe me when I tell you that neither the Count, the Countess nor Figaro sang; these parts were given to mere actors, and their principal songs, with some little alteration in the words, were sung by the other singers; to add to this, the gardener roared out some interpolated popular English songs, which suited Mozart just as a pitch-plaster would suit the face of the Venus de' Medici. The whole opera was, moreover, "arranged" by a certain Mr. Bishop (a circumstance which I had seen noticed in the bill, but did not understand until now)—that is, adapted to English ears by means of the most tasteless and shocking alterations.'[2]

Bishop's own so-called operas were numerous. *Angelina*, a little play with music, was produced at Margate in 1804 when he was barely eighteen; and during the next thirty years or so, many

[1] This was used as the basis for Berthold Goldschmidt's opera, *Beatrice Cenci* (composed 1950).
[2] Prince Pückler-Muskau, *A Tour in England, Ireland and France in 1828 and 1829*. London, 1832.

plays for which he provided music of more or less operatic quality were produced in London. It should be remembered, too, that he was one of the first English composers to write music for the ballet as a separate stage entertainment. A full list of his musical works for the stage comprises nearly a hundred items.

Three of his operas are specially to be remembered: *The Circassian Bride* because it was first performed at Drury Lane on February 23, 1809, the day before that theatre was burnt down; *Maid Marian* (1822) because Planché, his librettist, showed unusual initiative in basing it on one of Peacock's new satirical novels; and *Clari, or, The Maid of Milan* (1823) because it contained 'Home, sweet Home'. This tune had originally been published by Bishop as a so-called Sicilian Air in his set of *National Melodies of all Countries*; but it was his own composition and in its operatic guise became one of the most popular airs of the Victorian era and one that prima donnas were particularly fond of interpolating into other operas.

Even Bishop's own operas seem to have been open to some of the objections levelled against his adaptations of foreign operas. Thomas Dibdin, who wrote the book for *Zuma* (1818), complained that his text was 'so transformed, transposed, and altered in various ways, through all its incidents and situations, for the sake, no doubt, of improved musical subjects,—that it may not be improperly compared to the production of a provincial scene-painter, who having commenced the representation of a grove, was so assailed with hints, commands, and advice from every part of the theatre, that, in consequence of unavoidable acquiescence with all,—his intended landscape became gradually metamorphosed into a street'.[1]

A year after the Covent Garden production of *Clari* London succumbed to the fascination of Carl Maria von Weber's *Der Freischütz*. Here was a romantic opera after the hearts of the people. Kind's libretto, with such episodes as the casting of the magic bullets and the supernatural horrors of the Wolf's Glen, was right in the tradition of plays like 'Monk' Lewis's *The Castle*

[1] From the advertisement to *Zuma*, quoted in *The Reminiscences of Thomas Dibdin*.

SADLER'S WELLS

Water colour wash by Augustus Pugin (*circa* 1809). This was a preliminary sketch for a colour print by Rowlandson and Pugin.

COVENT GARDEN

The theatre as altered in 1792 from designs made by Henry Holland.

Gli Equivoci (1786)
Playbill of the first performance of Storace's opera in Vienna.

SIR HENRY BISHOP. Oil painting attributed
to G. H. Harlow (9 in. by 7 in.).

M. W. BALFE

Oil painting attributed to R. Rothwell (41 in. by 31 in.).

Bianca, or, The Bravo's Bride, as produced at Covent Garden, 1860.

The Daughter of St. Mark: design by the Messrs. Grieve for Act II Scene 3, showing the port of Famagusta seen through the battlements of the palace (1844).

Spectre; but never before had the English public heard so romantic a score. There was a quality in the music of Weber's *Singspiel* that brought with it something of the genuine freshness of nature—of the German landscape; and it is interesting to learn from Sir Julius Benedict, who about that time was Weber's pupil, that in composition 'his first transcriptions were generally penned on the return from his solitary walks' in the country.[1]

Six separate productions of *Der Freischütz* were given in various English translations in London during 1824. On February 26 it was played at the Royal Cobourg Theatre (later the Old Vic); on July 22 at the English Opera House (Lyceum); in August as an equestrian melodrama at Astley's; on September 6 in an adaptation by Edward Fitzball at the Surrey Theatre; on October 14 at Covent Garden; and on November 10 at Drury Lane. For this last production Bishop adapted the score and provided additional music.

The same autumn Weber received an invitation from Charles Kemble to write his next opera for Covent Garden. Despite his precarious state of health he accepted. The fee he was to be paid for the copyright of his new opera and for conducting various performances of *Der Freischütz* and *La Preciosa* was raised from £500 to £1,000. The subjects suggested were *Faust* or *Oberon* (the latter taken from Wieland's poem). Weber chose *Oberon*, and Planché supplied the libretto. The work of composition was for the most part completed in 1825. On March 6 the following year he arrived in London to superintend rehearsals; and the first performance took place on April 12. On returning from the theatre, he wrote to his wife: 'By God's grace and help I have tonight had such a perfect success as never before. It is quite impossible to describe the dazzling and touching effect of such a complete and cloudless triumph. God alone be praised for it! When I entered the orchestra the whole house rose as of one accord, and an incredible applause, cheers, waving of hats and handkerchiefs received me and was hardly to be quieted. . . . The splendour and perfection of the scenery pass all description, and I shall never see

[1] Sir Julius Benedict, *Carl Maria von Weber*, 1786–1826.

the like of it again. They say the expenses amounted to £7,000. Performances are to continue now every evening as long as the singers can hold out. I have undertaken to conduct the first twelve.'

Apart from Braham and Miss Cawse, the singers appear not to have been particularly good; but Weber's praise of the settings should not be overlooked, for on the spectacular side the English theatre at this date seems to have been outstanding. In any case, the vast size of the two patent theatres demanded big-scale display rather than an intimate style of production. Two years earlier, in a letter from Italy criticising the Paris Opera, Beddoes had said, 'The house is not nearly so commodious or elegant as Drury Lane, and the painting and mechanism of their scenery is not so dexterous and brilliant;'[1] and at the Scala, Milan, he found 'the scenery not equal to the best at our theatres.' Such was the opinion of a poet who, from the evidence of *Death's Jest Book*, might well have proved a first-rate librettist for a romantic composer, had a suitable opportunity arisen.

A record of the scenery and costumes, not of *Oberon* it is true, but of many of the operas and plays of the latter part of the eighteenth and early part of the nineteenth centuries is preserved in the attractive toy theatre sheets issued about this time by William West, the Hodgsons and other pioneer publishers of juvenile drama. Here, apart from popular foreign operas like *The Libertine* (an adaptation of *Don Juan*), *Der Freischütz* and *The Daughter of the Regiment*, one finds that 1d. plain and 2d. coloured sheets were issued for such English semi-operas as *Tom Thumb, Midas, Cymon, The Waterman, The Siege of Belgrade, The Virgin of the Sun, The Aethiop, The Law of Java, Maid Marian* and *Don Quixote*. In this way some idea of their original stage setting has been handed down to subsequent generations.

A few days after the first performance of *Oberon* the rival house at Drury Lane produced a new opera by Bishop, also on an oriental theme taken from the Arabian Nights. Weber attended this performance (April 29) and gave the following description of

---

[1] T. L. Beddoes, Letter to Bryan Waller Procter. Milan, June 8 (1824).

it in a letter: 'Yesterday was an interesting day; the first performance of my so-called rival's opera *Aladdin*. It was difficult to
obtain places: one of the proprietors of the theatre, however,
offered me his box, and for that purpose called on me in person.
No sooner had I stepped into the box and was seen than the whole
house rose and received me with the greatest enthusiasm. This, in a
strange theatre and on such an evening, testified clearly to the love
of the nation, and much moved and rejoiced me. The opera lasted
—well, from seven to half-past eleven. That is long enough to kill
the audience and the work. The applause was at first very great.
Bishop had the same reception as myself; the overture encored as
well as the first romance of Aladdin. But gradually the applause
became fainter, and I am sorry to say justly so, for it is a small
weak affair, which can scarcely claim the pretence of an opera. A
very pretty hunting chorus passed unobserved, and when it was
over they whistled in the pit the hunting chorus from *Der
Freischütz*. Bishop was not recalled, and the opera may be said
to have failed.'

Five weeks later Weber was dead. Brief though his English
visit had been, his posthumous influence had a considerable effect
on the course of English opera and of opera generally in this
country, and his example undoubtedly strengthened the general
romantic movement in the theatre. It is true that there was an
unsuccessful attempt to repeat the example of *Oberon* in 1831 when
Ferdinand Ries, whose opera *Die Räuberbraut* had proved
extremely popular in London in 1829, was commissioned to write
The Sorceress to a libretto by Edward Fitzball; but the following
year (as has already been mentioned) *Der Freischütz* achieved the
distinction of being included in the first London season of German
opera given in German, and this marked the end of a long period
during which Italian opera had enjoyed undisputed supremacy in
this country.

The 1830's also witnessed an important revival of English
opera. This had already been forecast at the end of the previous
decade (1828) by so astute an observer as the aged Earl of Mount
Edgcumbe, who considered that of recent years English theatrical

music had shown steady improvement, while Italian opera had entered on a decline.[1] The rebuilt Lyceum Theatre opened in July 1834 under the management of Arnold, as the English Opera House with a production of *Nourjahad* by Edward James Loder. This was followed by John Barnett's *The Mountain Sylph*, which has been described as the first true English opera since Dr. Arne's *Artaxerxes*, a work of charm and imagination in which 'the composer, almost for the first time since the days of Purcell, really loved his characters.'[2] Other operas produced at the English Opera House in the 1830's included John Thomson's *Hermann*, George Alexander Macfarren's *The Devil's Opera*, and a revival (in Italian) of Benedict's *Un Anno ed un Giorno* originally written for the Fondo at Naples. At the St. James's Theatre, the building of which had been financed by the celebrated tenor, John Braham, a considerable success was scored by a comic opera, *The Village Coquettes*, composed by the twenty-four-year-old John Hullah to a libretto by the twenty-four-year-old Charles Dickens who at the same time was engaged in writing the monthly numbers of the *Posthumous Papers of the Pickwick Club*. This operatic burletta (as it was described in contemporary playbills) ran for 16 nights in London and was being played at Edinburgh when a fire destroyed the theatre and all the music. But of all the composers who came into prominence during the 'thirties, the most important was undoubtedly Michael William Balfe, whose first English opera, *The Siege of Rochelle*, though originally intended for the English Opera House, was ultimately launched at Drury Lane on October 29, 1835.

Edward Fitzball, who had based the libretto of *Rochelle* on that of Ricci's opera *Chiara di Rosembergh* (1831),[3] has left an eye-witness's account of the excitements of that performance.[4] 'It was a glorious night, the first night of *The Siege of Rochelle*—one to wish your whole life long the first night of a new play or a new opera. The cram there was, the fashion, the delicious music, the enthusiastic

[1] Cf. Earl of Mount Edgcumbe, *op. cit*, Ch. VIII.
[2] Cecil Forsyth, *Music and Nationalism*, London, 1911.
[3] Text by G. Rossi, founded on Madame de Genlis's novel, *Le Siège de La Rochelle*.
[4] Edward Fitzball, *Thirty-five Years of a Dramatic Author's Life*.

applause, the double *encores*—never had I witnessed anything like it. . . . So carried away were even persons of the highest consequence by the enthusiasm created by this beautiful music (thought by many still to be Balfe's best composition), that people bent over, and nearly threw themselves from the side boxes, next to the orchestra, to congratulate and shake hands with the young composer. They crowned him with a wreath of flowers, and I question, amid all the numerous and brilliant successes of this great artist (Balfe), if he ever felt such a delighted heart as on the first night of *The Siege of Rochelle*. It ran nearly the whole season.' It should be added that the first time Queen Victoria went in state to the theatre it was to the Theatre Royal, Drury Lane, 'the "Siege of Rochelle" being performed by *special desire*. There is a celebrated portrait of her Majesty, by Paris, seated in the box'.

Balfe, who was born in Dublin in 1808, had shown a natural capacity for music from an early age. His first master was William Michael Rooke (O'Rourke), himself composer of an opera called *Amalie, or, The Love Test,* which had to wait nearly twenty years before it was ultimately produced at Covent Garden in 1837. At the age of fourteen Balfe left Ireland to continue his studies in London as the pupil of Charles Horn. The young Irish lad was gifted both as an instrumentalist and a singer and soon obtained a job as violinist in the Drury Lane Theatre orchestra. His first appearance on the lyric stage was about 1825, when he sang Caspar in *Der Freischütz* at Norwich. But his performance was apparently marred by stage fright; and a too realistic representation of the scene in the Wolf's Glen led to a false alarm of fire and a stampede among the audience. After this inauspicious début he might never have persevered with a stage career as a singer had not a chance meeting in London with Count Mazzara, who was amazed by Balfe's fortuitous resemblance to his dead son, led to an invitation to visit Rome as the Count's guest and a generous offer of financial help which would enable him to pursue his studies both there and in Milan. The parallel with Handel's Italian tour is obvious.

Balfe's tour abroad took him to France and Italy and gave him a chance to develop as singer, conductor and composer. By 1829, not only was he established as one of the chief baritones at the Théâtre des Italiens, Paris, singing leading parts in *Le Nozze di Figaro*, *Don Giovanni*, *La Gazza Ladra*, *L'Inganno Felice* and *La Cenerentola*, but he had also become the personal friend of Cherubini and Rossini. His career as a theatre composer had started in

Sketch of Queen Victoria and Prince Albert by W. M. Thackeray in a letter to J. R. Planché asking for seats for the Royal Command performance of Planché's Coronation masque, The Fortunate Isles (*music by Bishop*), *at Covent Garden Theatre, February 1840.*

1826, when he wrote a ballet score, *La Perouse,* for the Teatro alla Scala, Milan; and by 1831 three operas of his to Italian librettos had been produced at Palermo, Pavia and Milan. When, two years later, he returned to London he had already won a considerable reputation abroad; and the success of *The Siege of Rochelle* (1835) followed by the production of *The Maid of Artois* (1836) with

Madam Malibran in the title part, sealed his renown in this
country as an opera composer.

Isoline, Maid of Artois, was the last part played by Malibran
on any stage, and it appears to have been a great personal triumph.
Alfred Bunn, the author of the libretto and the then lessee of
Drury Lane, recounts[1] how on the first night when he went into
her dressing-room between the second and third acts to ask how
she felt, 'she replied, "Very tired, but" (and here her eye of fire
suddenly lighted up), "you angry devil, if you will contrive to
get me a pint of porter in the desert scene, you shall have an encore
to your finale." Had I been dealing,' Bunn continues, 'with any
other performer, I should perhaps have hesitated in complying
with a request that might have been dangerous in its application
at the moment; but to check *her* powers was to annihilate them.
I therefore arranged that, behind the pile of drifted sand on which
she falls in a state of exhaustion, towards the close of the desert
scene, a small aperture should be made in the stage; and it is a fact
that, from underneath the stage through that aperture, a pewter
pint of porter was conveyed to the parched lips of this rare child
of song, which so revived her, after the terrible exertion the scene
led to, that she electrified the audience, and had strength to repeat
the charm, with the finale to the *Maid of Artois*. The novelty of
the circumstance so tickled her fancy, and the draught itself was
so extremely refreshing, that it was arranged, during the subsequent run of the opera, for the negro slave, at the head of the
governor's procession, to have in the gourd suspended to his neck
the same quantity of the same beverage, to be applied to her lips,
on his first beholding the apparently dying *Isoline*.' This episode
led to a tradition that in this scene the singer should always at a
certain bar retire up stage and kneel down back to the audience.

There is no doubt that, as and when produced, the operas of
Balfe—old-fashioned, naïve and superficial though they may

[1] Alfred Bunn, *The Stage: both before and behind the Curtain*. Apparently, the sixteen
performances of *The Maid of Artois* during the 1836 season grossed £5,690 11s. 0d. (an
average of £355 a performance), as against nine performances of *La Sonnambula* and four
of *Fidelio* (in both of which Malibran also appeared), at averages of £333 and £317
respectively.

appear today—were considered by his contemporaries to mark a signal advance in English opera. Writing of the state of English opera in the early 1820's, Planché said that when in conjunction with Bishop he had made an attempt in his second opera, *Cortez*, 'to introduce concerted pieces, and a finale to the 2nd act more in accordance with the rules of true operatic construction, it had

Signor Balfi.

Sketch of Balfe in his opera The Siege of Rochelle *made by W. M. Thackeray from one of the Drury Lane boxes in the autumn of* 1835.

proved, in spite of all the charm of Bishop's melody, a signal failure. Ballads, duets, choruses, and glees, provided that they occupied no more than the fewest number of minutes possible, were all that the play-going public of the day would endure. A dramatic situation in music was "caviare to the general", and inevitably received with cries of "Cut it short!" from the gallery, and obstinate coughing and other significant signs of impatience

BALFE'S
GRAND OPERA, THE
DAUGHTER OF S^{T.} MARK,
IS
ONE BLAZE OF TRIUMPH
Throughout its entire Performance, and, in consequence thereof,
WILL BE PERFORMED EVERY EVENING.

All Privileges, excepting those of the Public Press, must be suspended.

This Evening, TUESDAY, Dec. 13th, 1844,
Her Majesty's Servants will perform (*for the 17th time*)

A GRAND OPERA SERIA,
(IN THREE ACTS) entitled the
DAUGHTER OF S_{T.} MARK

The Music by M. W. BALFE.	The Libretto by A. BUNN.
The Scenery by the Messrs. GRIEVE.	The Dances by Monsieur ALBERT.
The Mise en Scene by Mr. W. WEST.	The Properties by Mr. BLAMIRE.
The Costumes by Mr. PALMER & Mrs. BALLS.	The Machinery by Mr. SLOMAN.

The Mess. GRIEVE have Painted the following Scenery expressly for the occasion:

Festal Hall in the Villa Andrea,
In which is introduced a
BRIDAL DIVERTISSEMENT.
Catarina's Oratory.
APARTMENT IN
THE MONCENIGO PALACE.
BATTLEMENTS ^{OF}_{THE} CASTLE,
WITH A VIEW OF THE
PORT AT FAMAGOSTA,
ON WHICH IS SEEN, IN FULL MARCH,
THE CORTÈGE OF THE KING,
(*On a scale of Magnitude hitherto out of the power of even this Theatre to attain,*)
GARDENS of a CASINO
At NICOSIA, in CYPRUS,
WITH A
CHARACTERISTIC CYPRIOT AND VENETIAN DANCE,
Apartment in the King's Palace.

Part of a playbill advertising The Daughter of St. Mark *at the Theatre Royal, Drury Lane, 1844.*

from the pit.'[1] Such were the conditions that had prevailed during the greater part of Bishop's career. But even with his first English opera it was considered that Balfe had made a distinct artistic advance and progressed further in the region of dramatic expression than Bishop, Barnett or Loder. A responsible nineteenth-century critic[2] could write: 'All the concerted pieces in *The Siege of Rochelle* seem to grow out of the situations and exactly to express them, as well as to intensify them. The orchestra had work to do which required attention and could not be "simplified" or "guessed at". . . . In every place there was a respect for the demands of form.'

By 1838 operatic conditions had so far improved that Felix Mendelssohn Bartholdy agreed to write an opera for the London stage. Planché, who had already collaborated with Weber thirteen years previously, was the obvious choice as librettist, and in compliance with Mendelssohn's express wishes for an original, historical subject with gay and lively characters, he wrote *The Siege of Calais*. But Mendelssohn was dissatisfied by the libretto; his ardour cooled; and the opera was never composed. Years later, the same libretto was handed over to Henry Smart, who failed to complete the composition owing to trouble with his eyesight. Subsequently it was read by Balfe, who agreed with Mendelssohn in finding it unsuitable.

When Balfe started his operatic career, at the beginning of Queen Victoria's reign, the long-established tradition of spoken dialogue in English opera still prevailed, though in the earlier years of the century there had been one or two exceptions when native composers had insisted on following Italian models. For instance, *Zenobia,* composed by that amateur of opera, Lord Mount Edgcumbe, was produced for Madam Banti's benefit at the King's Theatre in 1800, the first work by an Englishman to be written for London's Italian Opera House since Arne's *Olimpiade*. Another amateur, Lord Burghersh, later the Earl of Westmorland, wrote a number of Italian operas during the period when he was

---

[1] *The Recollections and Reflections of J. R. Planché.*
[2] William Alexander Barnett in *Balfe: his Life and Work.*

envoy at Florence—*Bajazette* (1821), *L'Eroe di Lancastro* (1826), *La Fedra* (1828), *Il Torneo* (1829), *Caterina, ossia, L'Assedio di Belgrade* (1830) and *Lo Scompiglio Teatrale* (1836). An English version of *Caterina*, which was based on Cobb's libretto for Storace's *The Siege of Belgrade*, was publicly rehearsed by the students of the Royal Academy of Music, London, of which Lord Burghersh was the founder.

When *The Mountain Sylph*, the first important English romantic opera, appeared in 1834, it was found that Barnett had had the courage to discard spoken dialogue. Four years later Balfe was commissioned to write *Falstaff* as a thorough-composed opera to an Italian libretto for Her Majesty's (formerly the King's Theatre); and in 1844 he produced *The Daughter of St. Mark* as an English 'Grand Opera Seria'—the first of his English operas in which the whole of the action was expressed in music. Another English 'Grand Opera Seria' was planned in 1848 to a libretto based on Victor Hugo's *Le Roi S'Amuse*, the source of Verdi's *Rigoletto* (1851); but its composition was abandoned. How closely the idea of a thorough-composed opera was still bound up with Italian opera can be seen from the fact that in 1851 Balfe set all the spoken dialogue in Beethoven's *Fidelio* as recitative for its production in Italian at Her Majesty's; and the same year a special benefit performance of his *Les Quatre Fils Aymon* was given in Italian under the title of *I Quattro Fratelli* at the same theatre. His enormously successful opera, *The Bohemian Girl*, was produced in Italian as *La Zingara* (Her Majesty's, 1858) with specially written recitatives instead of the spoken dialogue; and Italian versions of operas by other composers—for instance, *Der Freischütz* (retitled *Il Franco Arciere*), *Oberon* and *Maritana*, with recitatives specially prepared by Costa, Benedict and Mattei respectively—were made at various times to suit the Victorian public's taste.

Comparatively early in his career Balfe conceived the idea of founding a national English Opera, and accordingly in 1841 he took the English Opera House (Lyceum) and formed a special company. His project was backed by a list of distinguished subscribers, headed by Queen Victoria and the Prince Consort, who were always his warm supporters. He himself prepared a new opera, *Keolanthe, or, The Unearthly Bride*, with a romantic Egyptian setting, which Fitzball, his librettist, described as 'one of my dream-revels with imagination—a flight across golden deserts with the Queen of Fancy'.[1] It was Balfe's intention to invite all the best-known English opera composers of the period to collaborate, including Barnett, Rooke, Lover, Macfarren and Benedict. Barnett got no further than thinking about his opera; Benedict, who was still German by nationality though he had settled in London in 1835, began to work on *The Brides of Venice*; and Macfarren, whose *El Malachor*[2] had been chosen to follow *Keolanthe*, started to compose a new opera entitled *Don Quixote*. But the grandiose scheme collapsed after the two months' run of *Keolanthe*, apparently because of the disloyalty of the artists. *The Brides of Venice* and *Don Quixote* were performed a few years later at Drury Lane, under the management of Alfred Bunn. As for Balfe, he left London for Paris, ostensibly to write a new opera for Madame Grisi. One of his first acts there was to call on Rossini, who was very indignant when he heard of the rejection of Balfe's plans. Shaking a fist in the air, he cried, as if he were addressing an imaginary English audience: '*Vous êtes des bêtes, des animaux.* You have got one of the greatest composers of the age, who has poured forth his soul in melody for you, and you would not have him. He deserved all honour; you have given him contempt. *Cochons d'Anglais, va!*'

Although *Elfrida*, the projected opera for Madame Grisi, fell through, Balfe was shortly afterwards commissioned to write a comic opera to a libretto by Eugène Scribe for the Opéra Comique, Paris. This was *Le Puits d'Amour* (1843); and its success in Paris was repeated in London the same year, when its English

---

[1] Edward Fitzball, *op. cit.*

[2] This opera is not mentioned in Appendix A because it was never produced. Written in 1838 to a libretto by the composer's father, George Macfarren, it was accepted by T. Cooke and Peake for production at the English Opera House the same year, by Bunn for Drury Lane in 1839, by Barnett for the St. James's in 1840, and by Balfe for the English Opera House in 1841; but all these arrangements ultimately fell through. Other unproduced operas by Macfarren were *Allan of Aberfeldy* (libretto by John Oxenford) written for Drury Lane in 1851, and *Kenilworth* written to an Italian libretto—probably in 1880.

49002

version, *Geraldine, or, The Lover's Well* was produced at the Princess's Theatre. *Le Puits d'Amour* was followed at the Opéra Comique by *Les Quatre Fils Aymon* (1844). This opera appears to have been inadequately cast both in Paris and in London, where it was given under the title of *The Castle of Aymon*; but after its production in Vienna as *Die Vier Haimon's Kinder* (1844) it attained considerable popularity in Central Europe, further productions being brought out at Prague, Frankfurt, Leipzig, Hamburg, Basle, Amsterdam and Berlin in the course of the next eight years.

Balfe wrote two other operas for production abroad: *L'Etoile de Séville* for the Paris Opéra in 1845, and *Pittore e Duca* which Ricordi commissioned for Trieste in 1854. The former was never heard in England; but the latter was given in an English translation by the Carl Rosa Opera Company at Her Majesty's in 1882 under the title, *Moro, the Painter of Antwerp*. His greatest success both at home and abroad, however, was undoubtedly *The Bohemian Girl*, first produced at Drury Lane in 1843. Alfred Loewenberg calls it 'the most successful English opera of the early nineteenth century and about the only one which made headway in other countries as well.'[1] How widespread was its popularity is shown by the following list of the main productions during the twelve years after its first performance:

1844	Dublin
	New York
	Philadelphia
1845	Madrid
1846	Sydney
	Vienna
	Hamburg
1847	Brünn
	Prague
1849	Stockholm
	Frankfurt
1850	Munich
	Berlin

[1] Alfred Loewenberg, *The Annals of Opera.*

1854   Trieste
Zurich
Bologna
Brescia
Bergamo
1855   Amsterdam
St. Petersburg (?)

With the exception of Sullivan's operetta, *The Mikado*, such an international success remained unique in the history of English opera until the appearance of Britten's *Peter Grimes* a century later.

It had originally been intended that *L'Etoile de Séville* should be followed by a new opera by Balfe at the Paris Opéra; but though the greater part of *Le Jour de Noël* was actually written to a libretto by Scribe, this plan had to be relinquished owing to Balfe's appointment as conductor at the Italian Opera at Her Majesty's, where Benjamin Lumley, the impresario, had just secured Jenny Lind's services at a fee of £2,500. On March 3, 1846, Balfe opened the season with the first performance in Great Britain of *Nabucodonosor* (retitled *Nino* for the occasion) by his Italian contemporary Giuseppe Verdi. This was followed two months later by *I Lombardi alla Prima Crociata*; and the next year, immediately after the production of his *Macbeth* at Florence, Verdi wrote *I Masnadieri* for Her Majesty's and visited London to conduct the first two performances.

Meanwhile, English opera continued to be presented at Drury Lane under the management first of Bunn, and later of the French conductor Louis Jullien. During the three years that Balfe was conductor of the Italian Opera he wrote two works for the rival house: *The Bondman* (1846) for Bunn and *The Maid of Honour* (1847) for Jullien. Victorian critics thought *The Bondman* remarkable because the repetition of the key melody 'Child of the Sun' was supposed to have anticipated Wagner's use of *Leitmotiv*. As for *The Maid of Honour*, some performances of which were conducted by Hector Berlioz, Balfe apparently considered it to be his most finished production.[1] But Sim Reeves, the tenor, thought

[1] Cf. Edward Fitzball, *op. cit.*

otherwise. In his autobiography, he wrote: 'Why was I made to sing a song about a chair, in no way connected with the opera, presumably introduced with the view of finding favour in the eyes of the music publishers? The sentimental song entitled "In this old Chair my Father sat," proved, all the same, one of the successes of the work; indeed, its only success.'[1]

About ten years later Balfe was associated with another English National Opera scheme. This time the initiative came from two singers, Miss Louisa Pyne and Mr. William Harrison, who entered into a partnership and got together a company for the performance of operas in English. After starting operations at the Lyceum Theatre they moved to Drury Lane and were soon promoted to Covent Garden where they gave regular seasons during the autumn and winter from 1857 to 1864. In the course of their comparatively brief existence, they presented translations of various Italian and French operas (including some by Auber) and fifteen new English operas, of which six were by Balfe; and they claimed that during their eight seasons they expended in artists' salaries, authors' fees and musical copyrights a total of about £200,000. In fact, for a short time they provided a home for English opera, and in reviewing Balfe's *Bianca, or, the Bravo's Bride* (1860), adapted from the play and novel of 'Monk' Lewis, *The Times* critic was moved to affirm that 'the star of English opera was clearly in the ascendant'.

Foremost among the other English opera composers whose works were produced by this company was Balfe's compatriot, William Vincent Wallace. In Ireland the young Wallace had been trained as organist and violinist; but when he left his native island in 1835 he went, not like Balfe to Italy, but to New South Wales. After various adventures in Australia, New Zealand, the South Seas, India, Mexico and the United States, he returned to England in 1845; and a chance meeting with Heyward St. Leger, who saw him in a private box of a theatre wearing 'a white hat with a very broad brim, a complete suit of planter's nankeen, and a thick stick in his hand' led to an introduction to Fitzball and the collaboration

[1] J. Sims Reeves, *My Jubilee*.

that produced *Maritana* (1845).[1] For the Pyne-Harrison Company
he wrote *Lurline* (1860), which was based on the legend of the
Lorelei and anticipated Wagner with a scene in the depths of the
Rhine; and at first this had an even greater success than *Maritana*.
Two years later on November 3, the same company produced
his new opera, *Love's Triumph*, at Covent Garden; and his
librettist, Planché, made an indignant protest against the barbarous
way, as soon as the Christmas holidays arrived, it was mutilated
to make room for the annual pantomime (which that year was
Harlequin Beauty and the Beast). 'The length of the dull, mon-
strous, hybrid spectacle,' he wrote, 'which has superseded the
bright, lively, and laughable harlequinade of my earlier days,
precluding the possibility of giving the opera before it, in its
integrity, not only were several airs omitted, but duets and concerted pieces cruelly hacked and mutilated, without reference to
the author or composer, to the injury of their reputation . . . and
this, remember, by a management which solicited the support of
the public for a national opera! . . . In France the author and
composer would have their remedy at law against any manager
guilty of such injustice.'[2] This treatment does not seem to have
deterred Wallace, for the following year he allowed the Pyne-
Harrison Company to produce his next opera, *The Desert Flower*
(1863), which turned out to be his last.

Other English operas produced by the company included
Victorine by Arthur Mellon, the company's conductor, *Ruy Blas*
by Howard Glover, *She Stoops to Conquer* by Macfarren, the
enormously popular *The Lily of Killarney* by Benedict, and a
revival (November 8, 1861) of Macfarren's *Robin Hood*, which
had originally been brought out by Mapleson at Her Majesty's.

'If English opera appeared to be successful under the régime of
the Pyne-Harrison Company,' said Barrett,[3] 'it was because the
works given were attractive to the public, and the managers were
careful to place them upon the stage in a manner fit for public

[1] According to Edward Fitzball (cf. *op. cit.*), Alfred Bunn wrote the words of two of
the songs: 'In happy moments,' and 'Scenes that are brightest.'
[2] J. R. Planché, *op. cit.*
[3] W. A. Barrett, *op. cit.*

The Beggar's Opera

Engraving after a painting by G. S. Newton
(*circa* 1838).

The Night Dancers as revived at the Royal English Opera, Covent Garden, 1860.

The Brides of Venice, Drury Lane, 1844.

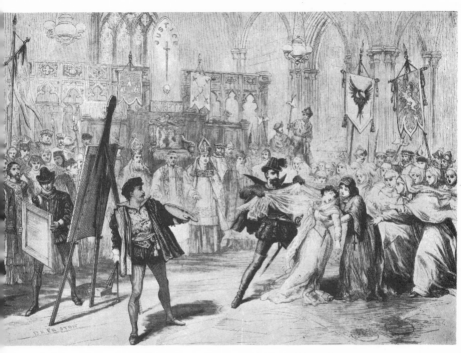

Moro, or, The Painter of Antwerp, Her Majesty's, 1882.

Lurline: the crystal dwelling of Lurline at the Covent Garden production of 1860.

COVENT GARDEN: destruction of the Opera House on the morning of March 5, 1856.

Mapleson's projected NATIONAL OPERA HOUSE (1875), as it was to be erected on the Thames Embankment.

acceptance.' But Harrison was ageing, and about this time his voice began to show signs of wear. Thomas Hardy, then in his early twenties and an assiduous frequenter of the half-crown amphitheatre at Covent Garden, was later heard to assert that Harrison's courage in singing his favourite parts, even when his voice had failed, 'might probably cause him to be remembered longer than his greatest success'.[1] But the public proved capricious; and although at first there had seemed to be a chance that a State subsidy might be forthcoming for the 'Royal English Opera', as the venture was called, the sudden death of the Prince Consort in 1861 effectively put an end to all such hopes, and a few years later the company collapsed for lack of financial support. Almost immediately an attempt was made (April 1864) to carry on its work by forming a joint stock enterprise called the English Opera Company Ltd.; but this proved equally unsuccessful, and the new company came to a sudden end early in 1866.

It is hard to assess exactly what English opera lost by the Prince Consort's early death; but the opinion of Luigi Arditi, the opera conductor, deserves quotation. Writing in 1896, he said:[2] 'The Prince Consort was a first-rate judge of music, and an accomplished amateur both as composer and executant. His frequent attendances at the operatic performances were always looked upon as a guarantee of the excellence of the music and its rendering alike. . . . The Prince Consort's death left a gap in the great patrons of the musical world which has never since been filled up.' It may or may not be coincidence, but within three years of his death the remarkable flow of English romantic operas dried up almost completely.

The following appraisal of Balfe's work by Barrett shows where his contemporaries considered the main virtues of his operas to lie and could easily be extended to apply to most of the other romantic operas of the 1834–64 period too. 'His melodies are of such a character that when the initial phrase falls upon the ear, the ear proposes the sequence. This sequence is so natural,

[1] Florence Emily Hardy, *The Early Life of Thomas Hardy*. London, 1928.
[2] Luigi Arditi, *My Reminiscences*.

that no other succession of notes but those which are written can satisfy the senses. There is no apparent effort of labour, no smelling of the lamp, no exercise of scientific contrivance thrust in by the neck and shoulders, as it were, for the same of pedantry. There is no finding out of a strange chord and building up a passage to exhibit it; there are no ugly progressions introduced for the sake of showing a contempt for the graces of art, and the position of superiority in the writer. His work is familiar, but never commonplace. . . . In the choice of subjects for his operas Balfe exhibited equally good taste. In not one is there any questionable situation or expression. The plots of his operas are all interesting, and some are exciting, but their interest and excitement are not due to actions or motives of which right-minded men scarcely dare to speak to each other. On the stage Balfe was by predilection a moral teacher. There is no sensuous swim in his music, no association with doubtful actions, or connection with words of equivocation, to carry the soul to regions of impurity. All is honest, tender, manly, straightforward, and true.'

By the end of the century the ingenuous, respectable, and often smug virtues of the Victorian romantic composers were beginning to become a serious liability; and the consensus of opinion of the new generation of critics was strongly arrayed against them. Yet even Bernard Shaw, reviewing revivals of *Lurline* and *Robin Hood* under his pseudonym of Corno di Bassetto in *The Star*, agreed that they possessed certain musical qualities of value. Of *Lurline* he wrote that to hear it once 'is enough, if not once too much. And yet there are several moments in the opera in which the string of hackneyed and trivial shop ballad stuff rises into melody that surges with genuine emotion'. The revival of Macfarren's *Robin Hood* at the National Standard Theatre, Shoreditch, he compared with Alfred Cellier's English opera, *Doris*, then newly produced at the Lyric Theatre (April 20, 1889), and came to the following conclusion: '*Doris* is the more aggravating of the two at first, because the music seems to interrupt the action until it becomes apparent that there is no action to interrupt. In *Robin Hood* the music generally advances matters: you feel that you are getting along, even though you are obviously in a no-thoroughfare.'[1] And twenty years later Cecil Forsyth, who boasted with obvious exasperation that he was 'one of the few living beings who had not only talked of but actually *read the works of the poet Bunn*'[2] and unmercifully attacked the jargon in which most of the English romantic opera librettos were written, had to admit that in the light of subsequent events Bunn and all his crew were avenged, since on the operatic stage 'a single "Ha, Ha!" aside (and in the right place) has more value than the finest string of poetical images and philosophical reflections (in the wrong place)'.[3]

During the first three decades of the twentieth century *The Bohemian Girl, Maritana* and *The Lily of Killarney* were still stock operas; but since about 1930 they have become so unfashionable that a new generation of opera-goers is growing up to whom these English romantic operas are completely unknown.

[1] Bernard Shaw, *London Music in* 1888–89 *as heard by Corno di Bassetto*. London, 1937.
[2] Cecil Forsyth, *op. cit.*
[3] *Ibid.*

CHAPTER V

Abortive National Opera Schemes
(Nineteenth Century)

1843 Theatres Act—Patent Theatres—Minor Theatres—Covent Garden—Her Majesty's—Drury Lane—Grand National Opera House—Gilbert and Sullivan Operas—Savoy Theatre—Royal English Opera House—Carl Rosa Opera Company—English Operas Produced by the Carl Rosa Company—Foreign Operas Produced by the Carl Rosa Company—Artistic Standards of the Carl Rosa Company—Moody-Manners Company

THE passing of the 1843 Act for Regulating Theatres was an important step in the reform of the theatre. Until then development had been cramped by the fact that under the restrictive Licensing Act of 1737 performances of Shakespeare and the stock repertory of tragedies and comedies had been confined in London to the two patent theatres of Drury Lane and Covent Garden, while Her Majesty's, formerly the King's Theatre in the Haymarket,[1] had been specially licensed for Italian operas since the beginning of the eighteenth century (and, subsequently, for ballets of action). This differentiation of function was adhered to quite strictly; and the Earl of Mount Edgcumbe recounts how when Paisiello's comic opera of *Nina* was performed at the King's Theatre with spoken dialogue, 'this way of acting it was deemed an infringement of the rights of the English theatres, and after a few nights it was stopped by authority, as unlawful at the opera'.[2]

The monopoly enjoyed by the three London theatres had led to their physical aggrandisement. For instance, Drury Lane, when rebuilt in 1794 by Holland for Sheridan, had a capacity of 3,611; and both Covent Garden and Drury Lane, when rebuilt after

---

[1] In 1837 the King's Theatre changed its style to Her Majesty's rather than the Queen's Theatre, because six years previously, during the management of George Macfarren, the father of the composer, the theatre in Tottenham Street (now known as the Scala) had assumed the title of the Queen's Theatre in honour of William IV's consort.

[2] Earl of Mount Edgcumbe, *op. cit.*

their fires of 1808 and 1809 respectively, seated over 3,000 people each. The King's Theatre, when rebuilt in 1791, had five tiers of boxes and a capacity of 2,500.

Meanwhile, the minor London theatres were growing in numbers and importance. According to Fitzball,[1] by the eighteen-thirties some of them had become so magnificent 'as to elicit both wonder and astonishment; the Surrey Theatre being, at one time, decorated with gold and velvet, a Genoa velvet curtain covering the stage. The Cobourg [later the Old Vic] . . . decorated with one sunny glitter of gold braided mirrors, with a superb looking-glass curtain, which drew up and let down in the sight of the audience, and reflected every form and face in that gorgeous house, from the topmost seat in the galleries, to the lowest bench in the pit'.

When the passing of the Theatres Act of 1843 enabled the minor theatres to put on straight plays without tricking them out with music, song and dance, Covent Garden found itself free to modify its policy by concentrating entirely on the presentation of opera. Accordingly, it reopened in 1847 with its interior redecorated and under the style of the Royal Italian Opera. In 1856 it was burnt down for the second time, but rebuilt within a few months; and by the end of the century it had become London's premier opera house, the word 'Italian' being dropped from its title in 1892 so that its policy could be directed towards the performance of operas in their original languages, whether Italian, French or German.

Her Majesty's was destroyed by fire in 1867, but, though rebuilt two years later, did not reopen for opera until 1877. Fifteen years later it was sold up, and the building demolished. A new theatre was erected and opened in 1897; but under the direction of Herbert Beerbohm Tree it completely abandoned its operatic policy, and so the tradition of presenting Italian opera on that particular Haymarket site, which had lasted for nearly two centuries, was finally ruptured.

During the whole of the century continual efforts were made to

[1] Edward Fitzball, *op. cit.*

establish some kind of National English Opera House. For a short period the Lyceum Theatre, originally built in 1798, functioned as 'The English Opera House'; but after Balfe's scheme of 1841 had collapsed it abandoned any consistent operatic policy and concentrated on melodrama instead.

It would be true to say that for the greater part of the first half of the century Drury Lane was virtually the home of English opera. Under the successive managements of Arnold, Elliston and Bunn, it became the centre for the operatic productions of Bishop, Balfe, Barnett, Benedict and Wallace. A good idea of its activity can be gained from Appendix A, where of the hundred odd English operas listed as having been first produced in this country during the first half of the nineteenth century, forty-one, or nearly half, were given at Drury Lane. Even so, it must be remembered that these operatic performances were never given in the form of a continuous season, but were interpolated between the plays that were the vehicle for Drury Lane's star actors such as Edmund Kean and William Charles Macready. In the latter half of the century the position changed insofar as the comparable figures in Appendix A show that only nine operas out of a total of ninety-one were given at Drury Lane and nearly all of these were due to occasional visits by the Carl Rosa Opera Company.

A Royal National Opera was launched at the St. James's Theatre in September 1871, with a revival of Balfe's *The Rose of Castile* conducted by Sullivan; but the project collapsed after a few weeks.

Of greater interest were the various schemes to build new opera houses.

In 1875 J. H. Mapleson, then the lessee of Drury Lane, conceived the idea of constructing a Grand National Opera House on the Thames Embankment at Westminster. It was his ambition to make it the leading opera house in the world. 'The building was entirely isolated,' he wrote;[1] 'and a station had been built beneath the house in connection with the District Railway, so that the audience on leaving had merely to descend the stairs and

[1] *The Mapleson Memoirs*, 1848–1888.

enter the train. In the sub-basement, dressing-rooms, containing lockers, were provided for suburban visitors who might wish to attend the opera. A subterranean passage, moreover, led into the Houses of Parliament; and I had made arrangements by which silent members, after listening to beautiful music instead of dull debates, might return to the House on hearing the division-bell. . . . There were recreation rooms, too, for the principal artists, including billiard tables, etc., besides two very large Turkish baths, which, it was hoped, would be of service to the manager in cases of sore throat and sudden indisposition generally. . . . Sir John Humphreys had arranged for the purchase of a small steamer to act as tug to a large house-boat which would, from time to time, take the members of the Company down the river for rehearsals or recreation.' But from the outset the work was dogged by misfortune. In the first place the foundations cost £33,000 instead of the £5,000 originally estimated; and then when about £103,000 had been laid out on the building another £10,000 was needed for the roof, after which (according to Mapleson) £50,000 could have been raised on mortgage. The £10,000 was not, however, forthcoming, and the roofless shell had to be sold for £29,000. Later, it was resold for £500; and ultimately a new building arose on the site to serve as the police headquarters now known as New Scotland Yard. Mapleson's sardonic comment was: 'With such solid foundations, the cells, if not comfortable, will at least be dry.'[1]

In the course of his career as impresario, both in Great Britain and the United States, he never showed great interest in English opera as such—in fact, the only new English operas produced under his management were Macfarren's *Robin Hood* (1860), Wallace's *The Amber Witch* (1861) and Balfe's posthumous *Il Talismano* (1874) in its Italianised form—so it was hardly surprising to find that (in the words of the Address to the Duke of Edinburgh when he laid the first stone of the Grand National Opera House) 'the production of the works of English composers, represented by English performers, both vocal and instrumental',[2]

[1] *The Mapleson Memoirs*, 1848-1888.   [2] *Ibid.*

was to have been secondary to the representation of Italian Opera in the spring and summer months.

London's next two opera house projects, however, were definitely intended for English opera, and both were built round the enormous success achieved by Sir Arthur Sullivan as an opera composer.

To the critic who considers Sullivan's comic opera music in relation to the romantic operas of the preceding fifty years it may seem that there is little or no reason to rank it much higher than the best of Loder, Barnett, Balfe, Macfarren and Wallace. How closely he kept to the material and style of his predecessors can be seen by comparing a tune like 'The sun whose rays are all ablaze', from *The Mikado*, with 'The cup is oak, the wine is gold' from Loder's *The Night Dancers*. Both songs are so closely related in line, metre and key that it is difficult to imagine that Loder's score was not in Sullivan's mind at the moment he composed that particular number. But whereas the earlier composers were usually handicapped by the low standard of the librettos they had to set, Sullivan had the good fortune to find as collaborator a man of genuine talent. In no other operatic partnership has the importance of the librettist been so fully recognised; and here he is always given precedence insofar as the operas of this collaboration are universally referred to as being by Gilbert and Sullivan rather than by Sullivan and Gilbert.

William Schwenk Gilbert was not only a sound theatrical craftsman, but also a meticulous versifier, with an extraordinarily wide command of metre, rhyme and assonance. The technical accomplishment of his lyrics was an unfailing stimulus to Sullivan and undoubtedly helped him to devote that extra degree of care to their setting that led to the perfect marriage of word and note which is the hallmark of the best Gilbert and Sullivan operas. Gilbert's satire has not always been appreciated at its proper value, perhaps because it is presented with such a sugary coat of nonsense that no one feels any serious effects after swallowing it. But even a comparatively unsuccessful opera like *Utopia Ltd.* has a libretto of great interest, and its pungent satire on English

Mad Margaret in Ruddigore: *costume sketch by W. S. Gilbert, 1886–7.*

institutions anticipates some of the more telling strokes in plays like Bernard Shaw's *The Apple Cart* and *The Simpleton of the Unexpected Isles.*[1]

Sullivan's first operatic essay, *The Sapphire Necklace* (1864), was left unfinished, because he was dissatisfied with the libretto by Henry F. Chorley; but shortly afterwards he obtained two well-written short farces from Sir Frank Burnand and composed *Cox and Box* and *Contrabandista*. The original performance of *Cox and Box* at the Adelphi Theatre on May 11, 1867, was given by amateurs; but on its first public performance at the Royal Gallery of Illustration on March 29, 1869, it appeared, prophetically enough, in the same programme as a piece by Gilbert called *No Cards*. Two years later Gilbert and Sullivan collaborated for the first time; but *Thespis*, 'an entirely original grotesque opera' as it was called, did not prove a striking success, and of the music only one song appears to have been preserved. It was the 'novel and original cantata' of *Trial by Jury* (1875), a one-act operetta with no spoken dialogue, that first caught the public's fancy and led the impresario Rupert d'Oyly Carte to decide that here was a theatrical partnership worth backing.

During the next two decades a dozen full-length Gilbert and Sullivan operas were written, all of which have preserved an unbroken popularity in Great Britain and in most English-speaking countries abroad, with the exception of the last two operas, *Utopia Ltd.* and *The Grand Duke*. Both of these were written after the celebrated quarrel between the two partners about the cost of the new carpet that D'Oyly Carte had laid down at the Savoy Theatre at the time of the run of *The Gondoliers*. The other ten all have their enthusiastic and faithful band of adherents, and at one time or another each has been awarded the palm. *The Mikado* (1885) has proved the most popular both at home and abroad; but in some ways it may be thought that *The Sorcerer* (1877), the first of the sequence, is also the best, for in it the contribution of each partner is at its freshest and most spontaneous. It is true that the

---

[1] 'The book has Mr. Gilbert's lighter qualities without his faults. . . . I enjoyed the score of Utopia more than that of any of the previous Savoy operas.'—Bernard Shaw, *Music in London*, 1890–94.

element of fantastication is not so pronounced as in, say, *Iolanthe* with its admixture of peers and peris, parliament and pastoral; but as a burlesque of certain typical characters of English country life it remained unsurpassed for many years, and not until the arrival of *Albert Herring* (1947) did Lady Sangazure and Dr. Daly, the vicar of Ploverleigh, meet their match in the imperious Lady Billows and bland Mr. Gedge, the vicar of St. Mary's, Loxford.

The Sorcerer's run of 175 performances at the Opéra Comique was followed by *H.M.S. Pinafore* and *The Pirates of Penzance* (with 700 and 363 performances respectively). *H.M.S. Pinafore* captured not only the London theatre-going public, but the whole of the Anglo-Saxon world. Its vogue in America was so great that shortly after its London première it was pirated in New York in over twenty different productions, professional and amateur, many of them running simultaneously. D'Oyly Carte decided to consolidate this decisive success by building his own theatre in London to be specially devoted to this type of operetta as presented by the D'Oyly Carte Opera Company. Accordingly, *Patience*, after an initial six months' run at the Opéra Comique, was transferred on October 10, 1881, to the new Savoy Theatre in the Strand, which thenceforth became the headquarters of the Gilbert and Sullivan operas.

The next few years brought an unbroken series of triumphs to the Savoy Theatre; but the partnership between Gilbert and Sullivan was not altogether an easy one. Sullivan, in particular, was dissatisfied with his success, both at home and abroad, as a composer of light operatic music. In the stolid Victorian world of oratorio he was revered for *The Prodigal Son* (1869), *The Martyr of Antioch* (1880) and *The Golden Legend* (1886); and he wanted to try his hand at serious opera too. The farthest Gilbert was prepared to go in this direction was *The Yeoman of the Guard* (1888), in which for once the plot was not constructed according to his usual topsy-turvy formula; but that did not satisfy Sullivan. In April 1889 Bernard Shaw wrote in *The Star*, 'Why Mr. Augustus Harris' (then the manager of the Royal Opera House, Covent Garden) 'does not get a grand opera out of Sir Arthur Sullivan, who is never dull, is one of the unaccountable things in modern management.'[1] Shortly afterwards Queen Victoria herself made the same suggestion; and this was tantamount to a royal command. Fortified by D'Oyly Carte's encouragement and backing, Sullivan chose a libretto by Julian Sturgis and spent May to December, 1890, composing *Ivanhoe*.

This was intended to inaugurate a series of 'grand' operas by native composers, to house which D'Oyly Carte built his second theatre, the Royal English Opera House in Cambridge Circus. The policy of the new house was based on D'Oyly Carte's experience at the Savoy Theatre; each opera was to be presented for a straight run, instead of being played in repertory. A double cast of British singers was engaged; and *Ivanhoe*, which opened on January 31, 1891, enjoyed the unprecedented run of 160 consecutive performances. Yet, a few months later, the whole scheme collapsed.

Herman Klein, one of the best known musical critics of those days, has given the following explanation of the *débâcle*:[2] 'The long run acted as a snare and a deception. Because *Ivanhoe* played to big houses and people went to hear it twice, thrice, or half a dozen times, Mr. Carte erroneously concluded that he would be in a position to imitate here his Savoy plan of running one successful opera at a time until it had exhausted its drawing power. He forgot that Sullivan might not go on writing successes for ever, or even attempt a second serious opera. He forgot that other English composers ought to have been commissioned in advance to write works for him, to enable him to provide the essential repertory for the foundation of a new school and a lasting home for native opera. In a word, the well-meaning manager killed the goose that laid him the golden eggs. He then completed the ruin of a splendid idea by trying to bolster it up with a French comic opera of Messager's, *La Basoche*, which failed where *Ivanhoe* had hit the mark, and so brought the whole venture to a disastrous ending.' D'Oyly Carte decided to cut his losses. He forthwith

[1] Bernard Shaw, *op. cit.*
[2] Herman Klein, *The Golden Age of Opera.*

disposed of the Royal English Opera House, and it was reopened shortly afterwards as the Palace Theatre of Varieties.

It is perhaps not quite fair to lay all the blame for this failure on D'Oyly Carte personally. Writing a few years later, Stanford said:[1] 'If Mr. Carte could have carried out his own views (which were broad, sound, and rational) the Opera House would not now be a music hall. He had not a free hand, and suffered in consequence.' In addition, there was the opera itself to consider. Reviewing it in *The World*, Shaw attacked Sturgis's libretto as fustian and considered Scott's original story and dialogue had been wantonly debased. Johnson Galloway, writing about the score, said:[2] 'The talent, skill and experience of Sullivan did not fail to produce some agreeable numbers, but they failed most egregiously to make grand opera. A perpetual sense of disappointment pervaded the piece; it never rose to the height demanded by the situation, save when that was comic, and occasionally the failure was absolutely painful. The music kept trying to soar, but was all the time chained by the leg.'

The fate of D'Oyly Carte's two theatres to some extent epitomised that of English opera at the end of the nineteenth century. While the Savoy Theatre prospered with works by Sullivan, Alfred Cellier, F. Cellier and Edward German—comic operas or operettas that could be looked on as the successors of the light operas of the previous century and a half—the disastrous collapse of the Royal English Opera House meant that practically no channel remained for the production of English serious operas except through the Carl Rosa Opera Company.

That company's inception was due to Carl August Nicolas Rose,[3] who was born in Hamburg in 1842. While still in his twenties, he went on a concert tour to the United States; and there he married Madame Parepa, the soprano, who was a member of the same concert party. In 1869 they set up the Parepa-Rosa English Opera Company, which toured opera in English throughout the United States for several seasons with Carl Rosa

---

[1] 'The Case for National Opera' in Stanford's *Studies and Memories*.
[2] *The Operatic Problem*, 1902.
[3] He subsequently changed his name to the phonetic form of Rosa.

himself as conductor and manager, and in 1873 transferred their activities to England. The first appearance of the Carl Rosa Opera Company in this country was at Manchester on September 1, 1873, when *Maritana* was given. The company's first novelty was *The Village Doctor* (formerly entitled *The Doctor of Alcantara*, 1862), the most popular of Eichberg's American comic operettas. This was played in Liverpool on October 21, 1873. The rest of the repertory of that opening season consisted of *The Bohemian Girl*, *The Marriage of Figaro*, *Il Trovatore*, *Don Giovanni* and *La Sonnambula*. The following year *Faust*, *Satanella* and *The Rose of Castile* were added; but the company's plans for a London season were upset by the death of Madame Parepa. When they ultimately came to the Princess's Theatre in September, 1875, the opening performance of *The Marriage of Figaro* made an excellent impression on the critics. Herman Klein wrote that 'Santley's masterly impersonation of Figaro was the gem of a performance universally acclaimed as the best that had ever been given in the vernacular.'[1] Santley himself, however, was critical of the production because Carl Rosa had insisted on omitting the sextet in the second act 'to make way for some silly dialogue'.[2] Other operas included in the company's repertory that season were *Faust*, *The Porter of Havre*,[3] *Fra Diavolo*, *The Bohemian Girl*, *Il Trovatore*, *The Water-Carrier*[4] and *The Siege of Rochelle*.

Up to Carl Rosa's death, in 1889, the company did its best to encourage English opera composers by producing a certain number of specially commissioned works. The earliest of these was Dr. Frederic Cowen's *Pauline* (1876), the libretto of which was based by Henry Hersée on Bulwer Lytton's *The Lady of Lyons*. Santley relates[5] how in agreeing to create the part of Claude Melnotte he made an error of judgment, for though Cowen made Melnotte a baritone especially to accommodate him, his impersonation of the character proved a complete failure.

[1] Herman Klein, *op. cit.*
[2] Charles Santley, *Reminiscences of my Life.*
[3] Cf. Appendix C.
[4] The Carl Rosa Company revived this opera in Glasgow on May 2, 1950, to celebrate the seventy-fifth anniversary of their first appearance in London.
[5] Charles Santley, *Reminiscences of my Life.*

Pauline was followed by Goring Thomas's *Esmeralda* (1883) and *Nadeshda* (1885), Sir Alexander Campbell Mackenzie's *Colomba* (1883) and *The Troubadour* (1886), Stanford's *The Canterbury Pilgrims* (1884), and Frederick Corder's *Nordisa* (1887). Of these, the operas of Goring Thomas and Mackenzie proved popular both at home and abroad. The music of the former was rather French in style—reminiscent of Gounod—and had considerable charm and grace. Mackenzie's *Colomba* was deemed to be an 'exceedingly clever and effective' score.[1] Although his later opera, *The Troubadour*, was a failure, Liszt apparently thought so highly of the music that after his death an unfinished fantasia on its themes was found in his desk.

The eighteen-eighties were perhaps the period of the company's greatest prosperity. From 1883 onwards Carl Rosa was closely associated with Augustus Harris, the manager first of Drury Lane (1887-8) and then of Covent Garden (1888-96); but although after Carl Rosa's death Harris for a moment took over the direction of the limited company, he found himself increasingly preoccupied with the fortunes of foreign opera at Covent Garden, and the following year he resigned his Carl Rosa directorship.

The frequency of new English works now began to decline. During the remainder of the century the company produced five new English operas, a revival and an adaptation. Stephen Philpot's *Dante and Beatrice* (1889) was followed by another commissioned opera by Cowen entitled *Thorgrim* (1890). Goring Thomas's posthumous comic opera, *The Golden Web*, was given in 1893. Two works were commissioned from Hamish McCunn, *Jeanie Deans* being produced at Edinburgh in 1894 and *Diarmid* (to a libretto by the Duke of Argyll) at Covent Garden in 1897. None of these achieved any real success. Meanwhile, Sullivan's *Ivanhoe* had been revived during the 1895 season; and four years later an unsuccessful attempt was made to adapt his oratorio, *The Martyr of Antioch*, as an opera.

In 1900 the company, which for a brief period (1899-1900) had been run as a commonwealth by some of the leading singers,

---

[1] R. A. Streatfeild, *The Opera.*

was taken over by a syndicate headed by Alfred and Walter Van Noorden. Shortly after Walter Van Noorden's death the company took over the Harrison-Frewin Company, then under the management of H. B. Phillips; and for a period of five years (1918–23) the parent Carl Rosa Company and the Phillips Section carried on as separate units, being afterwards merged into one company under the direction of H. B. Phillips. During the first two decades of the century no new English operas were produced; but after the first World War a few new works were given, including Alick Maclean's *Quentin Durward* (1920) and Reginald Somerville's *David Garrick* (1920). But this policy was pursued only spasmodically and met with no lasting success; and the production of George Lloyd's *John Socman* in 1951 marks the first occasion on which the company has given a new English opera since Joseph Holbrooke's *Bronwen* at Huddersfield in 1929.

Although the Carl Rosa Company has not been able to build up any consistent policy of presenting new English operas, it has shown considerable initiative in introducing foreign works to the British public, as can be seen from the impressive list of over fifty such operas in Appendix C. Since its inception it has realised the importance of Wagner; and its English productions of *The Flying Dutchman* (1876), *Rienzi* (1879), *Lohengrin* (1880) and *Tannhäuser* (1882) helped to set the seal on his popularity in this country. The 1876 production of *The Flying Dutchman* was the first performance of any of Wagner's operas in English; and Santley scored a great success in the title role. J. A. Fuller-Maitland wrote in *A Doorkeeper of Music*, 'the magic of Santley's personality as Vanderdecken impressed itself so deeply that after half a century I cannot forget the thrill of seeing him appear on the threshold, under his own picture—all the Guras, Scheidemantels, and the rest that I have seen have never dimmed that memory'. *The Mastersingers* and *Siegfried* were given in 1897 and 1901 respectively.

The company introduced English versions of three of Verdi's later operas—*Aïda* in 1880, *Othello* in 1892 and *La Forza del Destino* in 1909—and its first English production of *Carmen* at Her

SIR ARTHUR SULLIVAN (1888)

Oil painting by Sir J. E. Millais ($45\frac{1}{2}$ in. by $34\frac{1}{4}$ in.).

The Canterbury Pilgrims, Act III, Drury Lane, 1884.

Ivanhoe: showing the tournament scene at Ashby-de-la-Zouch with Ben Davies
in the title part, 1891.

A Village Romeo and Juliet

Drawing by Steven Spurrier, A.R.A., R.B.A., showing Walter
Hyde and Miriam Licette in the Fair Scene of the 1920 revival
at Covent Garden.

SIR CHARLES STANFORD
Drawing by Sir Leslie Ward ('Spy').

Majesty's in 1879 created such interest that by 1891 an extra Carl Rosa Company had to be formed for the express purpose of touring that opera alone.

One of the company's most memorable acts was to mount the first performance in Great Britain of *La Bohème*. Covent Garden, though it had produced *Manon Lescaut* in 1894, showed no interest in Puccini's new opera, when it was first brought out at the Teatro Regio, Turin, in 1896. Accordingly, Puccini's publisher, Tito Ricordi, decided to take a risk and placed it with the Carl Rosa Company for production in English. Both composer and publisher came over to Manchester for the first performance on April 22, 1897, of what the original English vocal score (but not the advertisements or the programmes) described as *The Bohemians*. Herman Klein, who joined them there in his capacity as critic of *The Sunday Times*, wrote: 'I never saw two young men in a more despondent frame of mind or more certain of failure. Rehearsals had been going badly and it was impossible that the opera should succeed. However, their doleful anticipations were not to be realised. On the following morning we all travelled back to Euston in a saloon carriage that the railway company had courteously placed at the disposal of the musicians and journalists. We had with us a very different Puccini now—a merry, smiling fellow, with a plentiful supply of Italian jokes, and radiant with the recollection of genuine Lancashire cheering. . . . The performance had, after all, been a good one, as Puccini frankly acknowledged; and beyond question it laid the foundation for the success which the company gained for the new opera during its subsequent autumn season at Covent Garden.'[1]

There is no doubt that during its early seasons great hopes were placed on the company. For instance, in 1879 Sir George Grove wrote: 'The careful way in which the pieces are put upon the stage, the number of rehearsals, the eminence of the performers and the excellence of the performances have begun to bear legitimate fruit, and the Carl Rosa Opera Company bids fair to become a permanent English institution'. Bernard Shaw was more

[1] Herman Klein, *op. cit.*

critical, however. Writing of the 1890 Drury Lane season a year after Carl Rosa's death, he warned the members of the company that they were 'saddled with a heavy national responsibility'.[1] He considered 'the company has yet to recover from the effects of what was in many respects a bad start. Carl Rosa was a sensible, pertinacious, shrewd man of business, with a turn for music, but without that quick keen sympathy with the artistic instinct in its human vehicles—that confidence, power, and tact in developing it and stimulating it to courageous action, which made the really able impresario. . . . In the old times I never saw in the Carl Rosa Company much more than a fortuitous assemblage of middle-class amateurs competing with one another for applause under a certain factory discipline. Of artistic discipline there was very little. The singers were allowed to play to the gallery by introducing such alterations and interpolations as their vanity and ignorance suggested. They were allowed to take sham Italian names,[2] and to sing broken English that would not have imposed on a moderately intelligent cockney poodle. . . . Carl Rosa could have checked it if he had cared to: there is never any difficulty in checking practices that do not pay. As they were not checked, I think it is fair to conclude that he had no adequate sense of the mischief they did in his company.'

It is only fair to point out that Bernard Shaw is here applying the highest standards of metropolitan criticism to a company that has never attempted to make London its headquarters or to do more for opera in England than to play it in the vernacular and tour it regularly every year throughout the length and breadth of the provinces. Although the wear and tear that this involves has imposed an extraordinary strain and standards of performance have naturally varied, the company has managed to achieve an astonishing degree of permanence. To be able to point to an uninterrupted record of over three-quarters of a century in presenting opera in English and English opera is something that no other organisation in this country has succeeded in doing—as yet.

[1] Bernard Shaw, op. cit.
[2] E.g. Signor Campobello for Mr. Campbell.

Of the many other opera touring companies that flourished at the beginning of the twentieth century, two in particular should be mentioned here.

The Moody-Manners Company, named after two opera singers, Fanny Moody and Charles Manners (whose real name was Southcote Mansergh), was founded in 1897 with the aim of producing grand opera in English. After a modest start it increased in efficiency so rapidly that by 1902 it had three different companies on the road, of which the principal one appeared at Covent Garden in 1902 and 1903, and at Drury Lane the following year. In 1904 and 1906 it ran special opera festivals in Sheffield, the profits from which were diverted to the foundation of Sheffield University; and in the latter year Manners's campaign to increase public interest in opera led to the creation of the Glasgow Grand Opera Society, one of the most enterprising amateur opera societies in Great Britain. At various times Manners offered prizes for British composers. Alick Maclean won £100 with his one-act opera *Petruccio* (1895); and MacAlpin's full-length *The Cross and the Crescent* won a £250 prize in 1903. Other new English operas produced were Maclean's *Maître Seiler* (1909) and Nicolas Gatty's *Greysteel* (1906) and *Duke or Devil* (1909); and Stanford's *Much Ado About Nothing* was revived. The company was dissolved in 1913 when Manners retired.

The Denhof Company was formed in 1910 to give performances in English of Wagner's *The Ring of the Nibelungs*. After three years' activity the organisation was merged in Sir Thomas Beecham's company.

CHAPTER VI

Exiles

(Nineteenth and Twentieth Centuries)

*English Operas Abroad—Hatton—Pierson—de Lara—d'Erlanger
—Influence of Germany—Stanford—English Operas in Germany
—Ethel Smyth and Her Early Operas—The Wreckers—Delius
—A Village Romeo and Juliet—End of the Period of Exile*

WHEN it was clear that no English opera house was in fact likely to be established and that the main function of a company like the Carl Rosa was certainly not going to be the production of English operas, composers had to look elsewhere for an outlet for their works. This was particularly serious since, according to Stanford,[1] such an enthusiasm and awakening in musical art started in this country in the 'eighties as had not been known for centuries. 'From folk-music to the most complex modern forms of composition, from great choral festivals with bodies of singers unrivalled in any other country, to the country competitions, which prove the interest felt throughout the land, every department of the art is advancing with the sole exception of the one branch which the rest of Europe has rated as the most important of all, dramatic music. . . . So it is that we are in danger, and imminent danger, of a set-back of the clock, of losing touch with the most ennobling, the most civilising (because it is the most far-reaching to all classes) of all the arts, just at the very moment when the country is at the highest point of enthusiasm for it. Throttle this enthusiasm now, and away goes England's chance for generations.' In this difficulty, where could English composers turn?

During a similar crisis in 1841, when Balfe had vainly tried to establish a National English Opera at the Lyceum, a number of letters had appeared in the press debating the merits of the

[1] C. V. Stanford, *op. cit.*

scheme, including one from Macfarren, 'whose publicly expressed persuasion was that English musicians would have no chance of attracting notice and patronage in their own country, unless they formed a colony in some foreign city, and, by publishing and performing their works there, obtained that stamp of approval from European criticism and success, under the warranty of which alone they would be accepted as deserving attention at home'.[1]

Shortly after this appeared J. L. Hatton, who had composed a romantic opera called *Pasqual Bruno* to a libretto by Fitzball and, being unable to get it represented in this country, took it over to Vienna and had it performed in German at the Kärntnerthor-theater. Its reception was frigid. *Bäuerle's Theaterzeitung* for March 4, 1844, published a scrupulously fair review, from which the following extracts are taken: 'Although we Germans may have to admit that we are unable to write good opera librettos, here is an English libretto which is almost worse than our German ones. The author must have a peculiar idea of what is called "the romantic" in art when he applies this term to such dramatic material as this. . . . Mr. Hatton may be a good knowledgeable musician, an experienced conductor—in England he may perhaps have written a great deal which has built up his reputation there—but his name is unknown to us, and we can only judge him as a composer by the work now presented to us here. To be frank, one must admit that the opera lacks the one really important thing that any composer must have if he is to create a work of art: namely, invention.' Fitzball relates how:[2] 'On returning [Hatton] brought me a play bill, thinking that I should be sufficiently delighted, and perfectly satisfied (as I was forced to be) at seeing my name Herr *Fix*ball inserted as the English author of the libretto.' *Pasqual Bruno* was never played in England; and Hatton's only other opera (*Rose*, produced at Covent Garden in 1864) was unsuccessful.

In 1845, the year after the production of *Pasqual Bruno*, H. H. Pearson, who for a short period had been Professor of Music at Edinburgh University, resigned his post and retired to Germany.

---

[1] Kenney's *Memoir of Balfe*.   [2] Edward Fitzball, *op. cit.*

There he spent the remainder of his life, composing (among other works) various operas under the name of Pierson, including *Leila*, *Elfensieg* and *Contarini*. None of them, however, was ever played in Great Britain, where today he is perhaps best remembered as the composer of 'Ye Mariners of England'.

Later in the century Isidore de Lara worked almost entirely to foreign librettos. After his sacred legend, *The Light of Asia*, had been given as an opera at Covent Garden in 1892,[1] he turned to France, and helped by the patronage of the Princess of Monaco, nearly all his remaining operas had their first performances on the Riviera or in Paris. This did not prevent them from being subsequently played in England; and, indeed, English versions of *Les Trois Masques*, *Les Trois Mousquetaires* and *Messaline* were produced by the Carl Rosa Company at various times after the first World War.

Frederic d'Erlanger used French librettos for the most part, though *Tess*, his operatic version of Thomas Hardy's novel, was composed to an Italian libretto written by Illica and performed for the first time at the San Carlo, Naples, in 1906. When it was brought to Covent Garden (July 14, 1909), Hardy found it Italianised to such an extent that he could hardly recognise it as his novel. 'Destinn's voice suited the title-character admirably,' laconically remarked Florence Emily Hardy in her biography of her husband; 'her appearance less so.'

Another English opera performed for the first time in Italy was Cowen's *Signa* (Milan, 1893). But, on the whole, it was to Germany rather than France or Italy that English composers, hoping to restore England's broken operatic tradition, looked for help in producing their operas.

The example of Germany herself was instructive. In the seventeenth century, while England, despite the momentary dislocation caused by the Commonwealth, had been able to enjoy a rich variety of experiment in various representational forms, Germany had been too distracted by the Thirty Years War and

---

[1] There is a review of it in Bernard Shaw's *Music in London*. Shaw seems to have been favourably impressed by the non-academic style of the music.

its aftermath to be able to follow any continuous policy. It was not until the beginning of the eighteenth century that German operatic conditions began to improve; and then it was partly to English models—particularly the ballad opera—that she looked for a lead in developing her own native style of *Singspiel*. A hundred years later she had completely outstripped this country and, thanks to works like Mozart's *Die Entführung aus dem Serail* and *Die Zauberflöte*, Beethoven's *Fidelio* and Weber's *Der Freischütz*, was consolidating a native tradition of her own. German opera now began to wield an important influence everywhere abroad, except in Italy; and this was confirmed in the latter part of the nineteenth century, as Wagner's theories about music drama became more widely known and performances of his works opened up new and astonishing vistas in the realm of opera. It is not too much to state that the first London productions of *Der Ring des Nibelungen*, *Die Meistersinger* and *Tristan und Isolde* in the 'eighties, together with the Carl Rosa Company's performances of English versions of *Rienzi*, *The Flying Dutchman*, *Tannhäuser* and *Lohengrin*, ended the long, undisputed supremacy of Italian opera in this country; and for those who agreed with Sullivan in comparing Italian opera with a 'great car of Juggernaut' which for a century and three-quarters had overridden and 'crushed all efforts made on behalf of native music',[1] the future now lay with Germany.

This was particularly the case with Stanford, himself one of the most important figures of the British musical renaissance of the 'eighties. His first opera, *The Veiled Prophet of Khorassan*, dated back to his student days in Leipzig, when the subject (based on Moore's *Lalla Rookh*) was suggested by his friend and companion, Raoul de Versan. The libretto was handed over to William Barclay Squire, then an undergraduate at Cambridge, and the score finished in 1878. Finding no immediate prospect of getting it produced in England, Stanford remembered that Ernst Frank, the chief conductor of the Frankfurt Stadttheater, had a reputation for accessibility; so he wrote to him out of the blue,

[1] From Sir Arthur Sullivan's lecture, 'About Music', delivered at Birmingham in 1888.

and Frank lived up to his reputation by inviting him to Frankfurt at once. Not only did he like the young Irishman's opera, but he went to some trouble to propose various alterations himself and to make a German translation. Before its production could be fixed, however, he had resigned from his post at Frankfurt, and Stanford had to look elsewhere for a theatre. He tried Berlin in vain; but by 1880 Frank had taken up a new appointment at Hanover, and there one of his first acts was to arrange for the production of *Der Verschleierte Profet* (as it was called) on February 6, 1881. Its success was instantaneous in Germany; but it took twelve years to reach Covent Garden, and then only for a single performance in an Italian translation.

After this, Stanford had no difficulty in getting his next opera, *Savonarola*, produced at Hamburg in April 1884, ten weeks before it was conducted by Hans Richter in London. But the Covent Garden production—also in German—was an unhappy one; and Stanford himself said that it was crippled from the start with 'maimed rites, a bearded hero, insufficient rehearsals and incompetent stage-management. In addition the owner of the libretto having refused to allow it to be sold in the theatre the public knew nothing of its meaning in a foreign tongue and I scarcely recognised the opera I had seen in Hamburg a few weeks before.'[1]

In *The Canterbury Pilgrims*, which was given by the Carl Rosa Company the same year as *Savonarola*, Stanford revealed his open admiration for Wagner—particularly *The Mastersingers*, which had made a tremendous impression on him during his student years at Leipzig. By the time he came to write his later operas—*Shamus O'Brien, Much Ado About Nothing, The Critic* and *The Travelling Companion*—he had developed a more individual and less derivative style.[2]

Towards the end of the nineteenth century other English operas were heard in Germany. Goring Thomas's *Esmeralda* was played at Cologne, Hamburg and Berlin, and his *Nadeshda* at Breslau; Mackenzie's *Colomba* at Hamburg and Darmstadt. Tours

[1] C. V. Stanford, *Pages from an Unwritten Diary*.
[2] In addition, Stanford wrote two unpublished operas: the first, *Lorenza*, to an Italian libretto; the second, an untitled work with the opus number 69.

of some of the Gilbert and Sullivan operas (in English) through Germany, Austria and other European countries led to productions in German (chiefly in Berlin and Vienna) of *The Pirates of Penzance*, *The Mikado*, *The Yeoman of the Guard* and *The Gondoliers*. Sullivan's *Ivanhoe* was given at the Berlin Opera House in 1895; and just after the turn of the century Stanford's *Much Ado About Nothing* was played at Leipzig (1902) and *Shamus O'Brien* (with recitatives instead of spoken dialogue) at Breslau (1907).

But Stanford, Goring Thomas, Mackenzie and Sullivan were no more than visitors abroad, whereas the first person who can with justice be called an operatic exile was Dame Ethel Smyth.

There have never at any time been many women composers; and she is the only one who has made a name for herself in the field of opera. She belonged to an age when women in this country were still denied their rights and debarred from many professions. Being intelligent, impetuous and militant by nature, she was naturally to the forefront in the struggle to demolish these barriers and lived to share in the triumph of the Women's Suffrage movement, of which she had been so passionate an advocate. The prejudices she fought against were just as powerful in the world of music as in other walks of life, and as rife abroad as in this country; and much of the time she should have devoted to composition had in fact to be spent in finding ways and means to overcome the prejudices of opera syndicates, intendants and conductors in an attempt to get her operas performed. Her attitude is well summarised in a letter she sent to Henry Brewster, who subsequently wrote the libretto for *Les Naufrageurs*. 'I feel I must fight for *Der Wald*,' she said,[1] 'also because I want women to turn their minds to big and difficult jobs; not just to go on hugging the shore, afraid to put out to sea. Now I am neither afraid nor a pauper, and in my way I am an explorer who believes supremely in this bit of pioneering.'

She herself was certainly never afraid to put out to open sea; and it was her good fortune to have powerful friends and allies in Germany, Italy and France, as well as England, to aid and abet

[1] Ethel Smyth, *What happened Next*.

her. Of these perhaps the most important as well as one of the most sympathetic was the exiled Empress Eugénie. Many a time the Empress appears to have come to the rescue when the harassed composer needed help for a performance or a publication.

The chequered course of her operas deserves to be recounted in some detail as being typical of the difficulties that faced any English opera composer of' that period. The composition of *Fantasio*, which was founded on de Musset's play of the same name, was finished by 1894; and Hermann Levi, conductor of the original *Parsifal* performance, having seen part of the score and realising that a woman composer would have little or no chance with the average German Kapellmeister, advised her to enter it for a certain operatic competition. She did so; but out of the entry of 110 operas three were adjudged to share the first prize, and seven (including *Fantasio*) were highly commended.

In the autumn of 1896, after Levi had commended *Fantasio* to Felix Mottl, the conductor at Carlsruhe, and the Empress Frederick, another of Ethel Smyth's personal friends, had written about it to Count Seebach, the intendant at Dresden, the composer embarked on a round journey, calling at Carlsruhe, Dresden, Leipzig and Cologne, the immediate result of which was that *Fantasio* was accepted for Cologne. But this decision was reversed when Hoffmann, the conductor, found he had no singer who could do justice to the part of 'Fantasio'. So early the following year Ethel Smyth made a further round journey to Hamburg and Wiesbaden—but without success; and it was not until later in the year that a chance suggestion sent her to Stavenhagen, the conductor at Weimar, where *Guntram*, Richard Strauss's first opera, had been put on in 1894 and where ultimately her opera was produced on May 24, 1898. Three years later it was given by Mottl at Carlsruhe.

The composer's own judgment on *Fantasio* is probably a fair one. She found there was too much passion and violence in the music for such a subject. Mottl himself agreed the libretto was weak, but thought the music well worth preserving.

At the suggestion of Mr. Harry Higgins, chairman of the

Covent Garden Syndicate, she took her next opera, *Der Wald* to
Paris in December 1900 and showed it to André Messager with a
view to its eventual production at Covent Garden. Shortly
afterwards, however, an interview with Count Seebach at Dresden led her to believe it had been definitely accepted for production there; but to her considerable disappointment a definite
rejection followed a few months later, due in all probability to the
growing Anglophobia in Germany caused by the Boer War.
Discovering that the members of the family of the then British
Ambassador in Berlin were friends of hers, she transferred her
attentions to that town; and Karl Muck, the conductor at the
Berlin Opera House, admired the score so much that he agreed to
produce it. The fantastic story of her attempt to get it put on
during the 1901-2 season, despite 'organised envy, malice, and all
uncharitableness'[1] is told at length in her book, *Streaks of Life*.
After many delays the first performance took place late in the
season on April 9, 1902. 'There had been slight hissing when the
curtain went up, but *before* it went down finally, organised booing
and cat-calls broke out simultaneously in three different parts of
the house.'[2] Nevertheless, *Der Wald* consolidated itself, and by the
time of its fourth performance all signs of opposition had disappeared. The operatic material was then withdrawn from Berlin
to prepare for a Covent Garden production (in German) that
July. According to the composer herself this was 'the only real
blazing theatre triumph'[3] she ever enjoyed. The opera was repeated at Covent Garden the following year; and there were also
productions at the Metropolitan Opera House (New York),
Boston and Strasburg.

When searching for a suitable theme for her next opera, she
recalled a visit she had paid in 1886 to the Piper's Hole on Tresco
in the Isles of Scilly. This cave near the sea, with its fresh-water
lake full of blind fish and its chained boat like Charon's ferry,[4]
made a deep impression on her at the time. Combining her
impressions of that visit with stories of the old Cornish wreckers,

[1] Ethel Smyth, *What happened Next.*
[2] *Ibid.*
[3] *Ibid.*
[4] Now, alas! sunk.

she asked her friend, Henry Brewster, to fashion a libretto out of this material. As it was then thought likely that Messager would be the next artistic director at Covent Garden, she readily agreed to Brewster's suggestion that the new opera should be written in French, that being the language he preferred when poetically disposed.

The score of *Les Naufrageurs* was finished by 1905; and Ethel Smyth then decided that Emma Calvé, whom it was thought Messager would be bringing to Covent Garden for the 1906 season, would be the ideal person to create the role of Thirza. But Calvé and Messager quarrelled; and though there was some talk of her doing the opera elsewhere—a season at the Waldorf Theatre was mentioned, and also a production at Monte Carlo— these plans came to nothing. After vainly trying the Théâtre de la Monnaie, Brussels, Ethel Smyth realised there was going to be no chance of getting *Les Naufrageurs* produced in its original French version and made up her mind to try Germany once more.

On showing the score to Artur Nikisch, she found to her amazement the work was immediately accepted for Leipzig. She accordingly arranged for the libretto to be translated into German under the title of *Strandrecht*; and although Nikisch was dismissed from his post as Kapellmeister before it could be put on, his successor, Hagel, agreed to honour his predecessor's undertaking, and the first performance was planned for the autumn of 1906.

Nevertheless, Ethel Smyth was uneasy. She rightly felt that Hagel could not be expected to show the same interest in the opera as Nikisch, and so she tried to see if she could arrange for other productions elsewhere. Of the three or four opera houses she approached, the most interested appeared to be Prague. The momentary scruples of its director, Angelo Neumann, who admired the work, but thought he ought to reject it because of his other commitments, were overcome by an extremely generous offer from the librettist who announced his intention of backing a production in that city to the extent of £1,000. Everything was accordingly fixed for a Prague production immediately after the Leipzig première.

The Leipzig production, which took place on November 15, 1906, was marred by the fact that, despite express assurances to the composer that no cuts would be made except with her consent, Hagel at the last moment cut the third act into an incomprehensible jumble. Nevertheless, the opera met with the approval of the public; there were thirteen curtain calls; and the composer, who was present, received a warm ovation. Later that evening, during a party given by the theatre director, she got agreement (as she thought) for a rehearsal with principals and orchestra to be held the following morning so that the cuts in the third act could be restored.

Early next day, however, she received two notes: one from Hagel to say that the opera must either be played as cut or not at all; the other from the director explaining that Hagel refused to do what she wanted, and he himself had had to go to Berlin for a few days, but hoped to see her on his return to Leipzig immediately after the second performance of her opera. Ethel Smyth sent express messages to both men, saying that unless her demands were met she would withdraw the opera. Receiving no reply, she wrote a letter to the *Leipziger Tageblatt* to explain the reason for her action, and on the third day after the first performance went down early to the theatre, removed all the orchestral material of *The Wreckers* from the orchestral pit, including the full score, and left at once for Prague.

It is doubtful whether this high-handed action improved her chances of getting her operas accepted in Germany; and unfortunately the production of *The Wreckers* at Prague on December 12, 1906, proved a particularly chaotic one. Neumann had had a stroke, and the work of preparation had been scamped. Maurice Baring, who came all the way from St. Petersburg on purpose to be present, said he had never heard a more disgracefully underrehearsed public performance. Nevertheless, the opera had good notices from those English critics who were present; and eighteen months later there were concert performances under Artur

Nikisch at the Queen's Hall, London, first of the Prelude to Act
II, 'On the Cliffs of Cornwall' (May 2, 1908), and then of Acts I
and II (May 28, 1908).

The first stage production in this country took place in 1909,
when it was played for a week at His Majesty's Theatre under Sir
Thomas Beecham. He also included it in the repertory for his
Covent Garden season the following year; but the production
seems to have been inadequately prepared, for the composer,
herself a great admirer of the conductor as appears from *Beecham
and Pharaoh*, called it 'a fiasco'. A production in Munich under
Bruno Walter was scheduled for February, 1915, but was cancelled immediately on the outbreak of the first World War.
Thereafter the opera lay dormant for some years; but a work of
such musical merit and dramatic intensity deserved revival, and
in 1939 it entered the repertory of the Sadler's Wells Opera
Company, to the great satisfaction of the composer herself, then
over eighty years of age, but unfortunately too deaf to hear the
performance.

During the years 1911–13 Ethel Smyth devoted herself to the
militant struggle for the vote that was being waged by the
Women's Social and Political Union and, like many other
suffragettes, was in course of time sentenced to a short term of
imprisonment. By the autumn of 1913, however, she had retired
temporarily from the fray, having made up her mind it was time
to write another opera. At first she flirted with the idea of using
J. M. Synge's *Riders to the Sea* as a libretto; but ultimately she
decided in favour of a cheerful subject and chose W. W. Jacob's
short story, *The Boatswain's Mate*. Having drafted the libretto
herself, she retired to Egypt to compose the music, which was
finished by spring 1914. It is characteristic of her state of mind at
the time that in the short gay overture she quotes her suffragette
composition, *The March of the Women*. During her journey back
to England, early that summer, she called at Vienna and left
Germany with two contracts in her pocket: one for the Munich
production of *The Wreckers* mentioned above and the other for
The Boatswain's Mate at Frankfurt-am-Main, also the following

February. But the outbreak of the war prevented both productions; and ultimately the first performance of *The Boatswain's Mate* was given by the Beecham Opera Company at the Shaftesbury Theatre (January 28, 1916) during Beecham's temporary absence in Rome.

So ended the long period of her operatic exile.

The other great operatic exile of the early part of the twentieth century was Frederick Delius. But whereas Ethel Smyth was an exile only insofar as she was forced by circumstances to seek opportunities abroad for the production of her operas, Delius was an exile in a wider sense. Born in Bradford, Yorkshire, he was sent as a young man by his parents to an orange plantation in Florida, and there he became familiar with negro music. Later he returned to England and after a period of study in Leipzig settled in France, where he lived for the rest of his life. Apparently, France was the only country where he could work and live at ease. Yet it was in Germany—not France or Great Britain—that his three operas were produced for the first time.

He wrote six operas in all and at various times thought of working on another two to be based on Emily Brontë's *Wuthering Heights* and Synge's *Deirdre of the Sorrows*. *Irmelin, The Magic Fountain* and *Margot-la-Rouge* remained unpublished and unperformed. It is true that *The Magic Fountain* was accepted for production at Weimar in 1893, but it was withdrawn at Delius's direct request. *Margot-la-Rouge* was written in 1902 for a Sonzogno one-act opera prize competition, and material from it was later reworked by him and his amanuensis, Eric Fenby, into an Idyll for soprano, baritone and orchestra (1930). A prelude salvaged from *Irmelin* was used as an orchestral intermezzo when *Koanga* was played at Covent Garden in 1935.

Each of the three operas that reached performance is based on a work of fiction: *Koanga* on the American novel, *The Grandissimes*, by G. W. Cable; *Romeo und Julia auf dem Dorfe* on the story, *Die Leute von Seldwyla*, by Gottfried Keller; and *Fennimore und Gerda* on *Niels Lynhe*, by the Danish novelist J. P. Jacobsen.

A Village Romeo and Juliet (to give it its English title) is generally accepted as Delius's operatic masterpiece. Originally produced at the Komische Oper, Berlin, in 1907, it was included in Beecham's Covent Garden season of 1910. Ten years later he revived it there and in 1934 (the year of Delius's death) conducted three student's performances of it at the Royal College of Music. The work had a chilly reception in 1910. Forsyth seems to have voiced a fairly general opinion when he wrote[1] 'Despite a certain poetical charm and an undoubtedly high level of musicianship, the work made little impression owing to its want of characterization and theatrical vitality. The peculiar inanity of a plot which might have collapsed at any moment after the first act (if the hero and heroine had seen the obvious and easy solution of their troubles in *marriage* instead of *suicide*) introduced into the performance what appeared to an English audience to be an element of irritation, and even of laughter.' It is only just to contrast with this criticism the considered judgment of Beecham, who has been a powerful advocate of Delius's music ever since his first meeting with the composer in 1907. Writing in 1944, he said:[2] '*A Village Romeo and Juliet* has the remotest kinship with melodrama; it is an idyll with something of the other-world or dream quality of a pastoral or fairy play. The characters are types rather than personages and express themselves with a brevity and reticence that is almost epigrammatic. . . . Purely orchestral episodes play almost as important a part in the narrative as the singing.' In any case it seems clear that a full-scale opera house like Covent Garden is not the right setting for an intimate lyrical opera such as this.

Koanga, on the other hand, proved unexpectedly successful when given its first English performance at Covent Garden in 1935, thirty-one years after its first production at Elberfeld. The scene is laid on an American plantation in one of the southern states; and the use of negro spirituals and creole dances helps to stiffen the somewhat enervating flaccidity of Delius's musical texture.

Fennimore and Gerda, first produced at Frankfurt in 1919, has never been performed in this country.[3]

[1] Cecil Forsyth, *op. cit.*
[2] Sir Thomas Beecham, *op. cit.*
[3] Eric Blom has written an excellent study of this opera under the title of 'A Musical Novel', which is included in his *Stepchildren of Music*. But, despite his enthusiasm, he

DAME ETHEL SMYTH

Charcoal sketch by J. S. Sargent.

The Wreckers: Act I of the revival at Sadler's Wells, 1939.

Hugh the Drover: the fight from Act I of the Sadler's Wells revival, 1950.

The Midsummer Marriage: page from the MS. score of Act I of Michael
Tippett's opera.

Dr. RALPH VAUGHAN WILLIAMS, O.M. (1948)

After the first World War there were still a few English operas
that received their first performances abroad. *Les Trois Mousquetaires*, the last of de Lara's operas, was brought out at Cannes in
1921. Three years later Le Théâtre Beriza produced Lord Ber-
ner's one-act opera, *Le Carosse du Saint-Sacrement*, at the Théâtre
des Champs-Elysées, Paris, in the same bill as Stravinsky's
L'Histoire du Soldat and Sauguet's *Le Plumet du Colonel*. Cyril
Scott's short opera, *The Alchimist*, was written in 1918 and should
have been produced in this country by Sir Thomas Beecham; but
when that proved impossible the composer turned to Germany,
and the opera was accepted by Wiesbaden. Unfortunately, the
opera house there was burnt down just before the opening night,
and eventually *Der Alchimist* was produced at Essen (1925). Four
years later Albert Coates's one-act opera, *Samuel Pepys*, was
played at Munich. Since those years at the turn of the nineteenth
century when Ethel Smyth had found it necessary to conduct an
exhausting campaign against foreign directors, intendants and
conductors in order to get her operas performed at all, the devotion of many idealists and amateurs[1] had helped to make it easier
for new English operas—especially those for which room could
not be found at our opera houses or in our touring companies—
to receive their first production at home. It is true that an opera
that breaks new ground, like Michael Tippett's *The Midsummer
Marriage*, may find a readier public in a country like Germany,
where operatic experiments are welcomed with interest; but there
is no reason why in future English operas should not be conceived
and written expressly for home production. The period of exile
is over.

---

seems doubtful whether the fastidious delicacy of the score could withstand the hazards
of stage performance.

[1] For details of the amateur effort see Appendix E.

CHAPTER VII

Seasons and Festivals
(Twentieth Century)

*Proposed Permanent London Opera House—Stanford as Advocate
—Hammerstein's London Opera House—Beecham's Opera Seasons
—Thomas Beecham Opera Company—British National Opera
Company—Gordon Craig as Producer—Boughton's Arthurian
Cycle—The Glastonbury Festival—The Immortal Hour—Bristol
Opera Season—Other West Country Festivals—The Glyndebourne
Festival—The Edinburgh Festival—The Aldeburgh Festival*

PLANS for a national opera by no means ended with the collapse of D'Oyly Carte's Royal English Opera House in 1891. On June 27, 1898, the following petition for a permanent opera house for London signed by one hundred and forty distinguished individuals was presented to the London County Council:

The humble petition of the undersigned sheweth as follows:

1. That in this, the richest capital in the world, there exists no means whereby the highest class of operatic music can be systematically brought within the reach of the great mass of the people.

2. That under existing conditions the very classes of the community which would benefit most constantly by the presentation of the greatest operatic masterpieces are now debarred from enjoying such a privilege, and the musical education of the public is thereby much restricted.

3. That, for this reason, little encouragement is offered to young artists to pursue the highest paths of their profession, and little opportunity is afforded for their advancement in them.

4. That the development of native operatic art is seriously hindered and discouraged by the lack of any permanent establishment where the works of native composers can be produced.

5. That in most of the important towns in Europe it has been found practicable, with the assistance of the public authorities and at no

great cost to the public exchequer, to make provision for the systematic representation of the best class of opera, which has thus, by long-established usage, become part of the life of the people.

6. That it would be possible for your Council, by an annual grant of money of no excessive amount, to bring about the establishment of a permanent Opera House in London, which would fulfil the requirements hereinbefore set forth and thereby promote the musical interests and refinement of the public and the advancement of the art of music.

Your petitioners therefore humbly pray as follows—

That your Council should take such steps as to them appear advisable to ascertain how the great want referred to above can be best supplied; and if deemed necessary, to obtain powers to devote some portion of their funds to assist in the maintenance of an Opera House for the promotion of the highest form of musical art.

And your petitioners will ever pray.

This petition was considered by the General Purposes Committee of the L.C.C., which expressed the view that 'the encouragement of the higher forms of musical art is greatly needed in London, and if accorded wisely, either by the State or the Municipality, it would be attended with very beneficial results to the whole community'. They went so far as to advise the reservation of a site for the erection of an opera house, but drew attention to the fact that the State, while providing for the visual arts, devoted hardly any of its funds to music, and suggested that it would be fair at least for it to co-operate in such a scheme.

In 1902 an anonymous benefactor wrote to *The Times*, offering £10,000 towards the foundation of a National Opera House, if others would bring the sum up to £500,000. The same year Johnson Galloway, M.P., published a little book in which he proposed that such a system should for the most part be subsidised by the appropriate local authorities. He explained that he borrowed this idea of municipal intervention all the more readily from Italy since 'the municipal element has become, of late, an all-important factor in the economy of our civic life, and seems all but indicated to take active part in a fresh phase of that life'.[1] In support of his

[1] W. Johnson Galloway, *op. cit.*

proposals he adduced the examples of foreign opera houses in Italy, Germany and France; and interest grew to such a point that, in conformity with an Address of the House of Commons dated March 2, 1903, all British diplomatic or consular officers in Europe, North and South America and Cairo were asked for returns concerning 'the financial support, whether in the form of Subsidies, Guarantees, or Buildings or Sites for Buildings, given from State or Municipal resources to Dramatic, Operatic, or Musical performances' in the countries to which they were accredited. The resulting White Paper[1] contained a varied assortment of interesting and sometimes entertaining information. In Italy, for instance, though most of the opera houses at that time were subsidised by the municipalities, no subventions were given by the State, whereas in Russia the equivalent of £300,000 was devoted by the Imperial Household in 1902 to the six Imperial Theatres in St. Petersburg and Moscow. In Switzerland, though some of the Cantons already subsidised theatres and orchestras, a suggestion by the Federal Council that it should extend to other branches of art the support it already gave to painting, sculpture and architecture, elicited a stern rebuke from the Canton of Berne, which, expressing a view diametrically opposed to that of the L.C.C., declared that 'music, the drama, and poetry do not enter the domain of political economy, and do not co-operate for the development of national well-being'. But in Great Britain the momentary spurt of interest in this question died down, and no further action was taken.

In 1908 Stanford returned to the charge with the publication of an excellently argued paper on 'The Case for National Opera'.[2] There were three prerequisites, he said: a site, a building and a subvention. The site should be 'central, and within reach of all, high and low, rich and poor'. As for the building, 'simplicity, dignity of design, comfortable seats, good acoustics, sufficiency of exits, are the main considerations'. In his view, the German Theatre at Prague was an ideal model. 'This fine house, which

[1] Miscellaneous. No. 6 (1903). H.M. Stationery Office.
[2] Included in *Studies and Memories*.

stands by itself in an open space, seats 1,800 persons and cost only £43,200 to erect. Allowing for increased seating accommodation, and for an addition of twenty-five per cent for English labour, the cost of such a building in London ought not to exceed £100,000.'

Arguing the case for a subvention, he gave examples of what was done at Brussels, Lyons, Bordeaux, Toulouse, Frankfurt, Breslau (where the German version of his *Shamus O'Brien* had been produced in 1907), and Geneva. His conclusion was that a grant of 'one-fourth of the expenses would be sufficient for the purpose of security'; and clearly he did not anticipate that in the case of the London opera house this would be more than £10,000 *per annum*. He took care to point out that this was a modest sum in comparison with what the State spent on the visual arts and ended his plea on the following note: 'What man has done, man can do. What Europe has done, England can do. The most difficult rock to surmount is prejudice, the fixed, innate dislike of Englishmen to make a new departure.'

Practical though Stanford's proposals were, they had no immediate effect on either the State or the L.C.C. Prejudice was still too strong. But suddenly in 1911, to everyone's surprise, the German-born American impresario, Oscar Hammerstein, known familiarly as 'the Barnum of Opera', decided to present London with an opera house on a site on the newly planned Kingsway. This was opened on November 13, 1911, with a performance of Nougués's *Quo Vadis?* The new company's repertory was mainly a French one and included *Guillaume Tell*, *Norma*, *Lucia di Lammermoor*, *Roméo et Juliette*, *Louise*, *Mignon* and three operas by Massenet—*Hérodiade*, *Le Jongleur de Notre Dame* and *Don Quichotte*. The only English opera was *The Children of Don*, a new opera by Joseph Holbrooke, the first part of a trilogy, *The Cauldron of Annwen*, based on Welsh legends. After nine months, the venture was bankrupt, and the building was later converted into a cinema. Apart from a brief Russian season in 1915, under Vladimir Rosing, opera did not return to the theatre until 1949, when Jay Pomeroy and the New London Opera Company ran a short season of Italian opera there.

Meanwhile, a determined attempt had been made by Beecham in 1910 to widen London's restricted operatic horizon. The brochure published in advance of his first Covent Garden season (February–March, 1910) set forth his aims as follows: 'Does there, or does there not, exist in England a public ready to take intelligent and continuous interest in music-drama *per se* if it had the chance? It is in order to find out what is the true answer to this question that the present enterprise—the Thomas Beecham Opera Season—has been inaugurated, for unless there is a real demand for opera, any attempt to found a permanent National Opera House in which the best works, new and old, native and foreign, shall be regularly and adequately performed, is at least premature.'

Beecham was young and wealthy. He could afford to by-pass conventions; and he did. The programme for his first Covent Garden season was made up of *Elektra* (the first performance of any opera by Richard Strauss in England), *Tristan und Isolde, Carmen, Hänsel und Gretel* and *L'Enfant Prodigue* (its first performance as an opera on any stage); and of English operas he revived *Ivanhoe* and *The Wreckers* and gave *A Village Romeo and Juliet* for the first time in England. The public, accustomed to the conventional German and Italian repertory of the usual Covent Garden season, was dazzled by such enterprise, but remained unconvinced.

Beecham followed up this first engagement without delay and took His Majesty's Theatre for an all-English season during the summer of 1910. This time the operas he presented were the *opéra comique* type and included first performances in English of Offenbach's *The Tales of Hoffmann*, Massenet's *Werther*, and Missa's *Muguette*, and a new English version of Johann Strauss's *Die Fledermaus*. There was also a short Mozart cycle consisting of *Il Seraglio, Le Nozze di Figaro, Così Fan Tutte,* and *Il Impresario.* Native works were represented by a revival of *Shamus O'Brien* and the first performance of *A Summer Night*, a one-act opera by G. H. Clutsam, the critic of *The Observer*. The main novelty of the season was Richard Strauss's *Feuersnot*. Out of this varied fare *The Tales of Hoffman* and *Die Fledermaus* proved the most popular with the public.

While his Opéra Comique season was still running at His Majesty's, Beecham made arrangements for another Covent Garden season in the autumn. The novelties were D'Albert's *Tiefland*, Leroux's *Le Chemineau* and Richard Strauss's *Salome*, while the programme included revivals of *Don Giovanni, Fidelio, Der Fliegende Holländer, Tristan und Isolde*, and Ambroise Thomas's *Hamlet*. This time English opera definitely took a back seat.

By the end of 1910 he had given about two hundred operatic performances in London; but the public response had proved so disappointing that he decided it would be courting disaster to continue the experiment along the same lines. The truth was that the public he had expected to take 'intelligent and continuous interest in music-drama' did not really exist. So well-informed an observer as Ethel Smyth was unable at this time to see 'how, in London at least—where people are always on the look-out for a new sensation, and where the same people who run to see *Elektra* would, as Mr. Beecham remarked, run with still more zeal to see an elephant standing on one foot on the top of the Nelson Column—a critical taste for operatic art is to be grown'. If it was to be done at all, it would take years of hard, patient, unspectacular and continuous spade-work.

But quite apart from the reactions of the general public, some of the critics confessed themselves baffled by the policy (or lack of policy) revealed by these three intensive seasons, which were described by Cecil Forsyth[1] as 'the promiscuous, polyglot, huddling-on of one opera after another. . . . Mr. Beecham,' continued Forsyth, 'has given us original English in the theatre: he has himself provided, and omitted to use, translations: he has engaged foreigners to sing in their own languages to English audiences: he has even affronted his audience by permitting a return to the "barbarous manner" of Handel's time when bilingual performances were tolerated: he has presented us with the spectacle of a company of nervous Anglo-Saxons, of whom perhaps only a couple were on more than nodding terms with the German language, struggling through a German opera in the original; and

[1] C. Forsyth, *op. cit.*

this has found its ludicrous counterpart in a performance before a London audience of an Italian version of a French opera based on the English of William Shakespeare'.

Although Beecham's indefatigable operatic activities continued during the next ten years, no consistent policy emerged. For a short time he joined the Covent Garden Grand Opera Syndicate and was responsible for the first production of *Der Rosenkavalier* there on January 1, 1913. In the spring of the same year he continued his self-imposed task of introducing Richard Strauss's music to the public by producing the original version of *Ariadne auf Naxos* at His Majesty's in conjunction with Sir Herbert Tree. Then, resigning his position at Covent Garden, he asked Diaghilev to bring over an opera company from St. Petersburg, which could appear at the same time as the ballet. He accordingly arranged for his father, Sir Joseph Beecham, to present Russian opera and ballet at Drury Lane in 1913 and 1914, both seasons being particularly memorable because of the appearance of Feodor Shaliapin. *Boris Godunov, Khovanshchina* and *Ivan the Terrible* were given during the 1913 season; *Prince Igor, May Night, Le Coq d'Or* and *Le Rossignol* the following year. And during the 1914 season he interpolated a single English opera, *Dylan, Son of the Wave*, being the second part of Holbrooke's Welsh trilogy *The Cauldron of Annwen*. Of this he has written that though much of the music was liked, 'without question both the story and the text were wholly beyond the comprehension of the Drury Lane audience'.[1]

After the outbreak of the first World War he formed a new opera company, which opened in October 1915 at the Shaftesbury Theatre, London, and brought out two English novelties; Stanford's *The Critic* (to the libretto by Sheridan) and Ethel Smyth's *The Boatswain's Mate*, early the following year. The Aldwych Theatre became this company's London headquarters, and Manchester its provincial centre. On his father's death in 1916, however, he became involved in financial complications that ultimately led to the collapse of his company in 1920 and the

[1] Sir Thomas Beecham, *op. cit.*

temporary cessation of his own personal operatic activities. Whatever may be the ultimate value of his contribution to the organisation of opera in this country, it must not be forgotten that his attitude during these early years as an impresario was a challenge to accepted conventions, his musical direction adventurous, and his standards as a conductor extremely high.

The traditions of the Thomas Beecham Opera Company were carried on for a few years (1922-9) by the British National Opera Company, which, apart from seasons at Covent Garden in 1923 and 1924, spent the greater part of its time touring the provinces. The artistic direction was in the hands first of Percy Pitt, and later of Frederick Austin. This company gave the first public performance of Ralph Vaughan William's *Hugh the Drover* and produced for the first time the following one-act operas: Ethel Smyth's *Fête Galante*, Gustav Holst's *The Perfect Fool* and *At the Boar's Head*, and Sir Alexander Mackenzie's *St. John's Eve*. It also revived Rutland Boughton's *Alkestis*, which had previously been heard at the Glastonbury Festival.

Beecham had the good fortune—at least in the earlier part of his career—to have sufficient money behind him to make it comparatively easy for him to put his ideals into practice. Other opera idealists were poor; but poverty did not necessarily deter them. Ways and means could usually be found of achieving their aims, often with the help of amateurs—true lovers of opera, though not professionally trained.[1]

As one of the effects of the industrial age had been to focus interest on revivals of works of art from earlier periods, partly because of their intrinsic value and partly as a means of escape from the present, it was natural that the activities of these amateurs should often be directed to revivals of seventeenth and eighteenth century works. In particular, the operas of Purcell were rediscovered. The 1895 performance of *Dido and Aeneas* by the students of the Royal College of Music under Stanford has already been mentioned. More important still, on May 17, 18 and 19, 1900, it

---

[1] Cf. Appendix E for a fuller account of the contribution by amateurs and students to English opera in the twentieth century.

K

was produced by Gordon Craig for the Purcell Operatic Society at the Hampstead Conservatoire (later the Embassy Theatre). The following year Craig produced *The Masque of Love* (from *The Prophetess*, by then generally known as *Dioclesian*) and repeated *Dido and Aeneas* for a week's run at the Coronet Theatre, Notting Hill Gate; in 1902 he put on Handel's *Acis and Galatea* (played with Mozart's additional accompaniments) together with *The Masque of Love* for a fortnight's run at the Great Queen Street Theatre; and *The Masque of Love* was revived again in 1904. In all these productions the musical direction was in the hands of Dr. Martin Shaw.

In view of the later charges of extravagance made against Craig as a producer it is interesting to remember that the 1900 production of *Dido and Aeneas* cost £379 and took £378, no salary being paid to either Craig or Shaw, and that the 1901 programme cost £534 and took £533.[1]

Craig's own description of his *Dido and Aeneas* production was as follows:[2] 'When I presented the opera in 1900, with my friend Martin Shaw, I had only a plain blue[3] background, which has become dreadfully popular since then. Lights from above placed on a "bridge" which we built—a grey proscenium, such as many of the German theatres have used since 1904—a colour scheme—very little movement.' In 1906 he did a fresh design for Act III, Scene 1, which was published later in *Towards a New Theatre*. Writing of this many years later, he said:[4] 'It has always been a habit of mine to recall verse and recall melodies. So, naturally, when in Berlin six years after doing *Dido* in London, and being gay and happy and rehearing this "Come away fellow sailors" song—it running in my mind, I sat me down and did the design. So with *Macbeth* over and over; whether I was in a village or on sea I would be doing design after design. Hunger, you know! hunger for what was denied me—a theatre of my own. For when

---

[1] Cf. Janet Leeper, *Edward Gordon Craig: Designs for the Theatre*. London (Penguin), 1948.

[2] Gordon Craig, *Towards a New Theatre*. J. M. Dent & Sons Ltd., London, 1913.

[3] W. B. Yeats and Henry Nevinson both refer to a *purple* backcloth or background. Cf. Janet Leeper, *op. cit.*

[4] From an unpublished letter to E. W. White dated January 6, 1950.

SORCERESS

Dido and Aeneas: *woodcut of the Sorceress by E. Gordon Craig, 1900.*

on the stage I *rarely* put pencil to paper—I do my sceneries by what's called sleight of hand—and to hell with all theories.'

Although Craig never reverted to opera production in later years, his example was not forgotten, and his influence was far-reaching.

As costs of metropolitan theatre production were rising, it was not surprising to find that other idealists looked outside London for a suitable setting for their operatic activities. Early in the twentieth century two of them planned to create an English counterpart to Bayreuth and *The Ring*. It might have been thought that without the backing of a contemporary Maecenas, like King Ludwig of Bavaria, such ambitious plans were doomed to failure. Yet, through the devotion of the promoters and their supporters, the festival was brought into being and ran successfully for twelve years; and through the composer's perseverance the cycle of music-dramas was completed.

Rutland Boughton and Reginald Buckley were the collaborators in question. They met about 1908 when Boughton himself was known as a composer of orchestral pieces, choruses and songs. His ambition, however, was to take up music-drama where Wagner had left off; but whereas Wagner had looked on the operatic chorus as something conventional and described it as 'scenic machinery made to walk and sing', Boughton wished to exploit the significance of the orchestral chorus (as he called it) as a means of expressing mass psychology as well as commenting on individual characters and their actions. He had already planned to write his own cycle of Arthurian dramas in imitation of *The Ring*, when he was offered a sequence of 'four poems, showing forth the coming of the Hero, his Manhood, the quest of the Grail and the ultimate fading away of those glorious days.'[1] These had been sent by Reginald Buckley, their author, first to Sir Edward Elgar, then to Sir Granville Bantock, and ultimately (on Bantock's advice) to Boughton himself.

The two artists immediately decided to work together. As a first step they published a book[2] in which they set forth their ideas

[1] Rutland Boughton and Reginald Buckley, *Music Drama of the Future*. London, 1911.
[2] *Ibid.*

on choral drama, their plans for a festival and for what they called 'the Temple Theatre' whose artists were to be members of an 'agricultural commune', and also the text of *Uther and Igraine*, the first of the Arthurian music-dramas, later retitled *The Birth of Arthur*. The next step was the composition of *The Birth of Arthur*; and in 1909 and 1913 orchestral excerpts were played at concerts at Leeds and Birmingham, and in August 1913 an experimental stage performance of a section of the work given at Bournemouth with the help of Sir Dan Godfrey. By this time it had been decided that Glastonbury, with its Arthurian legends, was the right place for the theatre and the festival; and a public appeal was launched accordingly. Although the financial response did not come up to expectations it was decided to hold a holiday school there in the summer of 1914; and this was the beginning of the Glastonbury Festival.

The Round Table, the second of the Arthurian music-dramas, was produced at Glastonbury in 1916 and proved one of the Festival's greatest box-office draws. The progress of the cycle was momentarily held up by Buckley's death in 1919; but early in the 'thirties Boughton decided, on Bernard Shaw's suggestion, to become his own librettist and accordingly wrote the books for the three remaining music-dramas. The complete cycle consists of *The Birth of Arthur* as prologue to *The Round Table, The Lily Maid, Galahad* and *Avalon*. Only the prologue and the first two parts of the cycle have so far been produced; but as the works are interconnected, both musically and dramatically, it will be impossible to assess their true value until a production of the complete cycle can be arranged.

The Glastonbury Festival was held annually between 1914 and 1925, with the exception of the years 1917, 1918 and 1923. In addition to the two first Arthurian music-dramas, four other operas by Boughton received their first performances there: *The Immortal Hour* (1914), *Bethlehem* (1915), *Alkestis* (1922) and *The Queen of Cornwall* (1924).

Of these, *The Immortal Hour* enjoyed the greatest success, not only at Glastonbury but also in London. It was given at the Old

Vic in 1920 by the Glastonbury Players, and two years later ran for 216 nights at the Regent Theatre when presented there by the Birmingham Repertory Company. The only comparable runs for English thorough-composed operas have been *Ivanhoe* (160 performances in 1891) and Britten's *The Rape of Lucretia* (eighty-three performances in 1946). The Celtic symbolism of Fiona MacLeod's play and the dim echoes of Debussy and Wagner in Boughton's music caught the fancy of the public, somewhat to the astonishment of the composer himself, who, writing quarter of a century later, confessed: 'Indeed I felt some shame when, at the height of its first success in London, I watched an audience greet the final curtain with an hysterical enthusiasm entirely out of keeping with the mood that I expected to be engendered by the work.'[1] But although *The Immortal Hour* has now lost that accidental quality that endeared it to the escapist public of those post-war years it still remains a moving parable of the testing and discarding of dreams and illusions, and the progress towards a fuller life of reality, expressed in terms of song.

Bethlehem, a musical setting of the Coventry Nativity Play, was, according to the composer, 'deliberately composed as a Folk-opera, the lyrical quality of the play being increased by the insertion at suitable moments of Early English Carols, either as choral interludes after the manner of Greek tragedy, or as part of the play itself—*e.g.* the two lullabies for the Virgin. Folk-tunes were generally used as a basis for the interludes, the exception being original tunes taken from the Arthurian cycle, for it has seemed worth while to link up our various operas not only in the arbitrary way of subject, but also by an interplay of actual musical theme. Besides the entracte-carols three other folk-tunes were incorporated in the body of the work. And of all our pieces I think that *Bethlehem* . . . is most suited to such amateur societies as enjoy operatic forms'.[2]

As has already been mentioned, *Alkestis* was later included in

[1] Cf. article by Rutland Boughton on *The Immortal Hour* in *Philharmonic Post*, March–April, 1949.
[2] Rutland Boughton, 'The Glastonbury Festival Movement', extracted from *Somerset and the Drama*. London, 1922.

the repertory of the British National Opera Company. *The Queen of Cornwall*, Boughton's setting of the tragedy originally written by Thomas Hardy as a play for mummers, has not yet been seen in a professional production.

But it must not be thought that only Boughton's works were performed at Glastonbury: Apart from a number of plays—some of Laurence Housman's *Little Plays of St. Francis* were given there for the first time—there were also three new one-act operas: *Oithona* (1915), by Edgar Bainton, to a libretto adapted from Ossian, *The Sumida River* (1916, revised 1919), by Clarence Raybould, to Marie C. Stopes's translation of the Japanese Nō play attributed to Motomasa, and *All Fools' Day*, a fantasy with music by Clive Carey (1921). *Oithona* was produced while Bainton was a prisoner-of-war at Ruhleben. Thirty years later it is interesting to find that the idiom of Bainton's opera phantasy, *The Pearl Tree* (first produced at Sydney, New South Wales, in 1944), recalls that of *The Immortal Hour*, but translates it from a Celtic to a Hindu setting

The Festival also revived Shirley's *Cupid and Death* (1919), and Blow's *Venus and Adonis* (1920 and 1922) for the first time since their original seventeenth-century productions. *Dido and Aeneas* was included in the Festival programmes for 1915, 1920 and 1921. The only foreign opera was Gluck's *Iphigenia in Tauris* (1916).

The organisers of the Glastonbury Festival admittedly showed great initiative in their choice of material; but it must be remembered that the actual performances were on a humble scale and were given in a small hall with piano accompaniment instead of an orchestra. 'The singing and acting was done by the villagers and by anyone else who would come,' wrote Bernard Shaw,[1] who was one of the Festival's staunchest supporters, 'and a surprising number of quite distinguished talents did come. On these terms performances were achieved which in point of atmosphere and intimacy of interest were actually better than the performances at the enormously more pretentious Festival Playhouse in Bayreuth, or its copy the Prince Regent Theatre in Munich.' And all

[1] Bernard Shaw, *The Perfect Wagnerite*, 4th Edition. London, 1922.

this was accomplished in the face of the most trying physical difficulties. Sir Steuart Wilson, who was one of the post-war performers at the Festival, has described some of these from the actors' point of view. 'The dressing-rooms, such as they were, were at the opposite end of the main building to the stage. You dressed and made up and then went down an outside staircase into a yard and up another outside staircase straight on to the stage. When it was fine there were two greyhounds in the yard who had some kind of walking-on part—they approached suspiciously and had to be diverted from barking. When it was wet, which it often was, it was better to tread with caution in an unpaved yard.'[1] The finest testimonial to the work done by Boughton at Glastonbury came from Dent, when he wrote: 'Nobody can go to Glastonbury as a spectator without feeling that here is a sense of poetry and idealism seldom to be met with elsewhere. Nobody can go to Glastonbury as a worker without learning something new about music and drama.'[2]

The discontinuance of the Festival after 1925 was due partly to difficulties of finance and management. Appeals for funds had been made at various times, but without sufficient response to enable the work to be consolidated or developed; and Boughton himself attributed some of these difficulties to his own 'incapacity as a business man'.[3]

Chief among the West Country towns occasionally visited by the Glastonbury Festival Players was Bristol, and here an attempt was made to present an independent opera festival—in 1924 and 1927 at the Victoria Rooms, Clifton, and in 1926 at the old Theatre Royal in King Street. The promoting spirit of these opera seasons was P. Napier Miles, himself a pupil and friend of Sir Hubert Parry and a composer of talent. His *Westward Ho!* an operatic adaptation of Kingsley's novel made by E. F. Benson, the third act of which is concerned with the great storm that swept up the Bristol Channel and caught the *Vengeance* off Lundy Island,

[1] Cf. article by Sir Steuart Wilson on *The Immortal Hour* in *Philharmonic Post*, March–April, 1949.
[2] *The Illustrated London News*, September 17, 1921.
[3] Rutland Boughton, *The Glastonbury Festival Movement*.

had been given at the Lyceum in 1913; and Boughton had included his choral ballet, *Music Comes*, in the 1920 and 1921
Glastonbury Festivals. At the 1924 Bristol season *Music Comes* was
revived, and Miles's one-act operas *Markheim* and *Fire Flies* were
performed for the first time. The rest of the two programmes was
made up with revivals of *Dido and Aeneas* and Vaughan Williams's
pastoral episode, *The Shepherds of the Delectable Mountains*, and the
first performance in England of Manuel de Falla's *Master Peter's
Puppet Show*.

Two years later all these were repeated at the three weeks'
season at the Theatre Royal, with the exception of *Music Comes*.
In addition there were the first public production of Ethel Smyth's
Entente Cordiale, a revival of Carey's *All Fool's Day*, which had
already been produced at the 1921 Glastonbury Festival, and performances of Vaughan Williams's ballet *King Cole*. The programme was stiffened by the inclusion of two full-length operas:
Così Fan Tutte under the title *The School for Lovers*, and Stanford's
last opera, *The Travelling Companion*.

These last two operas were repeated the following year during
a week's season at the Victoria Rooms, Clifton; but after that the
festival collapsed. This was the moment when Beecham was
trying to launch the Imperial League of Opera in an attempt to
raise sufficient money to provide an annual guarantee for opera in
London and the provinces; and it was apparently felt in Bristol
that such local support as might be forthcoming for opera should
be directed towards the larger scheme.

Although about 40,000 people subscribed, the funds raised
proved too small, and the League gradually fizzled out. Meanwhile, further efforts were made in the West Country (though
not in Bristol or Glastonbury) to revive the ideal of a festival of
English operas. Boughton attempted a come-back, first in 1934 at
Stroud, where *The Lily Maid* was performed for the first time and
The Immortal Hour revived, and then at Bath the following year
with a further revival of *The Immortal Hour* and the first performance of *The Ever Young*, a new music-drama composed
during 1928-9. Like *The Immortal Hour*, *The Ever Young* is a

development of Irish legend; but though there is a certain thematic relationship between the two works, the one is in no sense the sequel of the other. These Stroud and Bath festivals were isolated phenomena; and it was not until 1945 and 1948 that Cheltenham and Bath founded their respective annual festivals, in each case opera playing a prominent though not a predominant part in their programmes.

To the personal enterprise of John Christie was due the creation of the Glyndebourne Opera Festival in 1934. He built a small opera house in the grounds of his private house at Glyndebourne, Sussex, and saw to it that though the auditorium seated no more than 570, the stage had up-to-date technical equipment. The acoustics of the theatre proved excellent for operas which did not need a full symphony orchestra; and as the initial policy was to present not English opera nor even opera in English, but certain masterpieces of foreign opera sung in their language of origin by an international cast, the operas of Mozart proved an ideal basis for this festival's repertory. Beautifully situated in the lap of the South Downs, Glyndebourne looked for its audience, not to the immediate neighbourhood, but to London, just over fifty miles away. As nearly all its seats were priced at two guineas it had to rely for support on comparatively wealthy people who accepted it as a fashionable appendage to the London season and were prepared to spend three if not four times as much on their entertainment there as at Covent Garden.

Although Glyndebourne styled itself a festival there was little fundamental difference between it and the Covent Garden opera season that took place every summer. The season at the Royal Opera House set in London's overcrowded flower, fruit and vegetable market was longer, more varied and less expensive than the festival in the private opera house in the beautiful gardens of Glyndebourne; but both theatres chose their operas from the standard German and Italian repertories and drew their singers from the international pool. That is not to say that English singers were not employed; but their appearances were usually confined to the smaller parts. With Fritz Busch as musical director, Carl

Ebert as producer and Rudolf Bing as general manager, Glyndebourne had the advantage in that it was able to insist on more
careful preparation and longer periods of rehearsal for productions which in some cases were reproductions of productions that
had already been given with great success in pre-Nazi Germany;
but Covent Garden still managed occasionally to introduce a few
novelties in its German and Italian seasons and to interpolate an
occasional English opera such as Delius's *Koanga*, Albert Coates's
Pickwick, Eugene Goossens's *Don Juan de Mañara* and George
Lloyd's *The Serf*.

Glyndebourne has made two attempts to tackle the problem of
English opera. The first was when it toured *The Beggar's Opera*
and brought it to the Haymarket Theatre in 1940. The second
was when the Glyndebourne English Opera Group was formed to
launch Britten's first chamber opera, *The Rape of Lucretia*, just
after the second World War in 1946. By the following year, however, this Group had become independent of Glyndebourne, and
though they returned there in the summer of 1947 as visitors for
the first performance of *Albert Herring* and a revival of *The Rape
of Lucretia*, the link with Glyndebourne was effectively broken.

More enduring has been Glyndebourne's connection with the
Edinburgh Festival. Glyndebourne originally played an important part in the conception of this International Festival of
Music and Drama and became responsible for the general artistic
direction of the Festival and the provision of opera. This arrangement worked well since Glyndebourne Opera, having no deep
local roots, had nothing to fear from transplantation. As had been
the case at Glyndebourne before the war, the Edinburgh opera
programmes were generally made up of revivals. For instance
the 1947 Festival included a revival of Verdi's *Macbeth* as originally
produced by Ebert in Berlin in 1930 and played in England for
the first time at Glyndebourne in 1938. In 1948 Edinburgh enjoyed a revival of Ebert's 1935 Glyndebourne production of
Don Giovanni, and in 1949 a revival of his 1931 Berlin production
of *Un Ballo in Maschera*. But so far there has been no production
of English opera or even opera in English.

Indeed, the initiative for festival productions of English opera passed to the English Opera Group. Working at Aldeburgh in conditions that were nearly as primitive as those of the Glastonbury Festival, and with the whole-hearted support of the inhabitants of George Crabbe's ancient Borough to back them up, they succeeded in making English opera one of the main attractions of the Aldeburgh Festival. *Albert Herring*, an eminently suitable choice with its local East Anglian setting, was revived for the first Festival in 1948; and the following year Britten's entertainment for children, *Let's Make an Opera!* had its first performance in the Jubilee Hall. Since then there have been revivals of *The Rape of Lucretia* (1949) and *The Beggar's Opera* (1950).

The Group also appeared regularly at the Cheltenham Festival of British Contemporary Music and toured not only the provinces but also certain foreign countries: Holland in 1947 and 1948, Switzerland in 1947, Norway and Denmark in 1949. Until then English opera companies had rarely played in Europe. The appearance of English companies at St. Petersburg in 1773 and Hamburg in 1797, and the Central European tours of Gilbert and Sullivan operas that D'Oyly Carte sent out in the 1880's, have already been noticed; but the English Opera Group's tours abroad have been the only occasions—apart from the special performances of *Peter Grimes* given by the Covent Garden Opera Company in Brussels and Paris in 1948—on which foreigners have had a chance of enjoying thorough-composed English operas with British singers and British instrumentalists in their original productions. English opera has, in fact, for the first time become an important article of export abroad.

CHAPTER VIII

The Foundations are Laid
(Twentieth Century)

The Old Vic—Tableau Operas under Miss Cons—Extended Repertory under Miss Baylis—Sadler's Wells Theatre—Sadler's Wells Opera Company—Sadler's Wells Ballet Company—State Subvention for Broadcast Opera (1930–2)—Entertainments Duty Exemption—C.E.M.A.—The Arts Council of Great Britain—Opera in Wartime—Benjamin Britten's Peter Grimes—The Covent Garden Opera Trust—New London Opera Company—English Opera Group

QUITE apart from the various opera syndicates at Covent Garden, the touring companies like the Carl Rosa, and the special opera festivals that have already been mentioned, a different operatic scheme was developing in London, whose prime purpose was charitable in so far as it deliberately set out to provide 'high-class opera . . . suited for the recreation and instruction of the poorer classes'.[1] This was the Old Vic on the South Bank, which had opened originally as the Royal Cobourg Theatre in 1818.

The modern career of the Old Vic dates back to 1880, when Miss Emma Cons obtained a lease of the Victoria Theatre (as it was then called) and reopened it as the Royal Victoria Coffee Music Hall. Her prime interest was that of the social reformer fighting by every means to counteract the temptation of the poor to indulge in strong drink; and on her committee of philanthropists music was represented by Benedict, Carl Rosa and Sullivan. Regular ballad concerts were given, and once a fortnight the second half of the programme consisted of operatic excerpts in tableau form. This type of presentation was dictated by the fact that Miss Cons had only a music-hall licence; so any continuity

---

[1] Quoted from the Royal Victoria Hall Foundation Charity Commission Scheme dated September 11, 1925.

of stage presentation was impossible. In a notice[1] circulated to her audience she explained that the management were forbidden to act "even *one* entire scene from an Opera. Were they to take out a Dramatic Licence they would be obliged by the law to at once stop all smoking on the part of the audience. By simply having Selections from the music of the Opera, sung before a conventional background and illustrating the story by tableaux, the Management are able to give their audience some idea of the principal Operas without exceeding the limits of their Licence." The operas treated in this way included such romantic English favourites as *The Bohemian Girl*, *The Rose of Castile*, *Maritana* and *The Lily of Killarney*. The popularity of these tableau performances increased rapidly under the musical direction of Charles Corri, a descendant of Domenico Corri, the composer of *The Travellers* (1806); and notable landmarks were the productions of *Tannhäuser* (1904) and *Lohengrin* (1906).

Miss Cons died in 1912 and was succeeded by her niece, Miss Lilian Baylis, whom she had appointed as her Acting Manager fourteen years previously. At last the licensing difficulties were overcome; and by the time of the first World War the Old Vic had become the acknowledged 'home of Shakespeare and opera in English', performances of Shakespeare's plays being given regularly, and operas staged without the continuity of the action being incessantly broken by a drop curtain to satisfy the requirements of the original licence. The repertory was now extended to include Mozart; and this marked the beginning of Dent's connection with the Old Vic. His spirited translations of the librettos of *The Marriage of Figaro*, *Don Giovanni* and *The Magic Flute* were largely responsible for the rejuvenation of these operas when revived there after the War; and henceforth his counsels were to play an increasingly important part in the shaping of the Old Vic's opera policy.

Opera in the Waterloo Road was popular; but only by dint of the severest economies did it pay. Dent has described how the general policy was 'that operatic rehearsals should be avoided as

[1] Quoted in Edward J. Dent's *A Theatre for Everybody*.

far as possible, mainly on account of the ever-increasing expense of the orchestra. . . . Moreover, Miss Baylis was accustomed to pay her singers the lowest possible fees and this could only be excused on the ground that she always allowed them every possible opportunity of earning money by outside concert engagements.'[1] The orchestra was kept to a bare minimum and consisted of about eighteen players, including single woodwind, double string quintet, and one or two extra instruments—in fact, very much the same sort of chamber orchestra as was later chosen by Benjamin Britten for the English Opera Group's productions, except that the Group's orchestra had a solo instead of a double string quintet—but rather than allow the original scores merely to be cut down, Corri took pains himself to rescore some of the more important operas, and one of his greatest achievements was his reduction of *Tristan and Isolde*.

Of the English operas presented during the nineteen-twenties, *The Bohemian Girl*, *Maritana* and *The Lily of Killarney* continued regularly to fill the house. Nicholas Gatty's one-act *Prince Ferelon* was performed in 1921, and his setting of *The Tempest* was taken over the following year from the Surrey Theatre, where Messrs. Fairbairn and Miln ran an English opera season for a short period. Ethel Smyth's *The Boatswain's Mate* was revived, also in 1922.

The growing popularity of opera and drama at the Old Vic made it inevitable that sooner or later the Governors should consider a scheme of expansion. In North London the old Sadler's Wells Theatre, originally founded about 1680 as a pleasure garden after the discovery of a mineral spring, had fallen on evil days. It had first come into prominence as a theatre towards the end of the eighteenth century, when King was its manager and Charles Dibdin ran it as an Aquatic Theatre; and there was a large tank of water under the stage, in which nautical spectacles were performed. Dibdin's son, Thomas, the playwright, was made manager in 1825. With the passing of the 1843 Act for Regulating Theatres it became the headquarters of Phelps and his Shakespearean Company. But soon a decline set in—drama gave way

[1] Edward J. Dent, *A Theatre for Everybody*.

to melodrama, melodrama to music-hall, music-hall to films—
and in 1915 the theatre was closed altogether. From this state of
dereliction it was rescued by Miss Baylis and the Governors of the
Old Vic, who raised enough money to buy the site and rebuild
the theatre to roughly the same scale as that of the Old Vic in the
Waterloo Road.

The new Sadler's Wells Theatre reopened in January 1931 and
was at first run literally as an Old Vic for North London—that is
to say, opera and drama were performed alternately at each
theatre. But the principle of alternation was soon found to be
unworkable in practice; and finally it was decided by the Governors that opera and drama must be divorced from each other,
drama remaining at the Old Vic and opera at the Wells. This
meant that London had—more or less accidentally—acquired a
new opera-house.

Dent vividly describes the immediate reactions to this unexpected state of affairs. 'Miss Baylis herself,' he writes,[1] 'was utterly
unprepared for the new developments which the opening of
Sadler's Wells inevitably involved. When the first announcement
was made to the Governors that there would be alternate weeks
of opera and drama, I said myself, "Then I suppose that means
that we shall now have opera every night of the week for eight
months." Lord Lytton, the chairman, put the question to
Miss Baylis. She seemed completely taken by surprise. "Yes,
I suppose there will," she replied with a rather dazed look,
as if it had never occurred to her that the whole work of the
opera department would from now onwards be doubled if not
more.'

The musical direction of the new opera house was taken over
from Corri by Lawrance Collingwood. Popular operas like *The
Marriage of Figaro, Don Giovanni, The Barber of Seville, Il Trovatore, Rigoletto, Faust, Carmen, Cavalleria Rusticana, I Pagliacci, La
Bohème* and *Madame Butterfly* remained the hard core of the repertory; and considerable initiative was shown by the production of
such comparatively unknown works as Rimsky-Korsakov's *Snow*

[1] Edward J. Dent, *A Theatre for Everybody.*

Maiden and *Tsar Saltan*,[1] Mussorgsky's *Boris Godunov* in its original version, Chaikovsky's *Eugene Onegin*, Smetana's *The Bartered Bride* and Verdi's *Don Carlos*.[2] More ambitious were the productions of *The Mastersingers*, *The Valkyrie* and *Der Rosenkavalier*; but these proved out-of-scale for a house with a moderate-sized stage, a medium orchestra and a popular audience. As regards English operas, those old romantic favourites, *The Bohemian Girl*, *Maritana* and *The Lily of Killarney* were dropped; and in their place came revivals of *Dido and Aeneas*, *The Wreckers* (1939), *The Travelling Companion* (1935), *Greysteel* (1938),[3] *Savitri* (1935) and *Hugh the Drover* (1937). Collingwood's operatic version of *Macbeth* had its first performance at Sadler's Wells in 1934. By Miss Baylis's death, in 1937, over fifty different operas had been produced since the opening of the theatre six years previously.

During this period Sadler's Wells had also become the headquarters of a ballet company formed by Ninette de Valois. Its earliest productions date from 1931, and of these the most important was Vaughan Williams's *Job*, a masque for dancing with choreography by Ninette de Valois herself, which had been taken over from the Camargo Society. In 1934 *Giselle* was produced with the British-born Alicia Markova and Anton Dolin as guest artists, and later the same year the company gave the first performance outside Russia of *Swan Lake* in its entirety. A remarkable series of new short ballets with choreography by Ninette de Valois and Frederick Ashton followed; and in 1937 the company was invited by the British Council to dance at the Paris Exhibition. The reputation of the young dancers—particularly Margot Fonteyn and Robert Helpmann—was enhanced by the production of *The Sleeping Beauty*[4] in its entirety in 1939. As well as giving its own performances during this period, the company also provided the incidental ballets in some of the operas.

[1] Both of these operas had been first produced in Great Britain by the Swindon Musical Society. Cf. Appendix E.
[2] Cf. Appendix C.
[3] For this revival (March 23, 1938) Gatty's one-act opera was expanded into two acts.
[4] Then entitled *The Sleeping Princess*. This misnomer was due to Diaghilev's decision to adopt it for the 1922 London revival, to distinguish it in the mind of the public from *The Sleeping Beauty* pantomimes.

The nineteen-thirties were notable, not only because in this period London acquired a new opera house, a full-time instead of a part-time opera company and a new ballet company, but also because there then occurred the first signs of a State subvention for opera. As so often in this country, it came about in an apparently haphazard way. In 1930 the Treasury at the instigation of Viscount Snowdon agreed that if the B.B.C. spent £25,000 a year in fees for relaying opera from Covent Garden, £17,500 of that sum would rank for direct Treasury grant; but after the Treasury had made three payments of £17,500, £17,500 and £5,000—a total of £40,000—the grant was withdrawn by the Coalition Government at the end of 1932.

The next step was an indirect one—exemption from Entertainments Duty.

It was the Finance Act of 1916 that first imposed a general tax on entertainment; and for some years this was levied, with only limited exceptions, on all theatre and cinema performances. In 1934, however, the possibility of exemption being granted in certain approved cases was admitted by the Commissioners of Customs and Excise, the main conditions being that the applicant must be a charitable trust or properly constituted non-profit-distributing company, that the control of the trust or company must be in disinterested hands, and that the entertainment must be 'partly educational'—whatever that phrase might mean. In 1946 these conditions were modified in the sense that it was no longer necessary to show that each individual entertainment was 'partly educational'. Instead, the phrase was applied to the general activities of the company concerned. It is interesting to find that whereas between 1934 to 1946 the Commissioners of Customs and Excise were extremely cautious in their selection of exempted plays, during the same period not a single opera was faulted on 'partly educational' grounds. Perhaps Jeremy Collier's suspicions of the disarming effect of music in connection with stage performances were justified after all.

The Sadler's Wells Opera and Ballet Companies, run as they were by a charitable foundation, had no difficulty in qualifying for this exemption; and, indeed, they particularly needed it insofar as it was laid down by the Charity Commission scheme that their performances were to be given at such prices as would 'make them available for artisans and labourers'.

Covent Garden was not under the same obligation towards its public; but its need was just as great. The costs of an art-form that calls for full stage resources as well as a company of first-rate singers and a symphony orchestra are bound to be excessive when related to receipts derived from the sale of tickets which by custom the public—even the Covent Garden public—expects to be only a fraction above prevailing theatre and concert prices, and which in actual fact have hardly increased during the last century, despite a considerable all-over rise in costs.[1] The various syndicates that were responsible for running the international seasons at the Royal Opera House were continually getting into financial difficulties, from which they could be extricated only by calling on their private backers for help. Thanks partly to the Treasury grant given through the B.B.C., the Covent Garden Opera syndicate managed to continue its activities until 1933. The following year the Royal Opera House Co. Ltd. was formed, and the artistic direction was entrusted first to Sir Thomas Beecham and Geoffrey Toye jointly, and after 1935 to Beecham alone. Productions were financed through the London and Provincial Opera Society Ltd., and later through the Covent Garden English Opera Society, and these were the first Covent Garden companies to obtain entertainments duty exemption.

The Carl Rosa Opera Company did not qualify for this exemption until 1942, when a non-profit distributing company called Grand Opera Productions Ltd. was set up to present it. Unfortunately the benefit that accrued to Grand Opera Productions from this relief was to a great extent negatived by the fact that its constitution was not accepted by the Commissioners of Inland Revenue as qualifying for exemption from income tax as well, and large income tax payments had to be made by the company during the first few years of its existence.

[1] Cf. p. 204.

Other opera companies that in due course obtained entertainments duty exemption were Glyndebourne Productions, the English Opera Group, the London Music Art and Drama Society (New London Opera Company), Intimate Opera, the London Opera Club and the Covent Garden Opera Trust.

The indirect subvention of tax relief began to be supplemented by direct subvention shortly after the outbreak of the second World War. Whereas three centuries previously the approach of civil bloodshed had led to the closing of the playhouses for nearly eighteen years, now an international cataclysm with heavy bombing of London and many other towns in Great Britain resulted in an intensification of interest and activity in the theatre. Help given by the Pilgrim Trust in the early stages of the war led directly to the formation of a Committee (later a Council) for the Encouragement of Music and the Arts, known familiarly as CEMA, which secured Government backing for its work as early as April, 1940, grants to it being made on the vote of the Ministry of Education. From the beginning CEMA's policy covered the theatre, as well as music and the visual arts; and its first operatic subvention was a guarantee of £200 to Sadler's Wells in 1940–41.

When the war came to an end the Coalition Government agreed that the work of CEMA should be put on a permanent peace-time basis. An announcement to this effect was made by the 'Caretaker' Government in the early summer of 1945, and the decision was implemented by the Labour Government shortly afterwards, when CEMA became incorporated under Royal Charter as the Arts Council of Great Britain and was made the recipient of a direct annual grant from the Treasury (no longer through the Ministry of Education). Its terms of reference covered the encouragement and diffusion of the fine arts in Great Britain—as distinct from the activities of the British Council, which were directed to the propagation of British culture abroad —and it was of set purpose left free to work out a long-term policy for the arts that would not be subject to overriding political considerations. In this way it became the recognised channel of state-aid for the arts; and the change-over from private to public patronage was taken a step further when the Local Government Act of 1948 made it possible for any local authority (except county councils and parish councils) to spend up to the product of a 6d. rate on entertainment in their areas. In this way a complete system for the subvention of the arts from public funds was evolved, partly as a result of emergency measures improvised during the war.

The wartime history of opera in England is mainly a record of the survival and development of the Sadler's Wells and Carl Rosa Companies, for during that period the Royal Opera House, Covent Garden, was used as a dance-hall, and the Glyndebourne summer festival was closed. At the beginning of September, 1939, the members of the Sadler's Wells and Carl Rosa Companies found their contracts cancelled, and for some time no one knew whether it would be possible to continue to present opera in war-time or not. As the London public gradually became accustomed to black-out conditions, and the stagnation of the 'phoney' war induced a widespread feeling of boredom, demands grew for a resumption of theatrical activity, and the Sadler's Wells Company was gathered together for an experimental Saturday matinée performance of *Faust* (September 30, 1939). This proved so outstandingly successful that regular performances followed at the Wells—first once, then twice a week—until by the summer of 1940 both opera and ballet companies were playing every night of the week to record houses. Meanwhile, in January 1940, the Carl Rosa Company had managed to reopen, and during the following months they toured the main theatres in the provinces with remarkable success.

The London blitz brought the activities of both companies to a sudden end. *Faust* was performed at the Wells on the evening of Saturday, September 7; but when the audience came out into Rosebery Avenue after the fall of the curtain they found the night sky glowing fiercely with the reflection of the great fires raging in the city and the docks, and it was clear that further performances would be out of the question. The Wells was immediately turned into a rest centre for homeless people and the company once more disbanded. A few days later the Carl Rosa Company, which happened to be playing at the People's Palace, Whitechapel, lost their entire wardrobe and scenery.

During the ensuing winter theatrical life in London was at a standstill. But at this point a well-timed offer from CEMA made it possible for Sadler's Wells to keep together a nucleus of their personnel and so prevent the complete disbandment of the company. It was suggested that two or three operas should be taken out on tour; and *The Marriage of Figaro* and *La Traviata* were chosen for the start. 'The number of this experimental company was twenty-six, with members of the chorus doubling the jobs of stage-hands, electrician, and wardrobe staff. The scenery was two three-fold screens, designed by Motley . . .: the furniture, two chairs and a sofa.'[1] The operas were produced in the industrial areas of Lancashire, in towns where many of the audience had never had the opportunity of hearing an opera before. For this tour each member of the company agreed to become a 'jack-of-all-trades'. The conductor filled in the missing orchestral parts with a piano; members of the chorus undertook to scene-shift and to look after wardrobe and lighting; and most of the singers sang continually—one as many as twenty-seven performances in the first month of the tour. The success of this experiment was instantaneous. Under the direction of Joan Cross the company and orchestra were gradually enlarged; new operas were added to the repertory; and when the Lancashire experiment was over, a promise of financial support from the Carnegie United Kingdom Trust made it possible for the company to undertake further tours and ultimately to return to London, where the New Theatre became their temporary headquarters.

Meanwhile, it had taken the Carl Rosa Company eighteen months to recover from their disastrous losses; but by dint of grim perseverance they were able gradually to replace their cos-

[1] From 'An Experiment in Opera (1940–1945)', by Joan Cross in *Opera in English*. Sadler's Wells Opera Books, No. 1.

tumes and properties, to reassemble their company, and by March 1942 they went out on tour again to the provinces.

During the war years the Sadler's Wells Company was able to 'build up a complex and expensive organisation, pay off a heavy debt on its home theatre, and stage regular and increasingly elaborate new productions'.[1] Not only did it preserve the loyalty of its metropolitan audience, but it also won a new and enthusiastic following in the provinces. By 1945 it felt itself strong enough to tackle a new English opera. Benjamin Britten had returned from a short stay in the United States three years previously with a commission from the Kussevitzky Music Foundation to compose a full-length opera. He had chosen as his subject the 'Peter Grimes' story in Crabbe's poem *The Borough* and had asked Montagu Slater to write the libretto. The work of composition was completed by the beginning of 1945; and as Sadler's Wells Theatre had just been derequisitioned it was agreed the company should present the new opera there on the night the theatre reopened.

Britten's only previous operatic essay had been *Paul Bunyan*, an operetta to a libretto by W. H. Auden, which had been given a few performances in 1941 at Columbia University, New York. This work has never been published or revived. He threw himself with enormous enthusiasm into the composition of *Peter Grimes*; and, as he himself later admitted,[2] the qualities of the Sadler's Wells Company 'considerably influenced both the shape and the characterization'. Eric Crozier was chosen as producer. The first performance on June 7, 1945, which marked the company's return to its home after an absence of nearly five years, was an historic occasion. Not only was *Peter Grimes* an immediate success with its English audiences, but it excited considerable interest abroad. During the next few years it was produced at the following different places, thereby easily rivalling the previous record of Balfe's *The Bohemian Girl*[3]—in fact, no first opera written in the

[1] From 'An Experiment in Opera (1940–1945)', by Joan Cross in *Opera in English*. Sadler's Wells Opera Books, No. 1.
[2] From Benjamin Britten's 'Introduction' to *Peter Grimes*. Sadler's Wells Opera Books, No. 3.
[3] Cf. p. 101.

twentieth century by any other composer, British or foreign, has enjoyed such an instantaneous triumph:

1946   Stockholm
       Basle
       Zurich
       Tanglewood, U.S.A.
       Antwerp
1947   Brno
       Milan
       Copenhagen
       Budapest
       Hamburg
       Mannheim
       Berlin
       Graz
       London, Covent Garden (also Brussels, Paris, Liverpool, Leeds and Manchester on tour)
1948   New York, Metropolitan (also Los Angeles, Philadelphia and Boston on tour)
       Oldenburg
       Stanford University College, California (also San Francisco on tour)
1949   Helsinki
       Strasbourg
       Colmar

As is evident from the list given above, Britten at one stroke became an international figure, and his future output a matter of concern to the whole operatic world. *Peter Grimes* was universally recognised as a symbol of the renascence of English opera; and its success went far to break down the inferiority complex under which English opera had laboured for so many years.

All this happened at a moment when plans were being made for the reopening of the Royal Opera House, Covent Garden. Messrs. Boosey & Hawkes, one of the foremost firms of music publishers, took a short lease of the building at the end of 1945 and sublet it to the Covent Garden Opera Trust, which was specially set up under the Chairmanship of Lord Keynes (then also chairman of the Arts Council of Great Britain) for the purpose of

BENJAMIN BRITTEN (1947)

Peter Grimes: design by Kenneth Green for the original Sadler's Wells production, 1945.

Albert Herring: John Piper's design for the drop cloth, 1947.

Let's Make an Opera!
The finale of *The Little Sweep*, 1949.

Peter Grimes: Peter Pears and Joan Cross in the Covent Garden production, 1947.

Albert Herring: showing Peter Pears in the title part, 1947.

Kathleen Ferrier in *The Rape of Lucretia*, 1946.

The Beggar's Opera, arranged by Britten, 1948.

running it as a national lyric theatre for opera and ballet. The Trust's aims were to found a National Opera House which would be open to the public for the whole year at reasonable prices (instead of for a limited season at high prices as before the war), and to establish a national tradition of both opera and ballet. Mr. David L. Webster was appointed General Administrator. A limited measure of financial backing from the State was secured through the Arts Council. With the agreement of the Governors of Sadler's Wells, the Sadler's Wells Ballet was transferred to Covent Garden where it became the resident ballet company and presented a fresh production of Chaikovsky's *The Sleeping Beauty* at the gala reopening on February 20, 1946.

In the case of opera, a new company had to be formed from scratch; and for this purpose auditions were held all over England, Scotland and Wales in the summer of 1946. By December 12 the company was strong enough for its chorus and some of its principals to appear with the Sadler's Wells Ballet and an acting cast in an adaptation of Purcell's *The Fairy Queen* specially made by Constant Lambert. As Dent said,[1] 'the performance of a national classic was indeed the appropriate symbol of the new enterprise, a proclamation of our faith in the greatest of English musicians'. But the new company made its first independent appearance on January 14, 1947, when *Carmen* was produced under the musical direction of Karl Rankl.

Gradually the new company built up a varied repertory. In addition to *Carmen*, there were productions of *Manon*, *The Magic Flute*, *Der Rosenkavalier*, *Turandot*, *Il Trovatore* and *Rigoletto* in 1947; and *Peter Grimes*, which had been withdrawn from Sadler's Wells Theatre in March 1946 after nineteen performances, was added to the Covent Garden repertory on November 6 in a new production by Tyrone Guthrie. The following year[2] the company produced *La Traviata*, *The Mastersingers*, *The Valkyrie*, *Tristan und Isolde*, *Boris Godunov* (in the original Mussorgsky version), *Aida*, *La Bohème*, *Siegfried* and *Fidelio*; in 1949, *The Marriage of Figaro*, *Das Rheingold*, *Götterdämmerung*, *The Olympians*, *Salome*

---

[1] Preface to *Purcell's The Fairy Queen*, John Lehmann, 1948.   [2] Cf. Appendix D.

(for the first time in English)[1] and *Lohengrin*; in 1950, *Madam Butterfly*, *The Flying Dutchman*, *La Tosca* and *The Queen of Spades* (for the first time in English)[2]—making a total of twenty-eight operas in four years. A few of these were adapted from stock; but the majority were newly produced. All operas were presented in English, except for a few gala performances of *The Ring* and other operas by Wagner given in German. The production of Sir Arthur Bliss's *The Olympians* on September 29, 1949, was a world première.

During the four years 1947–50 the company gave five hundred performances in London.[3] It also carried out three extensive provincial tours and played *Peter Grimes* in Brussels and Paris in the summer of 1948—the first time an English opera company had ever appeared at the Théâtre de la Monnaie or the Opéra. At the same time there were visits to the Royal Opera House from the San Carlo (Naples) Opera Company (1946), the Vienna State Opera Company (1947), the English Opera Group (1947), the Opéra Comique, Paris (1949) and the Teatro alla Scala, Milan (1950).

When the Boosey & Hawkes lease expired at the end of 1949 the Ministry of Works took a forty-two-year lease of the Royal Opera House from Covent Garden Properties Ltd., the ground landlords, and rented the building direct to the Covent Garden Opera Trust, which was then reconstituted as the Royal Opera House, Covent Garden, Limited.

The post-war audience for opera in London, which was considerably swollen by ex-service men who had heard opera for the first time in Italy during the Italian Campaign, was offered a further attraction when Mr. Jay Pomeroy formed the New London Opera Company which presented opera in Italian for an unbroken period of two years at the Cambridge Theatre (1946–8), and later in 1949 for a short season at the Stoll Theatre, Kingsway. Mozart, Rossini, Donizetti, Verdi and Puccini were the composers chosen; and the production of *Don Pasquale* proved particularly popular. All productions were in Italian, with the exception of *La Bohème* which was sung in English.

[1] Cf. Appendix C.   [2] *Ibid.*   [3] Cf. p. 207.

Of great potential importance for the future of English opera was the formation of the English Opera Group by Britten and some of his collaborators. As was pointed out in Chapter VII, the Group has been primarily a festival company, and its appearances at Glyndebourne, Aldeburgh, Cheltenham, Scheveningen, Amsterdam and Lucerne come into that category. It has also had short seasons in London at Covent Garden, Sadler's Wells, the People's Palace and the Lyric Theatre, Hammersmith, and has toured the provinces extensively.

Its aims were set forth by its promoters in the following terms: 'We believe the time has come when England, which has never had a tradition of native opera, but has always depended on a repertory of foreign works, can create its own operas. . . . This Group will give annual seasons of contemporary opera in English and suitable classical works including those of Purcell. It is part of the Group's purpose to encourage young composers to write for the operatic stage, also to encourage poets and playwrights to tackle the problem of writing the libretti in collaboration with composers.' It was made clear that the Group's scope would cover concerts as well as opera performances; and the first three works written for it were accordingly two operas by Britten himself and a Stabat Mater by Lennox Berkeley. As regards the opera performances, Britten in his determination to plan on economical lines decided to do without a chorus and to reduce his orchestra to chamber dimensions: a string quintet, woodwind quartet, horn, harp and percussion—all solo players. As has already been pointed out, this orchestra closely resembled the one evolved by Charles Corri to meet the financial exigencies of the Old Vic.

The first work Britten wrote for the Group was *The Rape of Lucretia* to a libretto by Ronald Duncan after the stage play of André Obey; and this was produced at Glyndebourne in the summer of 1946. He followed this up with a thorough-composed comic opera, *Albert Herring*, to a libretto by Eric Crozier based on a short story by de Maupassant (Glyndebourne, 1947); and the next year he made a new arrangement and adaptation of *The Beggar's Opera*, which was produced by Tyrone Guthrie

(Cambridge, 1948). In 1949 the first performance of *Let's Make An Opera!*, an entertainment for young people which included *The Little Sweep*, a one-act opera with spoken dialogue, was given at the Aldeburgh Festival; and when brought to London for runs at Christmas 1949 and 1950, this proved the most popular of all the Group's productions. For the Festival of Britain, 1951, the Group prepared Purcell's *Dido and Aeneas* in a new edition with the thorough-bass realised by Britten, and also a new opera by Brian Easdale, *The Sleeping Children*, with libretto by Tyrone Guthrie.

The English Opera Group has experienced many difficulties in its brief existence; but if it can consolidate and broaden its position it should play an important part in developing English chamber opera.

On Covent Garden and Sadler's Wells, however, is bound to fall the main responsibility for maintaining the highest possible standards in presenting opera in English, including a proportion of English opera, while the Carl Rosa Company, and to a lesser degree the two metropolitan companies, must concentrate on spreading such opera far and wide through the country. Their spirit of initiative is shown by their plans for the Festival of Britain year, which include first performances of three new English operas: Vaughan Williams's *The Pilgrim's Progress*, George Lloyd's *John Socman* and Britten's *Billy Budd*.

PART TWO

The Position Today

CHAPTER I

The Composition of New English Operas

IT has often been stated that it is a fundamental condition for the creation of new operas that there should be close co-operation between composer and librettist. As Benjamin Britten says:[1] 'In the general discussion on the shape of the work—the plot, the division into recitatives, arias, ensembles and so on—the musician will have many ideas that may stimulate and influence the poet. Similarly when the libretto is written and the composer is working on the music, possible alterations may be suggested by the flow of the music, and the libretto altered accordingly.' While this is doubtless true, it must not be thought to imply that the two collaborators are equal partners. They are not. The librettist's task is subordinate to the composer's; and it is the composer's opinion which must ultimately prevail. Where he does not assert his authority, one gets conditions favourable for the creation of semi-opera—as in the cases of Dryden and Purcell, and Gilbert and Sullivan—rather than opera. Goethe was right when he said: 'A libretto should be a cartoon and not a finished picture.'[2]

The librettist may supply a preliminary sketch of the subject and action; but his treatment is going to be largely subject to musical considerations. An operatic score consists of vocal and instrumental music, some of which may be natural music—for instance, the dance music played by the stage bands in *Un Ballo in Maschera* and *Peter Grimes*, and songs like the serenade at the beginning of Act II of *Don Giovanni* and the round in the pub scene (Act I, Scene 2) of *Peter Grimes*—the remainder being artificial in the sense that it is written according to the operatic

[1] Foreword by Benjamin Britten to *The Rape of Lucretia*. The Bodley Head, London, 1948.
[2] '*Der Operntext soll ein Karton sein, kein fertiges Bild*'—Letter to Zelter dated May 19, 1812.

convention. The vocal music in an opera ranges from declamation and recitative to formal airs (or half-airs), ensembles and choruses. From the beginning the librettist must be fully conscious of what Britten calls 'the problem of continuity, or degrees of intensity'.[1] The delivery rate of the librettist's words will be the musical rate and not the normal rate of a stage-play; and their audibility (and therefore intelligibility) will vary according to whether they are set as recitative, or an air, or for an ensemble of voices.

Ronald Duncan, as a result of his work on *The Rape of Lucretia*, understands this clearly. 'I soon discovered,' he writes,[2] 'that a libretto is a distinct literary form. It should not therefore be judged by ordinary literary or dramatic standards. For a libretto is not a mere drama that is then set to music. It should be a drama which is written *for* music. That distinction describes the form itself. A libretto is a vehicle for music, for song. An opera is not music spread over drama. An opera is a marriage between words and music, an organic growth and not a compound.'

References to English opera, scattered about histories of British music or of opera generally, often contain the dreary refrain 'a failure because of the bad libretto'. The fact that this has never been said about *Il Trovatore* should help to expose the fallacy that underlies this sort of judgment with its implication that, if the opera in question has been unsuccessful, the fault is the librettist's. The blame for an inadequate libretto rests as much on the composer as on his collaborator: the credit for a successful opera is almost entirely his. If Boito's magnificent librettos for *Otello* and *Falstaff* had been set by Mancinelli instead of Verdi, it is doubtful whether they would ever be heard today. British musicians who wish to become successful opera composers must accordingly familiarise themselves with the contemporary stage and studio conditions in which opera is presented and not rely entirely on their librettists' stagecraft.

It must not be thought that because his task is subservient to the composer's, the librettist is therefore an inferior artist. Quite

[1] Britten, *op. cit.*
[2] Ronald Duncan's ' The Libretto: The Method of Work,' *ibid.*

the contrary. As Britten says,[1] 'if the words . . . match the music in subtlety of thought and clarity of expression it results in a greater amount of artistic satisfaction for the listener.' Davenant, Shadwell and Dryden wrote opera librettos in the seventeenth century: today J. B. Priestley writes *The Olympians* and E. M. Forster *Billy Budd*. Keats started to write an opera libretto in 1818. Only a few sketches remain; and there is no indication for whom it was intended. But it was one of the misfortunes of the nineteenth century that the operatic stage did not know how to attract the services of outstanding potential librettists like Beddoes, Browning, Tennyson and Hardy.

Right at the beginning of the collaboration between composer and librettist an important decision has to be made about the choice of subject matter. The serious operas of the seventeenth century dealt mainly with classical and mythological subjects. Dryden expresses the current attitude in his Preface to *Albion and Albanius*. 'The Persons represented in Opera's, are generally Gods, Goddesses, and Heroes descended from them, who are suppos'd to be their peculiar Care; which hinders not, but that meaner Persons may sometimes gracefully be introduc'd, especially if they have relation to those first Times, which Poets call the *Golden Age* . . . and therefore Shepherds might reasonably be admitted, as of all Callings, the most innocent, the most happy, and who by reason of the spare Time they had, in their almost idle Employment, had most leisure to make Verses, and to be in Love; without somewhat of which Passion, no *Opera* can possibly subsist.' Yet at that date (1685) English opera had already advanced to the point where historical subjects were admitted— e.g. *The Cruelty of the Spaniards in Peru, The History of Sir Francis Drake*. The implications of this extension were not fully realised until the romantic revival of the eighteenth and nineteenth centuries found matter of operatic interest in every period of history.

Whereas from the beginning contemporary themes have been legitimate subjects for comic opera, because it is through the

[1] Britten, *op. cit.*

M

manners of his day that the writer of comedy attacks the foibles of humanity, serious opera has always been chary of dealing with contemporary material. The example of *La Traviata* is typical. When first produced at Venice in 1853 as a lyric drama of contemporary manners it scandalised the audience and was subsequently made acceptable only when the action was antedated to the seventeenth century, so blunting its immediate impact. The importance of the Italian *veristi* at the turn of the nineteenth century in successfully applying operatic treatment to realistic contemporary themes has not always been fully appreciated; but a work like Puccini's *Il Tabarro* is a classic of its kind. The obvious danger of using contemporary material is that if its main interest depends on its actuality the work is doomed to become quickly out-of-date. This is what has happened to Krenek's *Jonny Spielt Auf* (1927) and Hindemith's *Neues vom Tage* (1930). Two recent English operas that have tackled this problem with some measure of success are Vaughan Williams's *Riders to the Sea* and Inglis Gundry's *The Partisans*.

In the last few years an approach to a broader and deeper way of treating contemporary material has been made by T. S. Eliot in his verse plays *The Family Reunion* (1939) and *The Cocktail Party* (1949). So far, the only English opera composer who has shown signs of following this important lead has been Michael Tippett, who is responsible for both words and music of *The Midsummer Marriage*. In the (as yet unpublished) Preface to this opera he writes, 'the theatre can afford to rediscover the dramatic material appropriate to one place and one time where many and different worlds of apprehension interact'. The characters of *The Midsummer Marriage* may be in one sense our contemporaries—the 'big business' tycoon, the personal private secretary, the mechanic, the holiday hikers—but at the same time they have a deeper significance. By fusing dream psychology with mythology and anthropology Tippett has attempted to evolve a new technique of operatic presentation.

Since Alban Berg's *Wozzeck* (written 1914–20, produced 1925), it has been evident that opera is one of the most suitable art forms for representing complex psychological states of mind. This is amply borne out by *Peter Grimes*, where Britten has shown great invention in discovering appropriate ways of expressing Grimes's maladjustment in musical terms.[1] Similar subtleties are to be found in his delineation of Herman Melville's *Billy Budd*, the 'Handsome Sailor', whose downfall was caused by his only blemish, a stutter liable to develop under strong provocation.

Specially important in operatic construction is the time factor. Of course, there are different kinds of time to be considered. There is the actual time supposed to have been taken by the action represented on the stage—and this is an ideal time because an imaginary one. There is the dramatic time, which is the time taken by the action when played by actors; and there is the operatic time when the same action is set to music. Operatic time tends to be slower than dramatic time; but music sometimes makes it possible to take short cuts and to compress action in a way that would not be possible in drama.

It should be remembered that in opera composer and librettist should have a special attitude towards the words of the libretto and their intelligibility. In a play there is no reason why every word should not be heard and understood by the audience, whatever the actors' speed of delivery; but in an opera there are degrees of fast fading intelligibility, passing from solo declamation and recitative to ensembles and choruses. Where it is musically necessary for the words to be submerged, one must see that they are of minor dramatic importance. Conversely, where it is dramatically necessary for the meaning of the words to be easily understood, the music must be kept down. This means that principles of musical construction have to be modified in the light of principles of dramatic construction, and *vice versa*, and out of the interaction of these two different principles is born the elusive operatic principle.

And what is to be the effect of all this on the public? It is not merely a question of arousing an audience's interest. Wagner's

[1] A special section is devoted to this problem in *Benjamin Britten: a sketch of his life and works*, by E. W. White.

music dramas do that. Yet the fact remains that they suffer so seriously from the besetting German weaknesses of lack of proportion and moral irresponsibility as to be completely suspect as operatic models. The conscious and subconscious feelings, thoughts and aspirations that are expressed through opera should be based on positive and humane values. It is the Greek spiritual ideal that should inform the work of opera composers and librettists today just as it did the Florentine Camerata at the beginning of the seventeenth century; and that particular inspiration is to be sought, not in Germany or Austria, but on the shores of the Mediterranean.

CHAPTER II

English Operas for Revival

FROM what has been said in the previous chapter, it is clear that time, intelligibility and intensity are operatic factors that can be judged, not in the study, but only in terms of actual stage performance. This at once exposes the great weakness of English opera. The conditions do not exist—and have never existed—for a comprehensive critical assessment of its aesthetic quality. The absence of a national opera house and national opera company has meant that nothing could be saved from the piecemeal experience of the past in order to build up a living tradition that could supply standards for judgment.

The policy of the past three centuries has, in fact, been one of waste and frustration. English operas and semi-operas have been produced in considerable quantities, but in nearly every case they have had to be discarded at an early date owing to the chaotic conditions governing the organisation of opera here. Even Purcell, who is now universally admitted to be one of the great opera composers of all time, has had few fully professional performances of his works in this country. *Dido and Aeneas* has been done at Sadler's Wells; but it has never secured a place in the regular repertory. *The Fairy Queen* was played by the Covent Garden Opera and Sadler's Wells Ballet Companies for a few weeks in 1946 and 1947; but it has not been revived since then. Without adequate performances of these and other English operas, no satisfactory critical assessment of the genus can be made, for while there are some skilled people who can read a play and visualise its stage effectiveness, and others who can read a music score and auralise its sound in performance, it is doubtful whether an armchair appreciation of an opera libretto and score has any absolute value at all. It is therefore essential to embark on a policy of rescue by reviving a certain number of English operas. Although not more than a small fraction of the output of the last three centuries is likely to merit revival, that attempt should certainly be made, because only in that way can a tradition be created, the treasures of the past revealed and the astonishing variety of English opera appreciated at its proper worth.

To do this, all our operatic resources must be mobilised; and it is here that the B.B.C. can help. It is true that ordinary broadcasts can do little beyond enabling listeners to become acquainted with operatic scores; but in the future television will probable have an important part to play. A medium that can broadcast opera without distorting the music or stage action should revolutionise the impact of opera on the general public, particularly on those who have not yet had a chance of becoming acquainted with live opera performances. Viewers will be many times more numerous than present audiences; and a judicious policy of combining outside broadcasts with studio broadcasts should strengthen the present companies and their repertories and also make it possible for the B.B.C. to explore unfamiliar ground. It is essential that a considerable part of this exploratory work should be directed to English opera.

When one talks about the repertory of existing companies one assumes that, apart from a specialist organisation like the English Opera Group, these companies are anxious to build up a repertory that consists partly of foreign and partly of English operas. If (for the sake of argument) a resident company functions with a repertory of about fifty operas, one might expect between a quarter and an eighth of these to be native operas. If its repertory be smaller, this proportion might still hold good. If such a company presents an average of four new productions or reproductions each year, one might expect one English opera to be included every year or every other year. Some of these would be new works: others revivals.

What is the potential repertory of English opera?

If the present companies can maintain their positions, they should be able to present all the current works of Benjamin Britten.

In the case of Vaughan Williams, his operas have gained public favour slowly but surely. Nearly all of them were originally produced by students and were taken up by professional companies only at a later date: *Hugh the Drover* (originally written in 1910) by the British National Opera Company in 1924 and Sadler's Wells in 1937 and 1950; and *Sir John in Love* by Sadler's Wells in 1946. His last opera, *The Pilgrim's Progress*, described as 'a morality with music', was completed in 1948 and includes as its penultimate scene *The Shepherds of the Delectable Mountains* (first produced separately in 1922). It is likely to play as unique a part in the repertory of English opera as *Job*, 'a masque for dancing', in British ballet.

Of Boughton, it is difficult to speak with any degree of certainty. The value of his major work, the Arthurian cycle of four operas and a prologue, cannot be assessed until it has been performed as a whole—an expensive and hazardous undertaking. *The Immortal Hour*, though immensely popular a generation ago, has not won a permanent place in the repertory. *Bethlehem* seems almost more suited to amateur than professional production. *Alkestis*, *The Queen of Cornwall* and *The Ever Young* should be tried out again.

Holst's fame as an opera composer is based on a few one-act operas. Although both *The Perfect Fool* and *At the Boar's Head* scored a considerable success when originally produced, neither appears to have kept the favour of the public; and it seems likely that the earlier *Savitri* (composed in 1908; produced in 1916) has the greater staying power. His little chamber opera, *The Wandering Scholar*, deserves to be more widely known.

Delius's operas are hardly likely to win a permanent place in the repertory. His reticent and fastidious talent was the reverse of dramatic. *A Village Romeo and Juliet* has best chance of success when produced in intimate conditions. *Koanga* is a robuster work. *Fennimore and Gerda* has never yet been produced in England. It should be.

Ethel Smyth's *The Wreckers* is now well on its way to becoming an established classic. *The Boatswain's Mate* is one of the best

English short operas; but it is not easy to find it the ideal partner. Perhaps some day it will be possible to hear an English version of *Der Wald*.

Stanford's *Much Ado About Nothing*, *The Critic* and *The Travelling Companion* should certainly be kept alive. Even some of his earlier operas, like *The Canterbury Pilgrims*, might be worth hearing again; and the interesting suggestion has been made (in R. A. Streatfeild's book, *The Opera*) that the Prologue to *Savonarola* should be produced separately as a one-act opera. Stanford's greatest operatic success was *Shamus O'Brien*. This was played by Joseph O'Mara and his company all over the world—particularly in Australia and America—and apparently it was a gold-mine to them and to the composer. If revived now, it should be played for preference by a visiting Irish national opera company.

Scotland should make a special point of rehearing MacCunn's *Jeanie Deans*.

When produced according to the formula of stage realism, Sullivan's *Ivanhoe* has caused considerable trouble. Sir Thomas Beecham recounts how 'tons of timber were ordered for the scenes of the tournament and the burning of the Castle of Torquilstone'[1] when the opera was being revived at Covent Garden in 1910; and even at the original production the critic of *The Graphic*[2] noted that it was 'necessary to drop the curtain for at least twenty minutes in order that the *debris* might be cleared away' after the latter scene. A less ambitious production, without the embarrassment of superabundant props, might well improve the opera.

The Gilbert and Sullivan operas remain copyright until 1961, and until then there is every reason to suppose they will continue to be controlled by the D'Oyly Carte Company. After that they will enter the public domain, and anyone who wishes may reproduce them. The D'Oyly Carte Company has made a special feature of preserving the original stage tradition of these operas. There is perhaps doubtful wisdom in elevating it into nearly as strict a convention as that governing the performance of the

---

[1] Sir Thomas Beecham, *op. cit.*   [2] Issue of February 7, 1891.

Japanese Nō. A change will be welcome and may offer a chance of broadening the basis of the English operetta repertory generally.

Of other late nineteenth-century operas, Mackenzie's *Colomba* certainly and Goring Thomas's *Esmeralda* and *Nadeshda*[1] possibly deserve revival.

To pass to the romantic opera composers of the first two-thirds of the nineteenth century—it seems unlikely that the operas of Bishop will ever prove worth reviving (though George Hogarth spoke highly of *The Maniac*).[2] But Weber's *Oberon*, having been originally written for London, should still occasionally be heard there; and some of the romantic operas of Loder, Barnett, Balfe, Benedict, Macfarren and Wallace would seem to merit revival. Just as present-day audiences are prepared to accept in ballet the romantic conventions of *La Sylphide* (1832) and *Giselle* (1841), so it seems reasonable to expect that their operatic equivalents, *The Mountain Sylph* (1834) and *The Night Dancers* (1846), and other typical romantic works such as *The Bohemian Girl, Maritana, King Charles II, The Rose of Castile, Lurline, Robin Hood,* and *The Lily of Killarney*, would hold the stage today, provided they were presented with as much imagination and sincerity as is the case in Italy, for instance, with the operas of Donizetti.

The genial burletta by Hullah and Dickens, *The Village Coquettes*, should not be forgotten. Although the original score and parts were lost by fire, a devoted work of reconstruction has been carried out by E. J. Chadfield in his Rustic Edition of the opera published some years ago for the Dickens Fellowship; and this should certainly form the basis of any future stage version.

At the end of the eighteenth century Storace scored a great success in London. Half a century later George Hogarth, having given as his opinion that Storace's 'strong sense and judgment enabled him to unite pure Italian melody to the prosody and accent of English poetry with a felicity which has never been excelled by any other composer',[3] particularly deplored the

---

[1] ' . . . The second act of *Nadeshda,* which is by far the best piece of work Goring Thomas ever turned out for the stage.'—Bernard Shaw, *Music in London,* 1890–94.
[2] Cf. George Hogarth, *Memoirs of the Opera,* 1851.
[3] *Ibid.*

neglect of 'these charming pieces'. *The Haunted Tower, No Song No Supper, The Pirates* and *Mahmoud* should be tried out—perhaps in the first instance by students or amateurs.

The only English opera from the eighteenth century that has remained continuously alive is *The Beggar's Opera* in a number of different versions and adaptations; but within recent years revivals of *The Gentle Shepherd, Lionel and Clarissa* and *The Duenna* have shown what attractive results a good producer can obtain from some of the other ballad operas and light operas of this period. *The Quaker's Opera, The Dragon of Wantley, Love in a Village, Cymon, The Padlock* and *Rosina* might also be worth reviving. This century is a happy hunting ground for one-act operas or short pieces by Charles Dibdin and other composers; and some of those with small casts are in the current repertory of Intimate Opera.

There remains the problem of Handel. His English opera, *Acis and Galatea*, which, in Charles Dibdin's view,[1] was 'by infinite degree' his best work, is perhaps the only one of his operas that can hold a permanent place in the English repertory.[2] Yet this country has a certain responsibility in connection with his Italian operas which cannot be ignored.

As has been pointed out, they cannot be performed today unless the *castrati* parts are either taken by women or transposed for men with the necessary adjustments that such a transposition involves. One solution is for the B.B.C. to make a special point of broadcasting them in an English translation with women to sing the *castrati* roles; and a start has already been made with *Giulio Cesare, Serse* and one or two others. Arne's *Artaxerxes* might perhaps be dealt with in the same way.

The B.B.C. can also help with the late seventeenth-century operatic versions of Shakespeare and Purcell's semi-operas. Indeed, it may prove easier and more effective to combine the acting, singing and dancing that are essential ingredients of these dramatic operas on the television screen than in the theatre.

[1] Charles Dibdin, *op. cit.*
[2] It is interesting to remember that William Hogarth invented an imaginary English opera by Handel called *The Rape of the Sabines*, which figures in one of *The Rake's Progress* paintings (1735).

Other seventeenth-century works like *Cupid and Death*, *Venus and Adonis* and *Dido and Aeneas* are by origin occasional pieces for chamber rather than theatre presentation; but there is no reason why they should not be taken into the repertory of companies like the English Opera Group and the Sadler's Wells Opera Company.

Stage editions should be prepared of some of the early jigs where it is possible to reconstruct the original tunes.

CHAPTER III

The Staging of English Operas

'THE scenery is the first object in an Opera that powerfully attracts the eye, that determines the place of action, and co-operates chiefly to the illusive enchantment, that makes the spectator imagine himself to be transported either to Egypt, to Greece, to Troy, to Mexico, to the Elysian Fields, or even up to Olympus.' So wrote Count Algarotti in his *Saggio sopra l'Opera in Musica*.

It has already been pointed out that *The Siege of Rhodes* was the first public stage production in England to employ scenery. Fortunately the name of the designer and his actual designs have been preserved. John Webb was a pupil of Inigo Jones, who had died in 1652 after designing most of the great masques of the reigns of James I and Charles I. When one considers the modest dimensions of the stage at Rutland House—the proscenium opening was about nineteen feet by nine feet high—his scenery was ambitious. Three pairs of wings were set at each side of the stage, and different back flats painted for the first, second and fifth 'entries'. The third and fourth entries were in 'releive', which seems to have meant that the back flats were withdrawn to reveal a kind of recess.

Without attempting to trace in detail the sequence of English opera designers, it is interesting to find that in the middle of the eighteenth century a painter like John Inigo Richards, an original member of the Royal Academy, was working at Covent Garden on *The Maid of the Mill* and other similar productions. In the early years of Queen Victoria's reign the scenery of the Messrs. Grieve (consisting of Mr. Grieve, Mr. T. Grieve and Mr. W. Grieve) was one of the great attractions of the romantic operas given at Drury Lane; and an echo of their spectacular style is still to be found in some of our pantomime scenery. This was the period when, largely as a result of the expert knowledge of Planché, historical accuracy in scenery and costume began to be considered essential. But at the end of the nineteenth century a reaction against realistic scenery set in. As regards Shakespearean production, William Poel had already led a return to the austerity of the Elizabethan stage. Historical accuracy was at a discount; and in the programme Foreword to the Purcell Operatic Society's production of *Dido and Aeneas* a special point was made of explaining that Gordon Craig, the Stage Director, who in this case was also responsible for the scenery and costumes, had 'taken particular care to be entirely incorrect in all matters of detail'. In recent years perhaps the most conscious and successful attempt to enlist the services of the scene painter as member of a team that includes composer, librettist and producer has been made by the English Opera Group. John Piper has so designed his sets and costumes for *The Rape of Lucretia* and *Albert Herring* that they have become an integral part of these two productions.

It will be noticed that, in connection with his work on *Dido and Aeneas*, Gordon Craig was described as Stage Director. This was a continuation of the Victorian practice of relying on the stage manager to bind together the different stage elements in an operatic presentation—not that this stage management was always very effectively carried out. Santley recounts how, when Massé's *Queen Topaz* was produced during Mapleson's season at Her Majesty's in 1860, 'there was no attempt at stage-management; we all wandered on and off and about the stage as we pleased. The effect produced was very curious—neither players nor audience seemed to have the remotest notion what it was all about'.[1] And when Wallace's opera *The Amber Witch* was put into rehearsal a few months later and Santley, who was playing one of the leading parts, pointed out to the stage manager a particularly fatuous mistake, that individual replied, 'How the devil should I know anything about it? I have never read the book!'

Sometimes, it is true, the element of improvisation led momentarily to a happy result. The following is Santley's description of

[1] Charles Santley, *Student and Singer.*

what happened when *Lurline* was being produced at Covent Garden for the Pyne-Harrison season in the winter of 1860. 'We had, as usual, a stage-manager, who did not deem it necessary to study the drama and prepare the situations. At one of the last rehearsals we all got into a muddle in the finale of the second act; nobody seemed to know what to do, so we all stood still, which gave promise of a most thrilling effect on the audience. Suddenly Harrison was seized with an inspiration. "Stop! stop!" he cried out. "Stirling!" "Yes, sir!" "Cannot we have a Huguenot rush here?" "Certainly, sir, the very thing I was thinking of myself!" "Now then, all of you, be ready," and at a given signal we all rushed down to the footlights as though we had been going to annihilate Mellon and the whole of the orchestra. It brought the house down every night we played the opera.'[1]

But towards the end of the century the position began to change. In the first place the standards set by Rupert D'Oyly Carte and W. S. Gilbert for operetta at the Savoy (in the words of Bernard Shaw) 'raised operatic inscenation to the rank of a fine art'.[2] And then, as Wagner's works and opinions began to be known, it was realised that opera production was something far more important and comprehensive than mere stage management. Abroad, Adolphe Appia showed the possibilities of applying modern technical methods when he made his new designs for *The Ring* about 1896; and Gordon Craig's theatrical productions both at home and abroad were a revelation in the early years of the present century. As the emphasis all over the world has now shifted from creations to revivals, the status of the opera producer has become increasingly important.

Some idea of the different attitudes of librettist and composer towards problems of staging may be gained by contrasting the stage directions for scenes from seven English operas chosen from various periods:

[1] Charles Santley, *Student and Singer*.
[2] Bernard Shaw, *Music in London*, 1890–94.

Example I: *Albion and Albanius* (1685)

Act I

The Curtain rises, and there appears on either side of the Stage, next to the Frontispiece, a Statue on Horseback of Gold, on Pedestals of Marble, enrich'd with Gold, and bearing the Imperial Arms of *England*. One of these Statues is taken from that of the late King, at *Charing-Cross*; the other, from that Figure of his present Majesty (done by that noble Artist Mr. *Gibbons*) at *Windsor*.

The Scene, is a Street of Palaces, which lead to the Front of the *Royal Exchange*; the great Arch is open, and the view is continued through the open part of the *Exchange*, to the Arch on the other side, and thence to as much of the Street beyond, as could properly be taken.

Mercury *descends in a Chariot drawn by Ravens.*

He comes to *Augusta*, and *Thamesis*. They lie on Couches, at a distance from each other in dejected postures; She attended by Cities, He by Rivers.

On the side of *Augusta's* Couch are Painted Towers falling, a Scarlet Gown, and Gold Chain, a Cap of Maintenance thrown down, and a Sword in a Velvet Scabbard thrust through it, the City Arms, a Mace with an old useless Charter, and all in disorder. Before *Thamesis* are broken Reeds, Bullrushes, Sedge, etc. with his Urn Reverst.

These directions are sufficiently detailed for the designer to take them as working instructions. The influence of the masque is still strongly felt; but one has the impression that the architectural stage design with its careful perspective and complicated machinery is likely to clog the stage pageantry with heavy symbolism.

Example II: *The Beggar's Opera* (1728)

Act I, Scene I

Scene: Peachum's House. *Peachum* sitting at a Table with a large Book of Accounts before him.

Example III: *The Duenna* (1775)

Act I, Scene I

The Street before *Don Jerome's* House. Enter *Lopez* with a dark lantern.

In contrast with Example I, these and indeed nearly all eighteenth-century libretto directions seem bare and uninstructive. They are straightforward, business-like and brief, and leave the designer a free hand.

A sidelight on eighteenth-century methods of production is to be found in a letter written by Sheridan (in London) to Linley (in Bath) a few weeks before the first performance of *The Duenna*. 'Unless you can give us three days in town, I fear our opera will stand a chance to be ruined. Harris (the Manager at Covent Garden) is extravagantly sanguine of its success as to plot and dialogue, which is to be rehearsed next Wednesday at the theatre. They will exert themselves to the utmost in the scenery, etc., but I never saw any one so disconcerted as he was at the idea of there being no one to put them in the right way as to the music.'

One point emerges from an examination of *The Duenna*: the principal singing parts in this opera (Don Carlos and Donna Clara) are the least important from the dramatic point of view. These were performed by professional singers, while the other main characters were represented by actors and actresses, who were not professed vocalists. This divorce between singers and actors became symptomatic of the English opera stage at the end of the eighteenth and beginning of the nineteenth centuries. Indeed, Weber struck the same difficulty when he came to write *Oberon* for Covent Garden in 1825. On receipt of the second act of the libretto, he wrote (in English) to Planché from Dresden:[1] 'The cut of the whole is very foreign to all my ideas and maxims. The intermixing of so many principal actors who do not sing—the omission of the music in the most important moments—all these things deprive our *Oberon* of the title of an opera, and will make him unfit for all other theatres in Europe, which is a very bad thing for me, but—passons là-dessous.' Planché's own comment on the situation was:[2] 'None of our actors could sing, and but one singer could act—Madame Vestris—who made a charming Fatime. . . . My great object was to land Weber safe amidst an unmusical public, and I therefore wrote a melodrama with songs,

[1] Letter dated February 19, 1825.   [2] J. R. Planché, *op. cit.*

instead of an opera, such as would be required at the present day.'

Example IV: *The Daughter of St. Mark* (1844)

Act II, Scene 3

The battlements of the Palace at Famagosta, in Cyprus, with a view of the port seen under them, guards stationed at various parts, and the stage thronged with the populace, sailors, etc.

(After a Divertissement and Chorus, the stage directions continue as follows:)

During this Chorus the fleet which accompanies the state-vessel, with *Catarina* on board, is seen to pass in the distance, firing a salute, which is returned by the guns of the port—bells are in full ring, and loud flourish of trumpets, etc. heard on all sides, and with a brilliant march, at first distant, then louder, the procession begins. The *King*, preceded by *Pages*, *Squires*, *Heralds-at-Arms*, and followed by all his *Court*, meets the *Archbishop* and *Clergy*—then enter a body of Knights and their respective banners—then the *King's* Body-guard, Officers of the Army and Navy, Equerries, Ministers of State, the Municipal Body, and a File of Soldiers. At a given point the state-vessel reaches the port, when Pages lay down a rich carpet the whole length of stage, and young girls strew it with flowers. *Catarina* then descends, led by *Andréa* on one side, and *Moncenigo* on the other (as Ambassador) and followed by a Deputation from the Venetian Senate. She is met by the *King*, who kneels at her foot, and kisses her hand—then rising, he leads her forward, and presents her to the people, who all bow before her.

(After a Solo by the King and a full Chorus, the stage directions conclude as follows:)

The procession continues streaming down the battlements—the dancing and sports are carried on in the distance—the vessels hoist their flags, and guns keep up an incessant firing, the bells still ringing —a deafening shout from the whole populace, and the waving of banners on the walls and all elevated parts never cease, until the Act drops.

The directions for this scene have been quoted at length because they refer to the scene of the Port at Famagosta as reproduced

N

facing p. 89. This was painted by the Messrs. Grieve[1] and advertised in contemporary playbills (cf. p. 97) as being 'On a scale of Magnitude hitherto out of the power of even this Theatre to attain'. The spectacle must have been very effective theatre.

Example V: *The Canterbury Pilgrims* (1884)

Act I

The scene represents the exterior of the Tabard Inn, Southward, as it appeared at about the close of the fourteenth century. L, with built porch, the principal guest entrance—in a line with this, and continuing to back of stage, the main block of the building, making with the right wing which forms the back of the scene two sides of a quadrangle, of which the third R is supplied by a wall pierced in the centre with a large gateway opening on to the road beyond. Background above this of limetrees in spring foliage. Right round the two sides of the Tabard a wooden balcony (roofed and supported on columns beneath) forms a double colonnade—the portion on the left above the porch being practicable. Table and rough benches R—L.C., and L.

As the curtain rises, the hour of five is striking, and Hubert and his fellow 'prentices headed by Wat and Will are discovered assembling in the courtyard of the Inn and sing a Madrigal, the parts of which some hold in their hands, while others are receiving them from Hubert who is distributing them; ranging the singers at the same time beneath Cicely's window.

This stage direction is definitely written with the stage manager in mind. The setting is a realistic one. Not only does the librettist, Gilbert à Beckett, definitely aim at historical accuracy, but he describes his scene with such literalness that it seems to call for a pre-Raphaelite vividness of presentation in which the brick courses of the walls of the inn would be clearly visible and the audience would not be surprised to find a flight of live pigeons nesting in the limetrees. (The *mise en scène* for this opera was by Augustus Harris.)

---

[1] 'The celebrated Mr. Grieve, and his two sons, Thomas and William, the most perfect scene painters in the world, as a combination; and the most perfect example of parental and filial affection I ever witnessed.'—Edward Fitzball, *op. cit.*

Example VI: *The Birth of Arthur* (published 1911)
Act I, Scene I—A Wayside in Cornwall

PRELUDE

Deep in the shadow of forgotten things,
Rising like mountains round it,
Is a Lake.
White mists o'erwhelm it till its look is mourant.
Deep are its Shadows and its Silences,
But white the foam of its black waters,
When the breathless oars of ghostly rowers break its surface calm.

. . . . .

O Lake of Wonder, roll your Mists away!
Strike through the Mist, O Sun,
And give us Day!

. . . . .

When Boughton decided to set Buckley's poem, *The Birth of Arthur*, from which some of the chorus's opening lines are here quoted, he had in mind a very different style of production from Example V. During the early years of the twentieth century Gordon Craig led a revolt against realistic theatrical tradition with far-reaching results. Boughton's own description (written in 1911, nine years before the opera's actual production) of how he wanted this prelude to be staged runs as follows:[1] 'The curtain will rise, with the first bar of the prelude, upon a scene of vagueness—a lake surrounded by high mountains, but the whole enveloped in opal mist, and nothing clearly seen. From time to time dark shadows pass over, alternating with rays of vari-coloured light. Now and again a strange, mysterious, silent white craft will sail over the lake and perhaps a large bird-like creature will fly across. At the word: "Strike through the mist, O sun, and give us day," the scene will quickly change to a typical English country lane on a summer forenoon, with every leaf ablaze with sunlight. Threats as of coming thunder gradually turn the living light to dead sultriness, showing how Uther's character is affected by natural phenomena as sensitively as the feelings of animals.'

[1] Cf. *Music Drama of the Future.*

Boughton's ideas were naturally modified in the light of his later experience; and for this particular scene at Glastonbury he simply used his chorus as living scenery. This proved to be one of his most successful choral experiments.

He has always considered that the chorus had a special part to play in music drama; and it is interesting to know how in later years he looked back on his various choral experiments. Writing in 1949, he said:[1] 'Before I left home in 1892 I had begun a cycle of Jesus-dramas based on my experience as a boy in the local choral society; the plan for them being a very small central stage with the usual tiers for choral singers on either side of it. That was inevitably shelved after I had seen real operas in London after that date. But I still intended somehow or other to relate dramatic art to the indigenous choral art of England. The choruses in *The Birth of Arthur* were an experiment in that direction which when tried out at Glastonbury proved well worth while. In *Bethlehem* the chorus was used both realistically and in Greek fashion. In the *Queen of Cornwall* it issued from the very stones of the castle setting. . . . In the third drama of the Arthurian cycle (*The Lily Maid*) I reverted to the plan of the discarded Jesus cycle, but with a quartet of singers instead of a chorus, the smaller body being more suited to the intimacy of the work with its small orchestra. . . . [This quartet] has sometimes to relate the drama that is visible to the drama that is purely internal, and sometimes to actual drama which, as in film-work, takes place elsewhere.'

No apology is needed for dwelling at length on this point. The intelligent use of the chorus should be one of the virtues of English opera; and British opera choruses should excel in performance. Purcell's use of the chorus is masterly. It was noted at the time of *Ivanhoe's* first production as one of that opera's defects that Sullivan had given the chorus far too little to do. In *Peter Grimes* Britten has shown great ingenuity in welding a realistic chorus into his score. In *The Rape of Lucretia* the male and female chorus, though soloists, have similar functions to those of the vocal quartet in Boughton's *The Lily Maid*. But the use of the chorus in

[1] From an unpublished letter to E. W. White dated November 14, 1949.

the second act of *The Olympians* marks a return to the choral society tradition and is nearer in style to oratorio than to opera.

The opening stage direction of *The Olympians* runs as follows:

Example VII: *The Olympians* (1949)
Act I

The time is the morning of Midsummer Day, 1836. The scene is a large room—half entrance-hall, half drinking-room—in the *Golden Duck*, an inn and posting house in Southern France. The architecture, decoration, and general atmosphere of this room suggest the South— massive but light-coloured walls, arches that offer glimpses of a brilliant blue sky, decorative wrought-iron work on stairs and landing; a cool room for a blazing hot morning like this. There is very little furniture about, only a small table and a few small chairs. On one side is an entrance leading to the courtyard where coaches arrive and depart. In the centre is a flight of stairs running up to a half-landing that runs round most of the room. It leads to various bedrooms, but also provides, at the back, an entrance to the inn on a higher level than that from the courtyard. Opposite to the main entrance is a small door opening on to the humbler parts of the inn.

This bright morning, the place is in a bustle. Porters are carrying heavy baggage to the main entrance. Several small groups of travellers are about to depart. Maids are brushing and dusting along the half-landing. Seated at the solitary table is the Curé, a small comfortable priest with a sense of humour. He bids goodbye to two elderly travellers, and then sits down again. Some porters, after disposing of the baggage return to stand at the door; others go upstairs to flirt with the maids. There are sounds of a coach departing. There is still plenty of noise and bustle, but not much work is being done. This fact is at once apparent to the landlady, Madame Bardeau, a hard-faced middle-aged woman, who comes in carrying a tray with two glasses and a bottle of fine old brandy. She falls to scolding at once, and does this with some authority.

All this is written with much of the circumstantial approach that a novelist uses to build up atmosphere. The characters are tagged with easily identifiable labels. Later in Act I the company of broken-down players is introduced so successfully that by the end of the act the audience is quite prepared to accept the apotheosis of these good companions into the immortals of Olympus.

But this apotheosis, when it comes in Act II, is found to contribute little or nothing to the action of either the mortals or the immortals, and from this vital flaw the opera never really recovers.

Here are brief flashes from seven English operas chosen arbitrarily from the hundreds that have been written and produced during the last three centuries. It may now be interesting to take one of these operas and examine some of its different revivals.

Since its first performance at Lincoln's Inn Fields, in 1728, *The Beggar's Opera* has been revived on numerous occasions. Some of these are mentioned in the sample lists of operas performed in London in 1732, 1791, 1851 and 1948 (Appendix D); and some are illustrated. Without taking up undue space one can do little more here than to outline a few of the outstanding characteristics of some of the revivals of the last thirty years.

The remarkable version produced by Sir Nigel Playfair in 1920 at the Lyric Theatre, Hammersmith, with the score arranged by Frederic Austin, had a record run of 1,463 performances and was itself frequently revived. It was the first time *The Beggar's Opera* had been played in London since Sims Reeves sang Macheath in the 1886 revival at the Avenue Theatre; so its impact was quite fresh. For this production Gay's libretto was diluted and revived by Arnold Bennett. Austin used some of the original tunes as the raw material for his score, but had no hesitation (in his own words) in adding 'to the original length of the various numbers, here and there turning solos into duets or more extended pieces, inserting dances, instrumental interludes, and so on'.[1] In this way he used forty-five of the sixty-nine original airs, scoring the whole for string quintet, flute, oboe and harpsichord, with occasional use of the viola d'amore and viola da gamba. Macheath's part was transposed for bass-baritone instead of tenor, and Lucy Lockit's for contralto instead of soprano. The poster-bright sets and costumes by C. Lovat Fraser, which were a considerable help in taming the fierceness of the original satire and presenting it as a mannered, inoffensively picaresque comedy, proved well suited to the taste of the audience of those post-war years; and its success

[1] Quoted in *The Story of the Lyric Theatre, Hammersmith*, by Nigel Playfair.

led to Playfair's revival of other eighteenth-century operas, including *Polly* (1922) and *The Duenna* (1924).

The 1940 revival of *The Beggar's Opera* by Glyndebourne—seen in London and on tour, but not at the Glyndebourne Opera House itself—used the Austin score, but discarded the Playfair production and the Lovat Fraser scenery and costumes in favour of a new production by John Gielgud and a somewhat more serious setting based on the early drawings of George Cruikshank. Although the production had various points of interest, there were disturbing vacillations in its style of presentation; and the occasional use of mime to imply the presence of invisible props and the way the musical numbers (in continuance of the Playfair tradition) crystallised into a succession of static tableaux seriously disturbed the flow of the action.

In 1941 Dent made a new version of the score at the request of Sadler's Wells. This was based on the original edition. He arranged all the songs as they were, adding only the barest minimum of introduction necessary to give the singer the note, except in two cases where he wrote optional introductions to suggest a parody of the serious opera style of performance. He also restored, wherever possible, the original melodies and harmonies of Purcell, Eccles and Handel where these occurred. In the event, his version was given for the first time not by the Sadler's Wells Company, but by a group of amateurs, the Birmingham Clarion Singers, in a straightforward production by Tom Harrison.

In 1948 Britten prepared a new realisation of the score for use by the English Opera Group. For this he too went back to the early sources and chose sixty-six out of the sixty-nine airs used in the 1728 version. He particularly admired the tunes of these popular songs because they had 'strong leaping intervals, sometimes in peculiar modes, and were often strange and severe in mood'. Although he presented them with the most scrupulous fidelity, the accompaniments he devised were remarkable for brilliance of invention and variety of instrumental colouring within the modest compass of his chamber orchestra.

Most of the numbers are short and direct. Twice he combined

two of the original numbers to make a duet and a trio. The scene in the condemned hold where Macheath tosses off glasses of wine and bumpers of brandy in an attempt to work up sufficient courage to face the hangman at Tyburn was planned so that a passacaglia binds together the broken snatches of the ten different airs he sings. (In the Dent version the complete original tunes are given to the orchestra as far as possible, and Macheath comes in with his fragments as they occur, the idea being that his head is full of these old tunes and words, but he voices them only at odd moments in the course of his actions so that the orchestra may be said to represent his unconscious mind.) The operatic nature of the score is emphasised by the tonal pattern of the numbers[1] and by the use of the chorus; and although, as the beggar boasts in the prologue, there is nothing so unnatural as recitative in the opera, there are occasional passages of melodrama where Gay's prose dialogue is spoken above music. This device helps to bind closely the text and musical numbers—a necessary procedure if the current of the action is to flow without hindrance—and in no other modern presentation of the opera has this vital problem been so successfully solved as here. For this the producer, Tyrone Guthrie, must take credit as well as the composer. This was indeed a *beggar's* opera—in Guthrie's own words, 'the expression of people made reckless, even desperate by poverty, but in whose despair there is none the less a vitality and gaiety that the art of elegant and fashionable people too often misses'. At the same time, Britten succeeded in giving it a greater operatic density than it had ever had before.

The fact that all these productions differed from each other nearly as completely as they must have differed from the original production gives no cause for dismay. An opera producer is working with three elements: the score (which includes words as well as music), the audience, and the medium, and of these only the first is constant. It is his primary duty to discover every intention of the composer and to transmit these with every means at

[1] There is a version of the Britten score in which Macheath's numbers are transcribed for baritone instead of tenor. This has the effect of making the opera more sombre in tone colour.

his disposal. As the theatre develops, as its shape and geography, its machinery and its conventions change, so production style must change with it. A production is only right at a given moment, and anything it asserts dogmatically today may well be wrong fifty years from now.

The last two sentences are literally quoted from an article by Peter Brook; and the two sentences before them have been slightly adapted from the same article. Though in its context this passage referred to Shakespeare's plays,[1] it is just as valid when applied to opera.

Imaginative use of colour, lighting and movement has distinguished such contemporary productions as Eric Crozier's *The Rape of Lucretia,* Frederick Ashton's *Albert Herring,* Tyrone Guthrie's *Peter Grimes* and *The Beggar's Opera,* and Peter Brook's *The Olympians.* But occasionally these factors arouse hostile criticism, for some people find it difficult to use their eyes as well as their ears and to correlate what they see with what they hear. Gordon Craig's own description of his *Dido and Aeneas* production has been referred to above,[2] and it will have been noticed that he specifically states there was 'very little movement' in it. At that point he goes on to say: 'This very little movement is a characteristic of the English temperament, and, being incomprehensible to other nations, is avoided by Germans, Russians and French.' But if English opera is to obtain universal currency and English productions are to offer an acceptable standard, this failing must be eradicated. Stagnation on the operatic stage leads towards the static condition of oratorio. Stage action demands movement in space, just as music postulates movement in time. The timing of operatic singers' gestures and movements is different from that of ordinary actors. It is as if the persons of an opera moved and had their being in a completely different element. But however their deportment is modified, whether in the direction of movements that are quicker or slower, more circumscribed or more extended, this axiom remains—an opera must flow.

[1] 'Style in Shakespeare Production' in *The Penguin New Writing,* No. 36, 1949.
[2] Cf. p. 146.

CHAPTER IV

Opera Houses, Companies, Finance

THE ability of a country to run opera and maintain opera companies must depend in the first place on the accommodation available. Such accommodation in Great Britain has grown up haphazard. Of London's present theatres, the Royal Opera House (Covent Garden), the Palace and the Stoll (Kingsway), were originally built for opera alone. Drury Lane and Sadler's Wells were built for opera and drama; and His Majesty's for drama, but on a site where an opera house had stood for the greater part of the previous two centuries. Of these, only the Royal Opera House and Sadler's Wells are at present used regularly for opera. Outside London, Glyndebourne was planned as an opera house and has always been used as such. The Manchester Opera House may have been intended for opera when it was built; but it has housed every kind of touring company in its time and continues to do so. Table I gives particulars of these theatres' approximate dimensions and capacity.

It should be noted that although the Royal Opera House is large in size, its capacity is relatively restricted. This is because the well-proportioned auditorium was originally built with tiers of boxes and although most of the box partitions have now been removed, and the sight-lines accordingly improved,[1] the depth of the tiers remains quite shallow.

There are three main companies that work all the year round: Covent Garden, Sadler's Wells and the Carl Rosa. Other companies that operate part-time and have to be brought together for

[1] It is interesting to find Mr. T. Welsh, then joint proprietor with Mr. Hawes of the Argyll Rooms, writing to Thomas Dibdin from Florence on January 21, 1825, after visiting the Scala, Milan, and the Pergola, Florence, and complaining about opera conditions in Italy. 'Even the construction of the theatres is bad: the pit is so flat, that on the third seat you cannot see; and in the boxes intended for six, two only can see the stage. Think of this for Florence, which travellers so extol! Liars!'—quoted in *The Reminiscences of Thomas Dibdin.*

TABLE I

Name of theatre and date of building	Width of proscenium opening	Height of proscenium opening	Depth from proscenium to back wall	Width between fly galleries	Height from stage to grid	Capacity of orchestra pit	Capacity of auditorium
	ft. in.	ft. in. (37)	ft. in.	ft. in.	ft. in.		
Covent Garden (1858)	44	24	77	84	76	95	2,040
Sadler's Wells (1931)	30	22 6	26	40	48	55	1,630
Drury Lane (1812)	42 6	31 6	77 6	77	72	50	2,600
His Majesty's (1897)	34 6	29	45 6	70	59 6	25	1,319
Palace (1891)	34	34	O.P. 41 P.S. 46 6	66	70	35	1,380
Stoll (1911)	45	(72)	78	65	73	40	2,087
Glyndebourne[1] (1934)	24[2]	21	95	70 to 148	61	60	560[3]
Opera House, Manchester	37	37	42 6	51	57	30	2,060

some express purpose include Glyndebourne Opera and the English Opera Group. Of these, the Covent Garden and Sadler's Wells Companies have their own opera houses in London where they spend the equivalent of about eight or nine months in the year. Both companies also tour the provinces: Covent Garden to large towns like Birmingham, Glasgow, Leeds, Liverpool and Manchester; Sadler's Wells more widely. The Carl Rosa Company has no theatre of its own, though at one period in the 1880's it made the old Court Theatre, Liverpool, its headquarters; and it spends the whole of the year on tour. The Glyndebourne Company has its own Opera House to perform in; but that is so situated that it can only be used for special festival purposes.

[1] This theatre has the most modern and complete lighting equipment in Great Britain.
[2] To be increased later to 30 ft.
[3] To be increased to 800 by enlarging the gallery.

Similarly with the English Opera Group—its work is closely allied with such festival centres as Aldeburgh and Cheltenham.

The normal price range at Covent Garden for opera is from 2s. 6d. (gallery) to £1 for a seat in the grand tier, and the monetary capacity at these prices is just about £1,000. (It is difficult to sell out, because the boxes, which are highly priced, are ill-placed for viewing the stage.) The normal price range at Sadler's Wells is from 1s. 6d. (gallery) to 10s. 6d. (stall); and the capacity at those prices is just above £400. At Glyndebourne the usual festival price has been two guineas, with a few seats at a slight reduction; and the financial capacity is about £1,000.

It may be of interest to compare present prices at Covent Garden with those of previous periods, though any such comparison is bound to be somewhat superficial, since there is no accurate basis for the assessment of the real value of money at different times.

On the night it first opened (December 6, 1732) the house was calculated to hold about £200 with box seats at 5s., pit 2s. 6d., gallery 2s. and 1s., and 10s. 6d. for a seat on the stage. In 1792, after the theatre had been almost entirely rebuilt, the shilling gallery was abolished, and seats in the boxes were increased to 6s. and in the pit to 3s. 6d., with the gallery at 2s. The shilling gallery, however, had to be restored a fortnight later. When the theatre was reopened after the fire of 1808 the prices were 7s. for seats in boxes, or 3s. 6d. after the second act of an opera or the third act of a play, 4s. for the pit (second price 2s), and lower and upper galleries 'at the old prices'. It was the increased number of private boxes and the increased pit prices that caused the celebrated O.P. riots. At the beginning of Queen Victoria's reign the current prices were (the second prices being given within parentheses): box seats 5s (2s. 6d.); pit 2s. 6d. (1s. 6d.); lower gallery 1s. 6d. (1s.); upper gallery 1s. (6d.).

Up to this time, of course, the theatre had been the home of legitimate drama as well as of occasional operatic performances. After it was remodelled as an opera house in 1847, however, its prices were drastically revised. In 1851 the prices for a whole box ranged from four guineas (grand tier) to one and a half guineas (third and fourth tiers), and seat prices from 15s. 6d. (orchestra stalls) to 6d. in the gallery. By the end of the century the price range for boxes was from seven guineas to two and a half guineas, and for single seats from one guinea to 6d.

Although the prices paid by the public for opera have increased comparatively little in the course of the last century, costs have risen considerably—especially in recent years—and the value of money has fallen. In any case opera is expensive, since the charges for maintaining a company of soloists, a chorus and an orchestra have to be met, in addition to the usual costs of production, administration, overheads, rent, etc. At Covent Garden at the beginning of 1950, for instance, there were a permanent orchestra of eighty-five and permanent chorus of eighty. Both Covent Garden and Sadler's Wells have full-scale resident ballet companies as well. This means that at Covent Garden the two companies can appear together or singly. At Sadler's Wells the Theatre Ballet at present appears twice a week regularly during the opera season; but although it also tours the provinces it is not yet strong enough to give a London season on its own. This means that the Covent Garden Opera Trust and the Sadler's Wells Foundation have to carry the charges for their respective ballet as well as opera companies.

It is difficult to give any useful information about production costs. One can hardly forget the extravagant sums spent on some of the seventeenth-century court masques: £21,000 seems excessive for *The Triumph of Peace*, even though there were two performances, instead of the usual one—the first on February 3, 1634, in the Banqueting Hall, Whitehall, and the second on February 11 at the Merchant Taylors' Hall. The average cost of a masque in those days is supposed to have been about £1,400. *Psyche*, which was produced for a run at a commercial theatre, cost £800. The numerous books of theatrical reminiscences published in the nineteenth century give many details of the extortionate fees exacted by the great singers, but little information about production costs, though one gathers from Weber that *Oberon* cost £7,000. The Music Report, published in 1949 by the

Arts Enquiry sponsored by the Dartington Hall Trustees, states that in 1948 the average cost of a new production at Covent Garden was £7,000, and at Sadler's Wells £3,000

So far the Covent Garden Opera Trust, the Sadler's Wells Foundation and the English Opera Group are the main recipients in the operatic field of grants from the Arts Council of Great Britain as well as entertainments duty exemption from the Commissioners of Customs and Excise; and the following table shows the Arts Council's grants to date:

TABLE II

Company	1945–6	1946–7	1947–8	1948–9	1949–50
Covent Garden Opera Trust	£ 25,000	£ 55,000	£ 98,000	£ 145,000	£ 145,000
Sadler's Wells Foundation	10,000	15,000	23,000	40,000	47,500
English Opera Group	——	3,000[1]	3,000	5,000	3,000

From the above figures it would appear that the 2,350,000 people who visited the Royal Opera House between its reopening in February 1946 and the end of March 1950 were subsidised to the extent of about 4s. a head. About two million people must have visited Sadler's Wells during the slightly longer period April 1, 1945, to March 31, 1950, and the subsidy there appears to work out at just under 1s. 6d. per head.

As the Arts Council's grant to Covent Garden is by far the largest grant given by that body to any of its associated organisations, it is worth while analysing it in further detail. It goes to help the Covent Garden Opera Trust keep the Royal Opera House open throughout the year for opera and ballet performances, and also to maintain the Covent Garden Opera and Sadler's Wells Ballet Companies whether they are appearing at

---

[1] Paid to Glyndebourne Productions Ltd. in respect of a guarantee against loss on the tour of *The Rape of Lucretia* as presented by the Glyndebourne English Opera Company.

the Royal Opera House or elsewhere. The following table shows the number of performances given by these two companies,[1] both at the Royal Opera House and on tour during the five years 1946 to 1950 (opera figures in roman: ballet in italic):

TABLE III

	Royal Opera House	On tour in Great Britain	On tour abroad	Total
1946	11 : *178*	0 : *65*	0 : *10*	11 : *253*
1947	111 : *132*	70 : *32*	0 : *35*	181 : *199*
1948	135 : *147*	0 : *40*	4 : *32*	139 : *219*
1949	138 : *132*	50 : *32*	0 : *82*	188 : *246*
1950	116 : *144*	56 : *0*	0 : *121*	172 : *265*

The opera figures include 11 performances of *The Fairy Queen* in 1946 and 12 in 1947

From this it would appear that the total audience in Great Britain reached by these two companies in the five years 1946–50 was over two and three quarter millions; and on this basis the Arts Council's subsidy would work out at about 3s. 6d. a head.

In most other European countries a state opera house has been accepted as a matter of course for many years; but though most of them have opera companies of distinction, few can boast so important a ballet company as the Royal Opera House, Covent Garden. This is one of the elements that makes it difficult to find a satisfactory basis for comparing the Arts Council's grants with state grants abroad. Perhaps Paris and Stockholm offer two useful examples. The French Government gives the Paris Opéra (with a capacity of about 2,156) and the Opéra Comique a combined grant, which in 1946 amounted to the equivalent of about £600,000. The Royal Opera at Stockholm, with a theatre seating no more than 1,170, receives an annual subvention of 250,000

[1] It is interesting to compare these totals with the number of opera representations at Covent Garden during the four best years of Augustus Harris's régime in the 1890's, years that Herman Klein calls the last 'golden' period in the nineteenth century 'grand opera':
1891 — 94
1892 — 88
1893 — 89
1894 — 92
1895 — 77

Swedish crowns from the City of Stockholm and two million crowns from the State, which is derived from the National Lottery (*Penninglotteriet*) and is consequently not subject to debate in the Parliament (*Riksdag*). These grants are roughly equivalent to £17,000 plus £138,000. In the light of these figures, the Arts Council's grants do not appear excessive.

If opera is to become established in this country, Covent Garden and Sadler's Wells must be helped to secure their rightful positions. There is no need to be too precise about a differentiation in function between the two houses—on the analogy of the Paris Opéra and Opéra Comique, for instance. Certain operas may be better suited to one house than the other—symphonic operas (particularly Wagner and Strauss) and spectacular operas such as *Boris Godunov*, *Aida*, *Turandot*, etc., to Covent Garden; operas that need intimacy in their presentation or rely for their effect on a strong, direct impact between singer and audience to Sadler's Wells—but the greater part of the international opera repertory is certainly common ground. If any differentation in function is needed, then it should be between Covent Garden and Sadler's Wells on the one hand, and a company like the D'Oyly Carte playing operettas on the other.

Covent Garden has a unique role to play as an opera house of internationally recognised status; Sadler's Wells as an opera house with special duties towards the citizens of London. While both are integral units in a national opera, and one would naturally expect the State to recognise its responsibility by offering grant-in-aid to both through the Arts Council of Great Britain, one would also expect the appropriate Local Authority or Authorities to show a special interest in Sadler's Wells. The petition of 1898[1] should not be forgotten.

That progress is slow should surprise no one. These companies are comparatively young; and it should be remembered that most continental companies have a long tradition behind them. It took even the Sadler's Wells Ballet eighteen years' hard work before it reached its present eminence.

[1] Cf. p. 138.

But national and metropolitan opera is not sufficient. Both the Covent Garden and Sadler's Wells Companies are seen for part of the year in the provinces; but the Carl Rosa Company, which for nearly eighty years has toured the provinces, month after month, year after year, and introduced an audience numbering well over forty millions to the stock operatic classics, needs to find a permanent base and security to consolidate and improve its work. The ideal arrangement would probably be for the company to have the chance to make its headquarters in one of the great provincial towns—for instance, Birmingham, Leeds, Liverpool or Manchester—to play there for several months of the year and to tour for the remaining months. Here is a great opportunity for municipal enterprise.

Neither Edinburgh nor Glasgow is mentioned in this connection, because it is taken for granted that Scotland will wish to make its own independent arrangements for opera in Scotland. And the same applies to the Irish Republic. A country that has supplied some of the best composers, librettists, singers and audiences for opera in the last two centuries or more ought certainly to have its own permanent opera house and opera company. In Wales, an attempt is already being made to build up a Welsh National Opera Company.

Training for opera must proceed concurrently with these developments. As Frank Austin said in a paper read to the licentiates of Trinity College as far back as March 1882;[1] 'You cannot, of course, create talent by any system of academic training; at the same time talent may lie dormant for lack of study, or be vitiated by injudicious training.' The training given by the Royal Schools and other schools of music is useful, but does not go far enough. An attempt to provide more advanced training is being made by the Opera Studio (founded in 1948).

The fact that only now is this country starting to establish what nearly all other European countries have had for years, if not centuries—namely, a national opera—should not necessarily prove a disadvantage. If our composers, librettists, producers,

[1] Frank Austin, *A National School of Opera for England.*

o

performers and audiences are unfettered by tradition, they should be all the better able to tackle this new job without hard and fast preconceptions. English opera is emerging from the difficulties and tribulations of the last three centuries with fresh vigour and confidence. Composer, poet, interpreter, listener—all now have the chance to help create a new and glorious age of opera.

PART THREE

Appendices

APPENDIX A

A Short List of English Operas and Semi-Operas and their First Performances

---

Notes: This list is selective, not exhaustive, and includes only operas that have been publicly performed. For its purpose an English opera or semi-opera has generally been taken to mean a stage action with instrumental and vocal music written by a British composer to an English libretto. Operas in which there is no spoken dialogue are marked with a star.

No attempt has been made to include all the semi-operas that can be covered by the terms 'light opera', 'ballad opera', 'comic opera', etc. In the case of a prolific composer like Bishop, whose works may more correctly be regarded as plays with incidental music than light operas, only a few representative items have been chosen.

Some operas have been composed by British composers to foreign librettos; others by foreign composers to English librettos. Where these are included, their entries are printed in italics. First performances of English operas given abroad in a foreign translation or to a foreign libretto are also italicised; and a separate entry is made for their subsequent first performance in Great Britain. Librettos in Italian are marked (It.), in French (Fr.), in German (G.), and in Erse (E.) after the name of·the librettist. Operas by foreign composers to foreign librettos which had their first performance in Great Britain are excluded, as are also operas by British composers who later accepted foreign nationality (e.g. Eugen d'Albert). Operas produced abroad and written by foreign composers who subsequently became British by naturalisation (e.g. Handel, Benedict and Costa) are given within square brackets. American composers and librettists are treated as foreign, *The Rake's Progress* by Stravinsky and Auden (for instance) being excluded.

The fact that in Great Britain the change to the Gregorian calendar took place in 1752,˙Wednesday September 2 being followed by Thursday September 14, should be borne in mind when comparing the pre-1752 dates in this list with those in Dr. Loewenberg's *Annals of Opera* where all dates are given according to the Gregorian style.

In the second column, where no name of a town is given, London should be understood.

An indication of the number of acts, and whether there is a prologue (Pr.) or epilogue (Ep.), is given in the last column.

Date of Production	Place and Theatre	Composer	Librettist	Number of Acts
		★ ROWLAND'S GODSON[1] (jig)		
About 1590	?	Anon	William Kemp (?)	I
		★ ATTOWELL'S JIG[2]		
1595 (?)	?	Anon	George Attowell	I
		★ SINGING SIMPKIN[3] (jig)		
Autumn, 1595 (?)	?	Anon	Richard Tarlton (?)	I
		THE BLACK MAN[4] (jig)		
About 1602	?	Anon	Robert Cox	I
		★ MICHAEL AND FRANCES[5] (jig)		
Christmas, 1602	Osmotherly, Yorkshire	Anon	Francis Mitchell	I
		★ LOVERS MADE MEN (masque)		
Feb. 22, 1617	House of the Rt. Hon. the Lord Hay	Nicolas Lanier	Ben Jonson	I

[1] On April 18 and 29, 1592, the two parts of 'Rowlandes godson moralized' were entered on the Stationers' Register to John Wolfe. The date of composition is likely to have been some years earlier. There is a reference to this farce jig in the Induction of Nashe's *Summer's Last Will and Testament*, probably written in 1592. The jig was sung to one tune: 'Loth to depart.'

[2] This was licensed to Thomas Gosson on October 14, 1595, as 'A pretie newe Jigge betwene ffrancis the gentleman Richard the farmer and their wyves'. The tunes are specified: 'Walsingham', 'the Iewish dance', 'Bugle Boe', 'goe from my window'.

[3] The date of this jig is probably fixed by the entry to Thomas Gosson on October 21, 1595, of 'a ballad called Kemps *newe Jygge* betwixt a souldiour and a Miser and Sym the clown'. Richard Tarlton may have performed or even written it. Kemp certainly played in it. It was sung to two tunes, which are not named in the printed text (Robert Cox's *Actaeon and Diana*—first edition undated; second edition 1656). Its vogue in England and on the continent lasted for a century.

[4] This jig was first printed by Francis Kirkman in a collection of skits entitled *The Wits, or, Sport upon Sport* (1673); and in the preface he mentions Robert Cox as its principal actor and contriver. The eight tunes are not specified. The text contains prose passages that were spoken.

[5] The title of this jig, which is untitled in the original manuscript, is due to S. J. Sisson, who in *Lost Plays of Shakespeare's Age* showed that after various amateur performances it was first given professionally—probably by the Egton Players—at Christmas 1602. All six tunes are specified, *viz.* 'ffiliday fflouts mee', 'ffortune', 'take thy old Cloake about thee', 'the Ladies of Essex Lamentacon', 'ffor her Aperne', and 'the Cobler'.

Date of Production	Place and Theatre	Composer	Librettist	Number of Acts
		*FOOL'S FORTUNE (jig)		
Summer, 1621	Claverly, Shropshire	Anon	Anon	I
		CUPID AND DEATH (masque)		
March 26, 1653	Private entertainment organised by Luke Channell	Matthew Locke, Christopher Gibbons	James Shirley	I
		* THE SIEGE OF RHODES		
Sept., 1656	Rutland House, Aldersgate St.	Henry Lawes, Henry Cook, M. Locke, Charles Coleman, George Hudson	Sir Wm. Davenant	5 entries
		* THE CRUELTY OF THE SPANIARDS IN PERU		
June, 1658	Cockpit, Drury Lane	?	Davenant	6 entries
		* THE HISTORY OF SIR FRANCIS DRAKE[1]		
June, 1659	Cockpit, Drury Lane	Locke and others	Davenant	6 entries
		* THE CHEATERS CHEATED[2] a representation in four parts to be sung		
About 1660	?	Anon	Thomas Jordan	I
		* ORPHEUS AND EURIDICE (masque) in Settle's Empress of Morocco		
Nov., 1673	Duke's, Dorset Garden	Locke	Elkanah Settle	I

[1] Referred to (apparently) as the 'Second Parte of Peru' by Sir Henry Herbert, Master of the Revels, in July 1662.

[2] This lengthy jig of over 600 lines was 'made for the Sheriffs of London' and published in Jordan's *Royal Arbor of Loyal Poesie* (1664). There are directions for nine changes of tune; but none of the tunes is specified.

Date of Production	Place and Theatre	Composer	Librettist	Number of Acts
		MACBETH		
1673 (?)	Duke's, Dorset Garden	Locke & Johnson	Davenant, after Shakespeare	5
		THE TEMPEST		
April, 1674	Duke's, Dorset Garden	John Bannister, Giovanni Battista, Draghi, Pelham Humfrey, Locke, Pietro Reggio	Thomas Shadwell, after Shakespeare	5
		PSYCHE		
Feb. 27, 1675	Duke's, Dorset Garden	Locke & Draghi	Shadwell	5
		CIRCE		
March, 1677	Duke's, Dorset Garden	John Bannister	Dr. Charles Davenant	
	THE LANCASHIRE WITCHES[1] AND TEGUE O DIVELLY THE IRISH PRIEST			
Sept. 1681 (?)	Duke's, Dorset Garden	?	Shadwell	
	★ VENUS AND ADONIS (masque)			
1682	?	John Blow	Anon	Pr., 3
	★ ALBION AND ALBANIUS			
June 3, 1685	Duke's, Dorset Garden	Grabu	John Dryden	3
	★ DIDO AND AENEAS			
Dec., 1689 (?)	Mr. Priest's School, Chelsea	Henry Purcell	Nahum Tate	3

[1] 'A kind of Opera'—W. Downes in *Roscius Anglicanus*. 'A tentative experiment in the direction of that mixed comic and fantastic opera which we should naturally associate rather with the German romantic movement of the nineteenth century.'—Edward J. Dent in *Foundations of English Opera*.

Date of Production	Place and Theatre	Composer	Librettist	Number of Acts
	THE PROPHETESS,			
	OR, THE HISTORY OF DIOCLESIAN			
June, 1690	Queen's, Dorset Garden	H. Purcell	Betterton, after Beaumont and Fletcher	5
	KING ARTHUR,			
	OR, THE BRITISH WORTHY (dramatic opera)			
1691	Queen's, Dorset Garden	H. Purcell	Dryden	5
	THE FAIRY QUEEN			
April, 1692	Queen's, Dorset Garden	H. Purcell	Anon, after Shakespeare	5
	THE INDIAN QUEEN			
1695	Queen's, Dorset Garden	H. Purcell[1]	Dryden and Howard	Pr., 5
	THE TEMPEST,			
	OR, THE ENCHANTED ISLAND			
1695	Queen's, Dorset Garden	H. Purcell	Shadwell, after Shakespeare	5
	BONDUCA,			
	OR, THE BRITISH HEROINE			
May, 1696 (?)	Drury Lane	H. Purcell	G. Powell, after Beaumont and Fletcher	
	BRUTUS OF ALBA,			
	OR, AUGUSTA'S TRIUMPH			
Oct., 1696 (?)	Queen's, Dorset Garden	Daniel Purcell	Powell	
	THE WORLD IN THE MOON (comic opera)			
May, 1697	Queen's, Dorset Garden	D. Purcell, J. Clarke	E. Settle	

[1] Act V is by Daniel Purcell.

Date of Production	Place and Theatre	Composer	Librettist	Number of Acts

CINTHIA AND ENDIMION,
OR, THE LOVES OF THE DEITIES

April 5, 1697[1]	Drury Lane		Thomas D'Urfey	

RINALDO AND ARMIDA

1698 (?)	Lincoln's Inn Fields	John Eccles	John Dennis, after Tasso	

THE ISLAND PRINCESS,
OR, THE GENEROUS PORTUGUESE

Feb., 1699 (?)	Drury Lane	D. Purcell, J. Clarke and R. Leveridge	P. Motteux	Pr., 5, Ep.

THE SECULAR MASQUE

1700		Daniel Purcell (?)	Dryden[2]	

THE GROVE,
OR, LOVE'S PARADICE (dramatic opera)

Feb. 19,[3] 1700	Drury Lane	Daniel Purcell	John Oldmixon	5

THE JUDGMENT OF PARIS (masque)

1701	Queen's, Dorset Garden	John Eccles	William Congreve	

THE VIRGIN PROPHETESS,[4]
OR, THE FATE OF TROY (dramatic opera)

May 15, 1701	Drury Lane		Settle	

★ [ALMIRA]

Jan. 8, 1705	Hamburg	Handel	Feustking (G.)	3

[1] This date is taken from Lady Morley's list of plays attended at the Theatre Royal, Drury Lane, quoted in L. Hotson's *The Commonwealth and Restoration Stage*, Harvard University Press, 1928.
[2] This was Dryden's last work for the stage.
[3] Cf., footnote 1 above.
[4] Later known as *Cassandra, or, The Virgin Prophetess* (1702) and *The Siege of Troy* (1707).

Date of Production	Place and Theatre	Composer	Librettist	Number of Acts
		★ ARSINOE, QUEEN OF CYPRUS		
Jan. 16, 1705	Drury Lane	Thomas Clay-ton, Nicolino Haym and Charles Dieu-part	Motteux, after Stanzani	3
		★ [NERO]		
Feb. 25, 1705	Hamburg	Handel	(G.)	
	THE BRITISH ENCHANTERS,[1] OR, NO MAGIC LIKE LOVE			
Feb 21, 1706	Queen's, Hay-market		George Gran-ville, Lord Lansdowne	
	WONDERS IN THE SUN, OR, THE KINGDOM OF THE BIRDS (dramatic opera)			
April 5, 1706	Queen's, Hay-market	Draghi, Eccles and Lulli	Thomas D'Urfey	
		★ ROSAMOND		
March 4, 1707	Drury Lane	Clayton	Addison	3
		★ [FLORINDO–DAPHNE][2]		
1708	Hamburg	Handel	(G.)	
		★ PRUNELLA[3] (interlude)		
Feb. 12, 1708	Drury Lane	various composers	Richard Estcourt	4
		★ [AGRIPPINA]		
Dec. 26, 1709	Venice, San Gio-vanni Crisostomo	Handel	Grimani (It.)	3

[1] According to Downes, this 'infinitely arrided both Sexes, and pleas'd the Town as well as any *English* Modern Opera'.

[2] According to Mattheson's *Grundlage einer Ehrenpforte* (Hamburg, 1740), this was originally written as *Octavia*; but owing to its length it was produced as two separate works, *Florindo* and *Daphne*. As is the case with *Nero*, the score is lost.

[3] Performed (apparently between the acts) during a revival of *The Rehearsal* by George Villiers, Duke of Buckingham.

Date of Production	Place and Theatre	Composer	Librettist	Number of Acts
		★ RINALDO		
Feb. 24, 1711	Queen's, Haymarket	Handel	Rossi and Hill, after Tasso (It.)	3
		★ CALYPSO AND TELEMACHUS		
May 14, 1712	Queen's, Haymarket	Galliard	Hughes	3
		★ IL PASTOR FIDO		
Nov. 22, 1712	Queen's, Haymarket	Handel	Rossi, after Guarini (It.)	3
		★ TESEO		
Jan. 10, 1713	Queen's, Haymarket	Handel	Haym (It.)	5
		★ AMADIGI DI GAULA		
May 25, 1715	Queen's, Haymarket	Handel	Heidegger (?) (It.)	3
		PAN AND SYRINX		
Jan. 14, 1718	Lincoln's Inn Fields		Lewis Theobald	1
		THE LADY'S TRIUMPH (comic-dramatic opera)		
March 22, 1718	Lincoln's Inn Fields	Galliard	Settle and Theobald	
		★ IL RADAMISTO		
April 27, 1720	King's, Haymarket	Handel	Haym (It.)	3
		★ IL MUZIO SCEVOLA		
April 15, 1721	King's, Haymarket	1st act by Mattei; 2nd by Bononcini; 3rd by Handel	Rolli (It.)	3
		★ IL FLORIDANTE		
Dec 9, 1721	King's, Haymarket	Handel	Rolli (It.)	3
		LOVE TRIUMPHANT, OR, THE RIVAL GODDESSES (pastoral opera)		
Easter Monday, 1722	Mrs. Bellamy's School		Daniel Bellamy, senior and junior	

Date of Production	Place and Theatre	Composer	Librettist	Number of Acts
* OTTONE, RE DI GERMANIA				
Dec. 1, 1723	King's, Haymarket	Handel	Haym (It.)	3
* FLAVIO, RE DE' LONGOBARDI				
May 14, 1723	King's, Haymarket	Handel	Haym, after Corneille (It.)	3
* GIULIO CESARE IN EGITTO				
Feb. 20, 1724	King's, Haymarket	Handel	Haym (It.)	3
* TAMERLANO				
Oct. 31, 1724	King's Haymarket	Handel	Haym, after Piovene (It.)	3
* RODELINDA				
Feb. 13, 1725	King's, Haymarket	Handel	Haym, after Salvi (It.)	3
* SCIPIONE				
March 12, 1726	King's, Haymarket	Handel	Rolli, after Zeno (It.)	3
* ALESSANDRO				
May 5, 1726	King's, Haymarket	Handel	Rolli (It.)	3
* ADMETO, RE DI TESSAGLIA				
Jan. 31, 1727	King's, Haymarket	Handel	Haym or Rolli (?), after Aureli (It.)	3
THE RAPE OF PROSERPINE				
Feb., 1727	Lincoln's Inn Fields	Galliard	Theobald	
* RICCARDO PRIMO, RE D'INGHILTERRA				
Nov. 11, 1727	King's, Haymarket	Handel	Rolli (It.)	3

Date of Production	Place and Theatre	Composer	Librettist	Number of Acts
	THE BEGGAR'S OPERA (ballad opera)			
Jan. 29, 1728	Lincoln's Inn Fields	Anon., arr. Pepusch	John Gay	3
	* SIROE, RE DI PERSIA			
Feb. 17, 1728	King's, Hay-market	Handel	Haym, after Metastasio (It.)	3
	* TOLOMEO, RE DI EGITTO			
April 30, 1728	King's, Hay-market	Handel	Haym (It.)	3
	THE QUAKER'S OPERA (ballad opera)			
Oct. 31, 1728	Little, Hay-market	Anon	Thomas Walker	
	THE GENTLE SHEPHERD (ballad opera) Scots pastoral comedy			
Jan. 29, 1729	Edinburgh, Taylor's Hall	Anon.	Allan Ramsay	5
	THE VILLAGE OPERA[1] (ballad opera)			
Feb. 6, 1729	Drury Lane	Anon	C. Johnson	
	THE BEGGAR'S WEDDING[2] (ballad opera)			
March 24, 1729	Dublin, Smock Alley	Anon	C. Coffey	
	FLORA, AN OPERA MADE FROM HOB, OR, THE COUNTRY WAKE (ballad opera)			
April 18, 1729	Lincoln's Inn Fields	Anon.	J. Hippisley	
	THE LOVER'S OPERA (ballad opera)			
May 14, 1729	Drury Lane	Anon.	W. R. Chet-wood	

[1] Cf. *Love in a Village*, 1762.
[2] Later in 1729, a one-act version, entitled *Phoebe*, was performed at Drury Lane.

Date of Production	Place and Theatre	Composer	Librettist	Number of Acts

THE CONTRIVANCES[1] (a comi-farcical opera)

| June 20, 1729 | Drury Lane | Carey | Carey | I |

DAMON AND PHILLIDA (ballad opera)

| Aug. 16, 1729 | Little, Hay-market | Anon. | Colley Cibber | I |

* LOTARIO

| Dec. 2, 1729 | King's, Hay-market | Handel | *after Salvi* (It.) | 3 |

* PARTENOPE

| Feb. 20, 1730 | King's, Hay-market | Handel | *Stampiglia* (It.) | 3 |

THE GENEROUS FREE-MASON,
OR, THE CONSTANT LADY, WITH THE HUMOURS OF
SQUIRE NOODLE, AND HIS MAN DOODLE
a tragi-comic-farcical ballad opera

| August, 1730 | Bartholomew Fair | Anon. | Chetwood | 3 |

SILVIA,
OR, THE COUNTRY BURIAL

| Nov. 10, 1730 | Lincoln's Inn Fields | Anon. | George Lillo | 3 |

* PORO, RE DELL' INDIE

| Feb. 2, 1731 | King's, Hay-market | Handel | *Metastasio* (It.) | 3 |

THE JOVIAL CREW (comic opera)

| Feb. 8, 1731 | Drury Lane | T. A. Arne | after Brome | 3 |

THE HIGHLAND FAIR,
OR, UNION OF THE CLANS (ballad opera)

| March 20, 1731 | Drury Lane | Anon [2] | Joseph Mitchell | |

[1] An earlier version, with little or no music, was given at Drury Lane on August 9, 1715.
[2] The music consisted of 'Select Scots Tunes'.

Date of Production	Place and Theatre	Composer	Librettist	Number of Acts

ORESTES (dramatic opera)

April 3, 1731	Lincoln's Inn Fields		L. Theobald	

THE WELSH OPERA,

OR, THE GREY MARE THE BETTER HORSE (ballad opera)

April 22, 1731	Little, Hay-market	Anon.	Fielding	

THE DEVIL TO PAY,

OR, THE WIVES METAMORPHOS'D[1] (ballad opera)

August 6, 1731	Drury Lane	Anon.	Coffey and J. Mottley	3

THE LOTTERY (ballad opera)

Jan. 1, 1732	Drury Lane	Anon.	Fielding	

★ EZIO

Jan. 15, 1732	King's, Hay-market	Handel	Metastasio (It.)	3

★ SOSARME, RE DI MEDIA

Feb. 15, 1732	King's, Hay-market	Handel	Noris (It.)	3

★ AMELIA

March 13, 1732	Little, Hay-market	J. F. Lampe	Carey	

★ ACIS AND GALATEA[2] (English pastoral opera)

May 17, 1732	Little, Hay-market	Handel	Gay	3

THE MOCK DOCTOR,

OR, THE DUMB LADY CUR'D (ballad opera)

June 23, 1732	Drury Lane	Anon.	Fielding	

[1] Cf. *The Devil's In It*, 1852, and *Letty the Basker-Maker*, 1871.

[2] William C. Smith's *Concerning Handel* (London, 1948) contains a well-documented account of the various early productions of *Acis and Galatea*, including its presumed first performance as a 'masque' before the Duke of Chandos at Cannons about 1720; its performance as a 'pastoral' at Lincoln's Inn Fields on March 26, 1731; and the series of performances as a 'serenata' without stage action given under Handel's direct supervision at the King's Theatre, Haymarket, starting on June 10, 1732. Its production as a 'pastoral opera' at the Little Theatre in the Haymarket (May 17, 1732) under Thomas Arne, the father of Dr. T. A. Arne the composer, was advertised as 'the first time it was ever performed in a Theatrical way'.

Date of Production	Place and Theatre	Composer	Librettist	Number of Acts
		* BRITANNIA		
Nov. 16, 1732	Little, Hay-market	Lampe	Lediard	
		TERAMINTA		
Nov. 20, 1732	Lincoln's Inn Fields	J. C. Smith	Carey	
		* ORLANDO		
Jan. 27, 1733	King's, Hay-market	Handel	Braccioli (It.)	3
	ACHILLES (ballad opera)			
Feb. 10, 1733	Covent Garden	Anon.	Gay	
		DIONE		
Feb. 23, 1733	Little, Hay-market	Lampe	Anon.	
		ROSAMOND		
March 7, 1733	Lincoln's Inn Fields	T. A. Arne	Addison	3
		ULYSSES		
April 16, 1733	Lincoln's Inn Fields	Smith	S. Humphreys	
	THE OPERA OF OPERAS, OR, TOM THUMB THE GREAT[1]			
May 31, 1733	Little, Hay-market	T. A. Arne	Mrs. Haywood, after Fielding	3
	THE OPERA OF OPERAS, OR, TOM THUMB THE GREAT			
Nov. 7, 1733	Drury Lane	Lampe	Mrs. Haywood, after Fielding	
		* ARIADNE IN CRETE		
Jan. 26, 1734	King's, Hay-market	Handel	Francis Col-man (It.)	3
	AN OLD MAN TAUGHT WISDOM, OR, THE VIRGIN UNMASK'D (ballad opera)			
Jan. 6, 1735	Drury Lane	Anon.	Fielding	

[1] Later revived in a one-act version.

P

Date of Production	Place and Theatre	Composer	Librettist	Number of Acts
		* ARIODANTE		
Jan. 8, 1735	Covent Garden	Handel	Salvi, after Ariosto (It.)	3
		* ALCINA		
April 16, 1735	Covent Garden	Handel	Marchi, after Ariosto (It.)	3
	THE HONEST YORKSHIREMAN (ballad opera)			
July, 1735	Goodman's Fields	Anon.	Carey	
	THE RIVAL MILLINERS, OR, THE HUMOURS OF COVENT GARDEN (Tragi-Comi-Operatic-Pastoral Farce)			
Jan. 19, 1736	Little, Hay-market	Anon.	Robert Drury	
		* ATALANTA		
May 12, 1736	Covent Garden	Handel	Anon. (It.)	3
		* ARMINIO		
Jan. 12, 1737	Covent Garden	Handel	Salvi (It.)	3
		* GIUSTINO		
Feb. 16, 1737	Covent Garden	Handel	Beregani (It.)	3
		* BERENICE		
May 18, 1737	Covent Garden	Handel	Salvi (It.)	3
	* THE DRAGON OF WANTLEY (a burlesque opera)			
Oct. 26, 1737	Covent Garden	Lampe	Carey	3
		* FARAMONDO		
Jan. 7, 1738	King's, Hay-market	Handel	Zeno (It.)	3
		* SERSE		
April 15, 1738	King's, Hay-market	Handel	Minato (It.)	3

Date of Production	Place and Theatre	Composer	Librettist	Number of Acts

* MARGERY,[1]
OR, A WORSE PLAGUE THAN THE DRAGON (burlesque opera)

Dec. 9, 1738	Covent Garden	Lampe	Carey	

NANCY,[2]
OR, THE PARTING LOVERS

Dec. 1, 1739	Covent Garden	Carey	Carey	

ROSALINDA (musical drama)

Jan. 4, 1740	Hickford's Room	Smith	John Lockman	

* IMENEO

Nov. 22, 1740	*Lincoln's Inn Fields*	*Handel*	*(It.)*	

* DEIDAMIA

Jan. 10, 1741	*Lincoln's Inn Fields*	*Handel*	*Rolli (It.)*	3

THE BLIND BEGGAR OF BETHNAL GREEN (ballad opera)

April 3, 1741	Drury Lane	T. A. Arne	R. Dodsley	

THE HAPPY CAPTIVE
with an Interlude in Two Comick Scenes, Betwixt Signor Capoccio, a Director from the Canary Islands, and Signora Dorinna, a Virtuosa

April 16, 1741	Little, Haymarket	Galliard	Theobald[3]	

THE KISS ACCEPTED AND RETURNED (an operetta)

April 16, 1744	Little, Haymarket	Lampe	James Ayres	

THE TEMPLE OF DULLNESS

Jan. 17, 1745	Drury Lane	T. A. Arne	Theobald[4]	

[1] A sequel to *The Dragon of Wantley.*
[2] This was later altered as *The Press Gang, or, Love in Low Life,* 1755.
[3] The text of this interlude was incorporated in *The Temple of Dullness,* 1745.
[4] *Cf.* preceding footnote.

Date of Production	Place and Theatre	Composer	Librettist	Number of Acts
	PYRAMUS AND THISBE (mock opera)			
Jan. 25, 1745	Covent Garden	Lampe	Anon.	
	KING PEPIN'S CAMPAIGN (burlesque opera)			
April 15, 1745	Drury Lane	T. A. Arne	Wm. Shirley	2
	* THE CHAPLET			
Dec. 13, 1749	Drury Lane	W. Boyce	M. Mendez	2
	DON SAVERIO			
Feb. 15, 1750	Drury Lane	T. A. Arne	T. A. Arne	
	ELIZA[1]			
May 29, 1754	Little, Haymarket	T. A. Arne	R. Rolt	
	* THE FAIRIES			
Feb. 3, 1755	Drury Lane	Smith	Smith, after Shakespeare	Pr., 3
	THE TEMPEST			
Feb. 11, 1756	Drury Lane	Smith	Garrick, after Shakespeare	
	* THOMAS AND SALLY, OR, THE SAILOR'S RETURN (a musical entertainment)			
Nov. 28, 1760	Covent Garden	T. A. Arne	Bickerstaffe	2
	MIDAS (burletta)			
Jan. 22, 1762	Dublin, Crow Street	Anon.	Kane O'Hara	3
	* ARTAXERXES (an English opera)			
Feb. 2, 1762	Covent Garden	T. A. Arne	T. A. Arne, after Metastasio	3

[1] This opera is said to have been given first in Dublin.

Date of Production	Place and Theatre	Composer	Librettist	Number of Acts
		LOVE IN A VILLAGE[1]		
Dec. 8, 1762	Covent Garden	T. A. Arne & others	Bickerstaffe	3
		THE FAIRY TALE		
Nov. 26, 1763	Drury Lane	J. Battishill & M. Arne	Colman, senr., after Shakespeare	2
		THE ROYAL SHEPHERD[2]		
Feb. 24, 1764	Drury Lane	Rush	R. Rolt, after Metastasio	3
		ALMENA (an English opera)		
Nov. 2, 1764	Drury Lane	Battishill and Rolt M. Arne		3
		THE GUARDIAN OUTWITTED (comic opera)		
Dec. 12, 1764	Covent Garden	T. A. Arne	T. A. Arne	
		⋆ **OLIMPIADE**		
1764	*King's, Haymarket*	*T. A. Arne*	*Metastasio* (*It.*)	
		THE MAID OF THE MILL		
Jan. 31, 1765	Covent Garden	Samuel Arnold	Bickerstaffe	3
		PHARNACES		
Feb. 15, 1765	Drury Lane	William Bates	T. Hull, after Lucchini	3
		CYMON (a dramatic romance)		
Jan. 2, 1767	Drury Lane	M. Arne	Garrick, after Dryden	5

[1] An altered form of *The Village Opera*, 1729. This comic opera is a *pasticcio* of music by seventeen different composers including Dr. Thomas Arne. For the next half century or longer, the *pasticcio* system flourished; and it must be realised, in the case of most of the operas from that period that are listed here, that the composer was also the arranger of music culled from many different sources.

[2] It was later altered as *Amintas* (Covent Garden, Dec. 15, 1769).

Date of Production	Place and Theatre	Composer	Librettist	Number of Acts
		LOVE IN THE CITY		
Feb. 21, 1767	Covent Garden	C. Dibdin	Bickerstaffe	
		THE ROYAL MERCHANT (comic opera)		
Dec. 14, 1767	Covent Garden	T. Linley, senr.	Hull, after Beaumont and Fletcher	
		LIONEL AND CLARISSA (comic opera)		
Feb. 25, 1768	Covent Garden	C. Dibdin	Bickerstaffe	3
		THE PADLOCK (comic opera)		
Oct. 3, 1768	Drury Lane	C. Dibdin	Bickerstaffe, after Cervantes	2
	THE EPHESIAN MATRON, OR, THE WIDOW'S TEARS (comic serenata)			
May 12, 1769	Ranelagh House	C. Dibdin	Bickerstaffe	1
		THE CAPTIVE (pasticcio)		
June 21, 1769	King's, Haymarket		Bickerstaffe	
	A SCHOOL FOR FATHERS (comic opera) (an alteration of LIONEL AND CLARISSA, 1768)			
Feb. 8, 1770	Drury Lane	C. Dibdin	Bickerstaffe	3
		THE REVENGE (a burletta)		
1770	Marylebone Gardens	Arnold	Thomas Chatterton	2
		THE COOPER (musical entertainment)		
June 10, 1772	Little, Haymarket	T. A. Arne	T. A. Arne	2
		THE ROSE (comic opera)		
Dec. 2, 1772	Drury Lane	T. A. Arne	T. A. Arne	2

Date of Production	Place and Theatre	Composer	Librettist	Number of Acts
	THE WEDDING RING (comic opera)			
Feb. 1, 1773	Drury Lane	C. Dibdin	Dibdin, after Goldoni's *Il Filosofo di Campagna*	
	THE GOLDEN PIPPIN (burletta)			
Feb. 6, 1773	Covent Garden	Anon.	K. O'Hara	
	ACHILLES IN PETTICOATS			
Dec. 16, 1773	Covent Garden	T. A. Arne	G. Colman, senr., after Gay	
	THE WATERMAN, OR, THE FIRST OF AUGUST (ballad opera)			
Aug. 8, 1774	Little, Haymarket	C. Dibdin	C. Dibdin	2
	THE COBLER, OR, A WIFE OF TEN THOUSAND (ballad opera)			
Dec. 9, 1774	Drury Lane	C. Dibdin	C. Dibdin	
	THE RIVAL CANDIDATES (comic opera)			
Feb. 1, 1775	Drury Lane	Thomas Carter	Sir Henry Bate Dudley	
	THE MAID OF THE VALE (a new version of Piccinni's LA BUONA FIGLIUOLA)			
1775	Dublin	M. Arne	Goldoni, trans. Holcroft	
	MAY-DAY, OR, THE LITTLE GIPSY (musical farce)			
Oct. 28, 1775	Drury Lane	T. A. Arne	David Garrick	
	THE DUENNA, OR, THE DOUBLE ELOPEMENT (comic opera)			
Nov. 21, 1775	Covent Garden	T. Linley, senr., & junr.	Sheridan	3

Date of Production	Place and Theatre	Composer	Librettist	Number of Acts

THE SERAGLIO (comic opera)

| Nov. 14, 1776 | Covent Garden | C. Dibdin | C. Dibdin | 2 |

POLLY (ballad opera, composed 1729)

| June 19, 1777 | Little, Hay-market | Pepusch and Arnold | Gay | 3 |

THE QUAKER (comic opera)

| Oct. 7, 1777 | Drury Lane | C. Dibdin | C. Dibdin | |

LOVE FINDS THE WAY (comic opera)

| Nov. 18, 1777 | Covent Garden | T. A. Arne, Sacchini and Fisher | Hudson, after A. Murphy | |

THE FLITCH OF BACON

| Aug. 17, 1778 | Little, Hay-market | William Shield | Sir Henry Bate Dudley | |

ROSE AND COLIN

| Sept. 18, 1778 | Covent Garden | C. Dibdin | C. Dibdin | 1 |

THE WIVES REVENGED

| Sept. 18, 1778 | Covent Garden | C. Dibdin | C. Dibdin | 1 |

THE CHELSEA PENSIONER (comic opera)

| May 6, 1779 | Covent Garden | C. Dibdin | C. Dibdin | |

SUMMER AMUSEMENT, OR, AN ADVENTURE AT MARGATE (comic opera)

| July 1, 1779 | Little, Hay-market | Arnold, Arne, Giordani and C. Dibdin | M. P. Andrews and W. A. Miles | |

THE SHEPHERDESS OF THE ALPS (comic opera)

| Jan. 18, 1780 | Covent Garden | C. Dibdin | C. Dibdin, after Marmontel | 3 |

Date of Production	Place and Theatre	Composer	Librettist	Number of Acts

THE WIDOW OF DELPHI,
OR, THE DESCENT OF THE DEITIES

Feb. 1, 1780	Covent Garden	Thomas Butler	Richard Cumberland	

THE ARTIFICE (comic opera)

April 14, 1780	Drury Lane	M. Arne	W. A. Miles	

FIRE AND WATER!

July 8, 1780	Little, Haymarket	Arnold	Andrews	

THE ISLANDERS

Nov. 25, 1780	Covent Garden	C. Dibdin	C. Dibdin	3

THE LORD OF THE MANOR

Dec. 27, 1780	Drury Lane	Wm. Jackson	Lieut. Gen. John Burgoyne, after Marmontel	3

THE BANDITTI,
OR, LOVE'S LABYRINTH[1] (comic opera)

Nov. 28, 1781	Covent Garden	Arnold	J. O'Keeffe	2

THE CONTRACT (comic opera)

May, 1782	Dublin, Smock Alley	Cogan and Sir John Stevenson	Robert Houlton	

THE FAIR AMERICAN (comic opera)

May 18, 1782	Drury Lane	T. Carter	Frederick Pilon	

ROSINA (comic opera)

Dec. 31, 1782	Covent Garden	Shield	Frances Brooke, after Favart	2

[1] Later revived as *The Castle of Andalusia* (Covent Garden, Nov. 2, 1782).

Date of Production	Place and Theatre	Composer	Librettist	Number of Acts

THE SHAMROCK,
OR, THE ANNIVERSARY OF ST. PATRICK[1] (comic opera)

April 7, 1783	Covent Garden	Shield	O'Keeffe	2

THE METAMORPHOSIS (comic opera)

Dec. 5, 1783	Drury Lane	Jackson	Jackson	

ROBIN HOOD,
OR, SHERWOOD FOREST (comic opera)

April 17, 1784	Covent Garden	Shield	L. MacNally	3

TWO TO ONE (comic opera)

June 17, 1784	Little, Hay-market	Arnold	G. Colman, junr.	

THE NOBLE PEASANT (comic opera)

Aug. 2, 1784	Little, Hay-market	Shield	Thomas Holcroft	

PEEPING TOM OF COVENTRY (comic opera)

Sept. 6, 1784	Little, Hay-market	Arnold	O'Keeffe	

FONTAINEBLEAU,
OR, OUR WAY IN FRANCE (comic opera)

Nov. 16, 1784	Covent Garden	Shield	O'Keeffe	

LIBERTY HALL,
OR, A TEST OF GOOD FELLOWSHIP (comic opera)

April 17, 1785	Drury Lane	C. Dibdin	C. Dibdin	

GLI SPOSI MALCONTENTI

June 1, 1785	Vienna, Burg-theater	Stephen Storace	Stephen Brunati (It.)	2

THE CHOLERIC FATHERS (comic opera)

Nov. 10, 1785	Covent Garden	Shield	Holcroft	

---

[1] Later revived as *The Poor Soldier* (Covent Garden, November 4, 1783).

Date of Production	Place and Theatre	Composer	Librettist	Number of Acts

THE STRANGERS AT HOME[1] (comic opera)

Dec. 8, 1785	Drury Lane	T. Linley, senr.	James Cobb	

PATRICK IN PRUSSIA,
OR, LOVE IN A CAMP[2] (comic opera)

Feb. 17, 1786	Covent Garden	Shield	O'Keeffe	

A MATCH FOR A WIDOW,
OR, THE FROLICS OF FANCY (comic opera)

April 17, 1786	Dublin, Smock Alley	C. Dibdin	Joseph Atkinson, after Patrati	

GLI EQUIVOCI

Dec. 27, 1786	Vienna, Burgtheater	Storace	da Ponte, after Shakespeare (It.)	2

HARVEST HOME (comic opera)

May 16, 1787	Little, Haymarket	C. Dibdin	C. Dibdin	

INKLE AND JARICO (comic opera)

Aug. 4, 1787	Little, Haymarket	Arnold	G. Colman, junr.	3

THE FARMER (comic opera)

Oct. 31, 1787	Covent Garden	Shield	O'Keeffe	

LOVE IN THE EAST,
OR, ADVENTURES OF TWELVE HOURS (comic opera)

Feb. 25, 1788	Drury Lane	T. Linley, senr.	Cobb	

MARIAN (comic opera)

May 22, 1788	Covent Garden	Shield	Brooke	

[1] An abridged version entitled *The Algerine Slaves* was performed at the King's Theatre in the Haymarket on March 17, 1792.
[2] A sequel to *The Shamrock*, 1783.

Date of Production	Place and Theatre	Composer	Librettist	Number of Acts
	THE HIGHLAND REEL (comic opera)			
Nov. 6, 1788	Covent Garden	Shield	O'Keeffe	
	THE ISLAND OF ST. MARGUERITE			
March 21, 1789	Drury Lane	Thomas Shaw	Hon. John St. John	
	THE BATTLE OF HEXHAM, OR, DAYS OF OLD			
Aug. 11, 1789	Little, Hay-market	Arnold	G. Colman, junr.	
	THE HAUNTED TOWER (comic opera)			
Nov. 24, 1789	Drury Lane	Storace	Cobb	3
	THE CZAR (comic opera)			
March 8, 1790	Covent Garden	Shield	O'Keeffe	
	NO SONG, NO SUPPER			
April 16, 1790	Drury Lane	Storace	Prince Hoare	2
	NEW SPAIN, OR, LOVE IN MEXICO			
July 16, 1790	Little, Hay-market	Arnold	J. Scawen	
	THE SIEGE OF BELGRADE (comic opera)			
Jan. 1, 1791	Drury Lane	Storace	Cobb	3
	THE WOODMAN (comic opera)			
Feb. 26, 1791	Covent Garden	Shield	Sir Henry Bate Dudley	
	THE CAVE OF TROPHONIUS			
May 3, 1791	Drury Lane	Storace	Hoare	
	THE SURRENDER OF CALAIS			
July 30, 1791	Little, Hay-market	Arnold	G. Colman, junr.	

Date of Production	Place and Theatre	Composer	Librettist	Number of Acts
DIDO, QUEEN OF CARTHAGE				
May 23, 1792	King's, Haymarket	Storace	Hoare	
THE PIRATES				
Nov. 21, 1792	Little, Haymarket	Storace	Cobb	3
THE MIDNIGHT WANDERERS (comic opera)				
Feb. 25, 1793	Covent Garden	Shield	W. Pearce	
OSMYN AND DARAXA				
March 7, 1793	Little, Haymarket	Thomas Attwood	James Boaden	
THE PRIZE, OR, 2, 5, 3, 8				
March 11, 1793	Little, Haymarket	Storace	Hoare	
THE MOUNTAINEERS				
Aug. 3, 1793	Little, Haymarket	Arnold	G. Colman, junr.	
THE CHILDREN IN THE WOOD				
Oct. 1, 1793	Little, Haymarket	Arnold	Morton	2
TRAVELLERS IN SWITZERLAND (comic opera)				
Feb. 25, 1794	Covent Garden	Shield	Sir Henry Bate Dudley	
THE GLORIOUS FIRST OF JUNE[1] (occasional entertainment)				
July 2, 1794	Drury Lane	Storace, Kelly and others	Sheridan and Cobb	1

[1] 'For the Benefit of the Widows and Orphans of the Brave Men who fell in the late Engagements under Lord Howe.' This entertainment was altered for production at Drury Lane in March 1797 under the title of *Cape St. Vincent, or, British Valour Triumphant*. Some of the lyrics were written by the Duke of Leeds, Lord Mulgrave, Mrs. Robinson, etc.

Date of Production	Place and Theatre	Composer	Librettist	Number of Acts
AULD ROBIN GRAY (a pastoral entertainment)				
July 29, 1794	Little, Hay-market	Arnold	Samuel James Arnold	
THE CHEROKEE				
Dec. 20, 1794	Drury Lane	Storace	Cobb	3
THE IRON CHEST				
March 12, 1796	Drury Lane	Storace	G. Colman, junr.	
MAHMOUD				
March 30, 1796	Drury Lane	Storace	Hoare	
THE WICKLOW GOLD MINES (comic opera)				
April 13, 1796	Covent Garden	Shield	O'Keeffe	
ABROAD AND AT HOME (comic opera)				
Nov. 19, 1796	Covent Garden	Shield	J. G. Holman	
THE SHIPWRECK (comic opera)				
Dec. 19, 1796	Drury Lane	Arnold	S. J. Arnold	
THE HONEY MOON (comic opera)				
Jan. 7, 1797	Drury Lane	William Linley	William Linley	
THE ITALIAN VILLAGERS				
April 25, 1797	Covent Garden	Shield	Hoare	
RAMAH DROOG, OR, WINE DOES WONDERS (comic opera)				
Nov. 12, 1798	Covent Garden	J. Mazzinghi and W. Reeve	Cobb	
LOVE IN A BLAZE				
May 29, 1799	Dublin, Crow Street	Sir John Stevenson	Atkinson	

Date of Production	Place and Theatre	Composer	Librettist	Number of Acts

THE CASTLE OF SORRENTO (comic opera)

| July 17, 1799 | Little, Haymarket | Thomas Attwood | Henry Heartwell and G. Colman | |

THE TURNPIKE GATE (comic opera)

| Nov. 14, 1799 | Covent Garden | Mazzinghi and Reeve | Thomas Knight | 2 |

PAUL AND VIRGINIA

| May, 1800 | Covent Garden | Mazzinghi and Reeve | Cobb | |

* ZENOBIA

| *May 22, 1800* | *King's, Haymarket* | *Earl of Mount Edgcumbe* | *Metastasio (It.)* | |

WILMORE CASTLE (comic opera)

| Oct. 21, 1800 | Drury Lane | J. Hook | Dr. R. Houlton | 2 |

VIRGINIA

| Oct. 30, 1800 | Drury Lane | Arnold | Mrs. Frances Plowden | |

IL BONDOCANI,
OR, THE CALIPH ROBBER (comic opera)

| Nov. 15, 1800 | Covent Garden | Attwood and Moorhead | T. J. Dibdin | |

THE BLIND GIRL,
OR, A RECEIPT FOR BEAUTY

| April 22, 1801 | Covent Garden | Mazzinghi and Reeve | Thomas Morton | |

THE BEDOUINS,
OR, THE ARABS OF THE DESERT (comic opera)

| May 1, 1801 | Dublin, Crow Street | Sir John Stevenson | Eyles Irwin | |

Date of Production	Place and Theatre	Composer	Librettist	Number of Acts

CHAINS OF THE HEART,
OR, THE SLAVE BY CHOICE (comic opera)

| Dec. 9, 1801 | Covent Garden | Mazzinghi and Reeve | Hoare | |

THE CABINET (comic opera)

| Feb. 9, 1802 | Covent Garden | Reeve, Moorehead, Davy, Corri and Braham | T. J. Dibdin | 3 |

ALGONAH
(revival of THE CHEROKEE, 1794)

| April 30, 1802 | Drury Lane | Storace, adapt. Kelly | Cobb | 3 |

FAMILY QUARRELS (comic opera)

| Dec. 18, 1802 | Covent Garden | Moorehead, Braham and Reeve | T. J. Dibdin | |

THE CARAVAN,
OR, THE DRIVER AND HIS DOG

| Dec. 5, 1803 | Drury Lane | W. Reeve | F. Reynolds | |

THE ENGLISH FLEET IN 1342 (an historical comic opera)

| Dec. 13, 1803 | Covent Garden | Braham | T. J. Dibdin | 3 |

THIRTY THOUSAND,
OR, WHO'S THE RICHEST? (comic opera)

| Dec. 10, 1804 | Covent Garden | Braham, Davy and Reeve | T. J. Dibdin | |

OUT OF PLACE,
OR, THE LAKE OF LAUSANNE

| Feb. 28, 1805 | Covent Garden | Reeve and Braham | Frederic Reynolds | |

Date of Production	Place and Theatre	Composer	Librettist	Number of Acts
	THE SOLDIER'S RETURN, OR, WHAT CAN BEAUTY DO? (comic opera)			
April 23, 1805	Drury Lane	J. Hook	T. E. Hook	2
	THE TRAVELLERS, OR, MUSIC'S FASCINATION			
Jan. 22, 1806	Drury Lane	Domenico Corri	Andrew Cherry	5
	FALSE ALARMS, OR, MY COUSIN (comic opera)			
Jan. 12, 1807	Drury Lane	Braham and M. P. King	J. Kenney	3
	KAIS, OR, LOVE IN THE DESERTS			
Feb. 11, 1808	Drury Lane	Reeve and Braham	Isaac Brandon	4
	THE EXILE, OR, THE DESERTS OF SIBERIA			
Nov. 10, 1808	Covent Garden	Mazzinghi and Bishop	F. Reynolds	
	THE CIRCASSIAN BRIDE			
Feb. 23, 1809	Drury Lane	Bishop	C. Ward	3
	SAFE AND SOUND (comic opera)			
Aug. 28, 1809	Lyceum	J. Hook	T. E. Hook	3
	THE MANIAC, OR, THE SWISS BANDITTI			
March 13, 1810	Lyceum	Bishop	S. J. Arnold	3
	GUSTAVUS VASA			
Nov. 29, 1810	Covent Garden		W. Dimond	

Q

Date of Production	Place and Theatre	Composer	Librettist	Number of Acts

THE KNIGHT OF SNOWDOUN

Date of Production	Place and Theatre	Composer	Librettist	Number of Acts
Feb. 5, 1811	Covent Garden	Bishop	Thomas Morton	3

THE AMERICANS

| April 27, 1811 | Lyceum | John Braham and M. P. King | S. J. Arnold | |

THE VIRGIN OF THE SUN

| Jan. 31, 1812 | Covent Garden | Bishop | Reynolds, after Kotzebue | |

THE AETHIOP,
OR, THE CHILD OF THE DESERT

| Oct. 6, 1812 | Covent Garden | Bishop | W. Dimond | |

THE MILLER AND HIS MEN

| Oct. 21, 1813 | Covent Garden | Bishop | Isaac Pocock | 2 |

NARENSKY,
OR, THE ROAD TO YAROSLAF (comic opera)

| Jan. 11, 1814 | Drury Lane | Reeve and Braham | Charles Armitage Brown | |

THE FARMER'S WIFE (comic opera)

| Feb. 1, 1814 | Covent Garden | Bishop | C. Dibdin, junr. | |

THE UNKNOWN GUEST[1]

| March 29, 1815 | Drury Lane | Kelly | Arnold | |

THE KING'S PROXY,
OR, JUDGE FOR YOURSELF (comic opera)

| Aug. 19, 1815 | Lyceum | T. Cooke | Arnold | |

[1] This is described as opera in *The Reminiscences of Michael Kelly*, though there seems no reason to suppose that it is in any way more of an opera than any of the other plays to which he wrote incidental music, sixty-two of which are listed in his book.

Date of Production	Place and Theatre	Composer	Librettist	Number of Acts

MY SPOUSE AND I (operatic farce)

| Dec. 7, 1815 | Drury Lane | Whitaker | C. Dibdin, junr. | |

THE PERSIAN HUNTERS,
OR, THE ROSE OF GURGISTAN

| Aug. 13, 1817 | English Opera House (Lyceum) | Horn | Anon. | |

ZUMA,
OR, THE TREE OF HEALTH

| Feb. 21, 1818 | Covent Garden | Bishop and Braham | T. J. Dibdin | |

DAVID RIZZIO (a serious opera)

| June 17, 1820 | Drury Lane | Braham, Attwood, Cooke, Reeve, C. Dibdin, junr. | R. Hamilton (songs by C. Dibdin, junr.) | 3 |

THE LAW OF JAVA

| May 11, 1822 | Covent Garden | Bishop | G. Colman, junr. | 3 |

MAID MARIAN,
OR, THE HUNTRESS OF ARLINGFORD (a legendary opera)

| Dec. 3, 1822 | Covent Garden | Bishop | Planché, after T. L. Peacock | 3 |

CLARI,
OR, THE MAID OF MILAN

| May 8, 1823 | Covent Garden | Bishop | Payne | 3 |

CORTEZ,
OR, THE CONQUEST OF MEXICO

| Nov. 5, 1823 | Covent Garden | Bishop | Planché | 3 |

NATIVE LAND,
OR, THE RETURN FROM SLAVERY

| Feb. 10, 1824 | Covent Garden | Bishop | Dimond | 3 |

Date of Production	Place and Theatre	Composer	Librettist	Number of Acts
	THE FROZEN LAKE			
Sept. 3, 1824	English Opera House (Lyceum)	Reeve	Planché, after Scribe	
	THE FALL OF ALGIERS			
Jan. 19, 1825	Drury Lane	Bishop	E. E. Walker, or J. H. Payne	3
	MASANIELLO, THE FISHERMAN OF NAPLES			
Feb. 17, 1825	Drury Lane	Bishop	Soane	5
	THE CAVERN (comic opera)			
1825	Dublin, Hawkins Street	Stevenson	Sarah Isdell	
	MALVINA (national ballad opera)			
Jan. 28, 1826	Drury Lane	Cooke	G. Macfarren, senr.	3
	OBERON, OR, THE ELF KING'S OATH			
April 12, 1826	*Covent Garden*	*Weber*	*Planché, after Wieland*	3
	* ALADDIN			
April 29, 1826	Drury Lane	Bishop	Soane	3
	ENGLISHMEN IN INDIA (comic opera)			
Jan. 27, 1827	Drury Lane	Bishop	Dimond	
	ISIDORE DE MERIDA OR, THE DEVIL'S CREEK (revival of THE PIRATES, 1792)			
Nov. 29, 1827	Drury Lane	Storace	Cobb	3
	AULD ROBIN GRAY (operetta)			
May 17, 1828	Surrey Theatre	A. Lee	G. Macfarren, senr.	
	* [MALVINA]			
Feb. 7, 1829	*Naples, San Carlo*	*Costa*	*(It.)*	

Date of Production	Place and Theatre	Composer	Librettist	Number of Acts
	★ [GIACINTO ED ERNESTO]			
1829	Naples, San Carlo	J. Benedict ‖	(It.)	
	★ I RIVALI DE SE STESSI			
Spring, 1830	Palermo	M. W. Balfe	(It.)	
	★ CATERINE, OR, THE AUSTRIAN CAPTIVE			
Nov. 6, 1830	Royal Academy of Music	Lord Burg-hersh	Cobb[1]	3
	★ [I PORTOGHESI IN GOA]			
1830	Stuttgart	Benedict	(It.)	
	★ UN AVVERTIMENTO DI GELOSI			
1830	Pavia	Balfe	(It.)	
	THE ROMANCE OF A DAY			
Feb. 3, 1831	Covent Garden	Bishop	Planché	
	THE SORCERESS			
Aug. 4, 1831	Adelphi	Ries	Fitzball	
	★ ENRICO QUARTO AL PASSO DEL MARNO			
1831	Milan, Scala	Balfe	(It.)	
	THE MAID OF SWITZERLAND (operetta)			
Jan., 1832	Queen's, Tottenham Street	G. A. Macfarren, junr.	Mrs. Cornwell Baron-Wilson	
	NOURJAHAD			
July 21, 1834	English Opera House (Lyceum)	Edward James Loder	S. J. Arnold	3
	THE DRAGON (comic opera)			
Aug. 4, 1834	English Opera House (Lyceum)	Lee	J. M. Morton	

[1] This opera was based on Cobb's libretto for *The Siege of Belgrade* (1791).

Date of Production	Place and Theatre	Composer	Librettist	Number of Acts

* THE MOUNTAIN SYLPH

Aug. 25, 1834	English Opera House (Lyceum)	Barnett	T. J. Thackeray	2

HERMANN, OR, THE BROKEN SPEAR

Oct. 27, 1834	English Opera House (Lyceum)	Thomson	Anon.	

THE RED MASK, OR, THE COUNCIL OF THREE

Nov. 15, 1834	Drury Lane	J. Templeton	Planché, after Cooper	

THE LORD OF THE ISLES, OR, THE GATHERING OF THE CLANS

Nov. 20, 1834	Surrey Theatre	G. H. Rodwell	Fitzball	2

SADAK AND KALASCADE, OR, THE WATERS OF OBLIVION (romantic opera)

April 20, 1835	English Opera House (Lyceum)	Packer	Mary Russell Mitford	2

THE SPIRIT OF THE BELL (comic opera)

June 8, 1835	English Opera House (Lyceum)	Rodwell	Kenney	

THE COVENANTERS (ballad opera)

Aug. 10, 1835	English Opera House (Lyceum)	Loder	T. J. Dibdin	

THE DICE OF DEATH

Sept. 14, 1835	English Opera House (Lyceum)	Loder	Oxenford	

THE SIEGE OF ROCHELLE

Oct. 29, 1835	Drury Lane	Balfe	Fitzball	2

THE MAID OF ARTOIS

May 27, 1836	Drury Lane	Balfe	Bunn	3

Date of Production	Place and Theatre	Composer	Librettist	Number of Acts
	* [UN ANNO ED UN GIORNO]			
Oct. 19, 1836	Naples, Fondo	Benedict	Andreotti (It.)	1
	THE VILLAGE COQUETTES			
Dec. 6, 1836	St. James's	Hullah	Charles Dickens	2
	[MALEK ADEL]			
Jan. 14, 1837	Paris, Théâtre-Italien	Costa	Pepoli, after Cottin (It.)	3
	FAIR ROSAMOND			
Feb. 28, 1837	Drury Lane	Barnett	Barnett	4
	CATHERINE GRAY			
May 27, 1837	Drury Lane	Balfe	G. Linley	3
	JOAN OF ARC			
Nov. 30, 1837	Drury Lane	Balfe	Fitzball	3
	AMALIE, OR, THE LOVE TEST (composed 1818)			
Dec. 2, 1837	Covent Garden	M. W. Rooke	Haines	3
	THE GYPSY'S WARNING			
April 19, 1838	Drury Lane	Benedict	Linley and R. B. Peake	2
	DIADESTE, OR, THE VEILED LADY			
May 17, 1838	Drury Lane	Balfe	Fitzball	2
	* FALSTAFF			
July 19, 1838	Her Majesty's	Balfe	Maggione, (It.)	2
	THE DEVIL'S OPERA			
Aug. 13, 1838	English Opera House (Lyceum)	Macfarren, junr.	Macfarren, senr.	2
	THE FORESTERS, OR, TWENTY-FIVE YEARS SINCE			
Oct. 19, 1838		Loder	Serle	

Date of Production	Place and Theatre	Composer	Librettist	Number of Acts
		FRANCIS I		
Nov. 6, 1838	Drury Lane	Loder	Anon.	
	FARINELLI (serio-comic opera)			
Feb. 8, 1839	Drury Lane	Barnett	Barnett	2
	HENRIQUE, OR, THE LOVE PILGRIM			
May 2, 1839	Covent Garden	Rooke	Haines	3
	FRIDOLIN (burletta)			
Nov. 26, 1840	Prince's (St. James's)	F. Romer	Mark Lemon	
	KËOLANTHE, OR, THE UNEARTHLY BRIDE			
March 9, 1841	English Opera House (Lyceum)	Balfe	Fitzball	2
	THE DEERSTALKERS, OR, THE OUTLAW'S DAUGHTER			
April 12, 1841	English Opera House (Lyceum)	Loder	Lemon	
	THE STUDENTS OF BONN (operetta)			
March 21, 1842	Drury Lane	Rodwell	Rodwell	
	THE QUEEN OF THE THAMES, OR, THE ANGLERS (operetta)			
Feb. 25, 1843	Drury Lane	Hatton	Fitzball	
	LE PUITS D'AMOUR			
April 20, 1843	*Paris, Opéra Comique*	*Balfe*	*de St. Georges and Scribe* (Fr.)	3
	GERALDINE, OR, THE LOVER'S WELL (English version of LE PUITS D'AMOUR)			
Aug., 1843	Princess's	Balfe	Trans. à Beckett	3

Date of Production	Place and Theatre	Composer	Librettist	Number of Acts
THE BOHEMIAN GIRL				
Nov. 27, 1843	Drury Lane	Balfe	Bunn	3
PASQUAL BRUNO				
March 2, 1844	Vienna, Kärntner-tortheater	Hatton	von Seyfried, from Fitzball (G.)	3
THE BRIDES OF VENICE				
April 22, 1844	Drury Lane	Benedict	Bunn, after La Gypsy, a ballet by de St. Georges	4
DON CARLOS				
June 20, 1844	Her Majesty's	Costa	Tarantini (It.)	3
LES QUATRE FILS AYMON				
July 15, 1844	Paris, Opéra Comique	Balfe	de Leuwen and Brunswick (Fr.)	3
THE CASTLE OF AYMON (English version of LES QUATRE FILS AYMON)				
Nov. 20, 1844	Princess's	Balfe	Trans. à Beckett	3
★ **THE DAUGHTER OF ST. MARK**				
Nov. 27, 1844	Drury Lane	Balfe	Bunn, after de St. Georges	3
THE ENCHANTRESS				
May 14, 1845	Drury Lane	Balfe	Bunn, after de St. Georges	3
THE FAIRY OAK				
Oct. 18, 1845	Drury Lane	Henry Forbes	Cope, adapt. Fitzball	3
MARITANA				
Nov. 15, 1845	Drury Lane	Wallace	Fitzball, after d'Ennery and Dumanoir	3

Date of Production	Place and Theatre	Composer	Librettist	Number of Acts

* L'ETOILE DE SEVILLE

Date of Production	Place and Theatre	Composer	Librettist	Number of Acts
Dec. 17, 1845	Paris, Opéra	Balfe	Lucas (Fr.)	3

AN ADVENTURE OF DON QUIXOTE

Feb. 3, 1846	Drury Lane	Macfarren, junr.	Macfarren, senr.	2

THE CRUSADERS

Feb. 26, 1846	Drury Lane	Benedict	Bunn	3

THE NIGHT DANCERS

Oct. 28, 1846	Princess's	Loder	Soane	2

LORETTA, A TALE OF SEVILLE

Nov. 9, 1846	Drury Lane	Lavenu	Bunn	3

THE BONDMAN

Dec. 11, 1846	Drury Lane	Balfe	Bunn, after de St. Georges	3

THE SEVEN MAIDS OF MUNICH, OR, THE GHOST'S TOWER

Dec. 19, 1846	Princess's	Rodwell	Rodwell	

MATILDA OF HUNGARY

Feb. 22, 1847	Drury Lane	Wallace	Bunn	3

THE FOREST MAIDEN AND THE MOORISH PAGE

May 31, 1847	Surrey Theatre	Tully	Fitzball	

THE MAID OF HONOUR

Dec. 20, 1847	Drury Lane	Balfe	Fitzball	3

LEILA

Feb. 22, 1848	Hamburg	H. H. Pierson	C. Leonhardt-Lyser (G.)	3

Date of Production	Place and Theatre	Composer	Librettist	Number of Acts

ROBIN GOODFELLOW,
OR, THE FROLICS OF PUCK (ballad opera)

| Dec. 6, 1848 | Princess's | Loder | Loder | |

QUENTIN DURWARD

| *Dec. 6, 1848* | *Covent Garden* | *Laurent* | *Fitzball* | |

KING CHARLES II

| Oct. 27, 1849 | Princess's | G. A. Mac-farren | Ryan | 2 |

THE SLEEPER AWAKENED

| Nov. 15, 1850 | Her Majesty's | Macfarren | Oxenford | |

* I QUATTRO FRATELLI
(Italian version of LES QUATRE FILS AYMON, 1844)

| *Aug. 11, 1851* | *Her Majesty's* | *Balfe* | Trans. Mag-gioni (It.) | |

THE SICILIAN BRIDE

| March 6, 1852 | Drury Lane | Balfe | Bunn, after de St. Georges | 3 |

THE DEVIL'S IN IT
(revived in 1871 as LETTY THE BASKET-MAKER)

| July 26, 1852 | Surrey | Balfe | Bunn | Pr., 3 |

PIETRO IL GRANDE

| *Aug. 17, 1852* | *Covent Garden* | *Jullien* | Ryan, trans. Maggioni (It.) | 3 |

* PITTORE E DUCA

| *Nov. 21, 1854* | *Trieste* | *Balfe* | Piave (It.) | Pr., 3 |

BERTA,
OR, THE GNOME OF THE HARTZBERG

| May 26, 1855 | Haymarket | Smart | Fitzball | |

RAYMOND AND AGNES (romantic opera)

| Aug. 14, 1855 | Manchester | Loder | Fitzball | 3 |

Date of Production	Place and Theatre	Composer	Librettist	Number of Acts
		THE ROSE OF CASTILLE		
Oct. 29, 1857	Lyceum	Balfe	A. Harris and E. Falconer	3
		*LA ZINGARA		
	(*Italian version of* THE BOHEMIAN GIRL, 1843)			
Feb. 6, 1858	Her Majesty's	Balfe	Adapt. Mapleson (*It.*)	3
		AULD ROBIN GRAY		
	(an alteration of AULD ROBIN GRAY, 1828)			
April 19, 1858	Surrey Theatre	T. Mackinlay, after Lee	Fitzball, after G. Macfarren, senr.	
		SATANELLA,		
		OR, THE POWER OF LOVE		
Dec. 20, 1858	Covent Garden	Balfe	Harris and Falconer, after Le Sage	4
		VICTORINE *		
Dec. 19, 1859	Covent Garden	A. Mellon	Falconer	3
		LURLINE		
Feb. 23, 1860	Covent Garden	Wallace	Fitzball	3
		*OBERON		
	(*Italian version of* OBERON, 1826)			
July 3, 1860	Her Majesty's	Weber (recitatives by Benedict)	Planché, trans. Maggioni (*It.*)	3
		ROBIN HOOD		
Oct. 11, 1860	Her Majesty's	Macfarren	John Oxenford	3
		BIANCA,		
		OR, THE BRAVO'S BRIDE		
Dec. 6, 1860	Covent Garden	Balfe	Palgrave Simpson, after M. G. Lewis	4

Date of Production	Place and Theatre	Composer	Librettist	Number of Acts
		THE AMBER WITCH		
Feb. 28, 1861	Her Majesty's	Wallace	H. F. Chorley, after Meinhold	4
		RUY BLAS		
Oct. 24, 1861	Covent Garden	Glover	Glover, after Victor Hugo	3
		THE PURITAN'S DAUGHTER		
Nov. 30, 1861	Covent Garden	Balfe	C. Bridgeman	3
		THE LILY OF KILLARNEY		
Feb. 8, 1862	Covent Garden	Benedict	Oxenford and D. Boucicault	3
		LOVE'S TRIUMPH		
Nov. 3, 1862	Covent Garden	Wallace	Planché	3
		BLANCHE DE NEVERS		
Nov. 21, 1862	Covent Garden	Balfe	J. Brougham	4
		THE ARMOURER OF NANTES		
Feb. 12, 1863	Covent Garden	Balfe	Bridgeman	3
		THE DESERT FLOWER		
Oct. 12, 1863	Covent Garden	Wallace	A. Harris and T. J. Williams after de St. Georges and de Leuven	3
		JESSY LEA (opera di camera)		
Nov. 2, 1863	Gallery of Illustration	Macfarren	Oxenford, after Scribe	2
		SHE STOOPS TO CONQUER		
Feb. 10, 1864	Covent Garden	Macfarren	Fitzball	
		THE SOLDIER'S LEGACY		
July 10, 1864	Marylebone Theatre	Macfarren	Oxenford	

Date of Production	Place and Theatre	Composer	Librettist	Number of Acts
		THE SLEEPING QUEEN (operetta)		
Aug. 31, 1864	Gallery of Illustration	Balfe	Farnie	1
		HELVELLYN		
Nov. 3, 1864	Covent Garden	Macfarren	Oxenford, after Rosenthal	4
		ROSE, OR, LOVE'S RANSOM		
Nov. 26, 1864	Covent Garden	Hatton	H. S. Edwards	
		THE BRIDE OF SONG (operetta)		
Dec. 3, 1864	Covent Garden	Benedict	Farnie	1
		COX AND BOX OR, THE LONG-LOST BROTHERS		
May 11, 1867	Adelphi	A. Sullivan	F. C. Burnand, after Morton	1
		KEVIN'S CHOICE (operetta)		
Dec. 2, 1867	St. George's Hall	T. A. Wallworth	Miss F. Hazlewood and H. Paulton	2
		THE CONTRABANDISTA, OR, THE LORD OF THE LADRONES		
Dec. 18, 1867	St. George's Hall	Sullivan	Burnand	2
		LETTY, THE BASKET-MAKER (revised version of THE DEVIL'S IN IT, 1852)		
June 14, 1871	Gaiety	Balfe	Rewritten by Palgrave Simpson	Pr., 3
		THESPIS, OR, THE GODS GROWN OLD		
Dec. 26, 1871	Gaiety	Sullivan	W. S. Gilbert	2

Date of Production	Place and Theatre	Composer	Librettist	Number of Acts
		CONTARINI,		
	ODER, DIE VERSCHWÖRUNG ZU PADUA			
		(written 1853)		
April 16, 1872	Hamburg	Pierson	M. E. Lindau (G.)	5
		IL TALISMANO		
	(originally written in 1866 as THE KNIGHT OF THE LEOPARD)			
June 11, 1874	Drury Lane	Balfe	A. Matthison, trans. Zaff.ra (It.)	3
		★ TRIAL BY JURY		
March 25, 1875	Royalty	Sullivan	Gilbert	1
		THE ZOO		
June, 1875	St. James's	Sullivan	B. C. Stephenson	
		★ PAULINE		
Nov. 22, 1876	Lyceum	F. H. Cowen	H. Hersee, after Bulwer Lytton	4
		BIORN		
Jan. 17, 1877	Queen's	Rossi	F. Marshall, after Shakespeare	5
		★ MARITANA		
March 4, 1877	Dublin	Wallace (recitatives by Mattei)	Fitzball (It.)	3
		THE SORCERER		
Nov. 17, 1877	Opéra Comique	Sullivan	Gilbert	2
		H.M.S. PINAFORE,		
	OR, THE LASS THAT LOVED A SAILOR			
May 25, 1878	Opéra Comique	Sullivan	Gilbert	2
		BLODWEN		
June 20, 1878	Swansea, Music Hall	J. Parry	Rowlands	3

Date of Production	Place and Theatre	Composer	Librettist	Number of Acts

THE PIRATES OF PENZANCE,
OR, LOVE AND DUTY

Dec. 30, 1879	Paignton, Bijou Theatre	Sullivan	Gilbert	2

* DER VERSCHLIERTE PROFET
(*German version of* THE VEILED PROPHET OF KHORASSAN)
(*a romantic opera*)

Feb. 6, 1881	Hanover	C. V. Stanford	Barclay Squire, trans. Frank (G.)	3

PATIENCE,
OR, BUNTHORNE'S BRIDE

April 25, 1881	Opéra Comique	Sullivan	Gilbert	2

MORO,
OR, THE PAINTER OF ANTWERP
(English version of PITTORE E DUCA, 1854)

Jan. 28, 1882	Her Majesty's	Balfe	Piave, trans. Wilson Barrett	Pr., 3

IOLANTHE,
OR, THE PEER AND THE PERI

Nov. 25, 1882	Savoy	Sullivan	Gilbert	2

* ESMERALDA

March 26, 1883	Drury Lane	Thomas	Marzials and Randegger, after Victor Hugo	4

* COLOMBA

April 9, 1883	Drury Lane	A. C. Mac-kenzie	F. Hueffer, after P. Méri-mée	4

PRINCESS IDA,
OR, CASTLE ADAMANT

Jan. 5, 1884	Savoy	Sullivan	Gilbert	2

Date of Production	Place and Theatre	Composer	Librettist	Number of Acts
* SAVONAROLA				
April 18, 1884	Hamburg	Stanford	G. A. à Beckett, trans. Frank (G.)	Pr., 3
THE CANTERBURY PILGRIMS				
April 28, 1884	Drury Lane	Stanford	à Beckett	3
THE MIKADO, OR, THE TOWN OF TITIPU				
March 14, 1885	Savoy	Sullivan	Gilbert	2
* NADESHDA				
April 16, 1885	Drury Lane	Thomas	Julian Sturgis	4
* THE TROUBADOUR				
June 8, 1886	Drury Lane	Mackenzie	Hueffer	
DOROTHY				
Sept. 25, 1886	Gaiety	A. Cellier	B. C. Stephenson	3
RUDDYGORE, OR, THE WITCH'S CURSE				
Jan. 22, 1887	Savoy	Sullivan	Gilbert	2
* NORDISA				
Jan. 26, 1887	Liverpool, Court Theatre	F. Corder	F. Corder	3
THE YEOMAN OF THE GUARD, OR, THE MERRYMAN AND HIS MAID				
Oct. 3, 1888	Savoy	Sullivan	Gilbert	2
DORIS				
April 20, 1889	Lyric	Cellier	B. C. Stephenson	

R

Date of Production	Place and Theatre	Composer	Librettist	Number of Acts

★ DANTE AND BEATRICE

Nov. 25, 1889	Brixton, Gresham Hall	Philpot	Miller	3

THE GONDOLIERS,
OR, THE KING OF BARATARIA

Dec. 7, 1889	Savoy	Sullivan	Gilbert	2

★ THORGRIM

April 22, 1890	Drury Lane	Cowen	Joseph Bennett	4

THE KNIGHT OF THE LEOPARD
(English version of IL TALISMANO, 1874)

Jan. 15, 1891	Liverpool	Balfe	A. Matthison	3

★ IVANHOE

Jan. 31, 1891	Royal English Opera House	Sullivan	Sturgis, after Scott	5

THE MOUNTEBANKS (comic opera)

Jan. 4, 1892	Lyric	Cellier	Gilbert	

★ THE LIGHT OF ASIA (sacred legend)

June 11, 1892	Covent Garden	de Lara	W. Beatty-Kingston, after Sir Edwin Arnold	3

HADDON HALL

Sept. 24, 1892	Savoy	Sullivan	S. Grundy	

★ CAEDMAR

Oct. 18, 1892	Crystal Palace	Granville Bantock	Granville Bantock	1

★ IRMENGARDA

Dec. 8, 1892	Covent Garden	L. Emil Bach	Beatty-Kingston	

Date of Production	Place and Theatre	Composer	Librettist	Number of Acts

THE MAGIC OPAL
(later THE MAGIC RING)

Jan. 19, 1893	Lyric	Albeniz	A. Law	2

LANSDOWN CASTLE,
OR, THE SORCERER OF TEWKESBURY (comic opera)

Feb. 7, 1893	Cheltenham, Corn Exchange	Gustav Holst	Major A. C. Cunningham	

THE GOLDEN WEB

Feb. 15, 1893	Liverpool, Court Theatre	Thomas	F. Corder and B. C. Stephenson	3

★ AMY ROBSART

July 20, 1893	Covent Garden	de Lara	A. Harris and F. E. Weatherley, after Scott, trans. Milliet (Fr.)	3

★ THE VEILED PROPHET OF KHORASSAN
(Italian version of DER VERSCHLIERTE PROFET, 1881)

July 26, 1893	Covent Garden	Stanford	Squire, trans. Mazzucato (It.)	3

★ JEHAN DE SAINTRÉ

Aug. 1, 1893	Aix-les-Bains	F. d'Erlanger	J. and P. Barbier (Fr.)	2

UTOPIA (LIMITED),
OR, THE FLOWERS OF PROGRESS

Oct. 7, 1893	Savoy	Sullivan	Gilbert	2

★ SIGNA[1]

Nov. 12, 1893	Milan, Teatro dal Verme	Cowen	A'Beckett, H. A. Rudall and Weatherley after Ouida, trans. Mazzucato (It.)	3

[1] Reduced to two acts for the Covent Garden performance (in Italian) on June 30, 1894.

Date of Production	Place and Theatre	Composer	Librettist	Number of Acts

* THE LADY OF LONGFORD

| July 21, 1894 | Covent Garden | L. Emil Bach | Harris and Weatherley, trans. Mazzucato (It.) | 1 |

* JEANIE DEANS

| Nov. 15, 1894 | Edinburgh, Lyceum | H. MacCunn | J. Bennett, after Scott | 4 |

THE CHIEFTAIN

(a revised and enlarged version of THE CONTRABANDISTA, 1867)

| Dec. 12, 1894 | Savoy | Sullivan | Burnand | |

* HAROLD, OR, THE NORMAN CONQUEST

| June 8, 1895 | Covent Garden | Cowen | Sir Edward Malet | 3 |

SYLVIA

| Aug. 12, 1895 | Cardiff | J. Parry | M. Parry | 3 |

* PETRUCCIO

| July 25, 1895 | Covent Garden | Alick M. MacLean | Anon. | 1 |

SHAMUS O'BRIEN (romantic comic opera)

| March 2, 1896 | Opéra Comique | Stanford | G. H. Jessop and Stanford, after Le Fanu | 2 |

THE GRAND DUKE, OR, THE STATUTORY DUEL

| March 7, 1896 | Savoy | Sullivan | Gilbert | 2 |

* THE LADY OF LONGFORD

(first performance in English of THE LADY OF LONGFORD, 1894)

| April 20, 1896 | Drury Lane | L. Emil Bach | Harris and Weatherley | 1 |

THE GEISHA

| April 25, 1896 | Daly's | Sidney Jones | O. Hall and H. Greenbank | 2 |

Date of Production	Place and Theatre	Composer	Librettist	Number of Acts
		* HIS MAJESTY, OR, THE COURT OF VIGNOLIA		
Feb. 20, 1897	Savoy	Mackenzie	Burnand and R. C. Lehmann	
		* MOINA		
March 14, 1897	Monte Carlo	de Lara	Gallet (Fr.)	2
		* INÈS MENDO		
July 10, 1897	Covent Garden	d'Erlanger	Decourcelle and Liorat, after Mérimée (Fr.)	3
		* DIARMID		
Oct. 23, 1897	Covent Garden	MacCunn	Campbell	4
		* FANTASIO		
May 24, 1898	Weimar	Smyth	Smyth, after de Musset (G.)	2
		* MESSALINE		
March 21, 1899	Monte Carlo	de Lara	Silvester and Morand (Fr.)	4
		ROYAL VAGRANTS, a story of conscientious objection (comic opera)		
Oct. 27, 1899	Forest Gate, Earlham Hall	H. Waldo-Warner	Cyril Hurst	2
		THE ROSE OF PERSIA, OR, THE STORYTELLER AND THE SLAVE (comic opera)		
Nov. 29, 1899	Savoy	Sullivan	B. Hood	
		* MUCH ADO ABOUT NOTHING		
May 30, 1901	Covent Garden	Stanford	Sturgis, after Shakespeare	4
		MERRIE ENGLAND		
April 2, 1902	Savoy	E. German	B. Hood	2

Date of Production	Place and Theatre	Composer	Librettist	Number of Acts
	⋆ DER WALD			
April 9, 1902	Berlin, Königliches Opernhaus	Smyth	Smyth (G.)	Pr., 1, Ep.
	⋆ PRINCESSE OSRA			
July 14, 1902	Covent Garden	Bunning	Bérenger, after Hope (Fr.)	3
	SARRONA			
Aug. 3, 1903	Bruges	Howland	Howland (Fr.)	Pr., 1
	⋆ THE CROSS AND THE CRESCENT			
Sept. 22, 1903	Covent Garden	MacAlpin	Anon., after Coppée	4
	⋆ KOANGA			
March 30, 1904	Elberfeld	Frederick Delius	C. F. Keary, after Cable, trans. F. Delius (G.)	Pr., 3, Ep.
	THE KNIGHTS OF THE ROAD			
Feb. 27, 1905	Palace	Mackenzie	Lytton	
	FIORELLA			
June 7, 1905	Waldorf Theatre	Webber	Sardou and Gheusi, trans. Macchi (It.)	1
	⋆ SANGA			
Feb. 21, 1906	Nice	de Lara	Moraud and de Choudens (Fr.)	3
	GREYSTEEL,[1] OR, THE BEARSARKS COME TO SURNADALE			
March 1, 1906	Sheffield	Gatty	R. Gatty	1
	⋆ DIE LIEBESGEIGE			
[Easter] 1906	Mayencee	MacLean	(G.)	

[1] Revived at Sadler's Wells on March 23, 1938, in an expanded two-act version.

Date of Production	Place and Theatre	Composer	Librettist	Number of Acts
		★ TESS		
April 10, 1906	Naples, San Carlo	d'Erlanger	Illica, after Hardy (It.)	4
	★ STRANDRECHT (LES NAUFRAGEURS)			
Nov. 11, 1906	Leipzig	Smyth	H. Brewster, trans. Decker and Bernhoff (G.)	3
	★ ROMEO UND JULIA AUF DEM DORFE			
Feb. 21, 1907	Berlin, Komische Oper	F. Delius	Jelka Delius, after Keller (G.)	Pr., 3
	★ SHAMUS O'BRIEN (first performance with recitatives)			
April 12, 1907	Breslau	Stanford	Jessop, trans. Anon. (G.)	2
	★ SOLÉA			
Dec. 19, 1907	Cologne, Opera House	de Lara	J. Richepin, trans. O. Neitzel (G.)	4
	THE STRANGER			
1908	His Majesty's	Holbrooke	Grogan	2
	★ THE ANGELUS[1]			
Jan. 27, 1909	Covent Garden	Naylor	Thornely	Pr., 4
	★ THE WRECKERS (first English performance of LES NAUFRAGEURS, 1906)			
June 22, 1909	His Majesty's	Smyth	Brewster, trans. Smyth and Strettell	3
	MAÎTRE SEILER			
Aug. 1909		MacLean		
	PIERROT AND PIERRETTE (lyrical music drama)			
Nov. 11, 1909	His Majesty's	Holbrooke	Grogan	2 Sc.

[1] Awarded the Ricordi Prize for the best English opera.

Date of Production	Place and Theatre	Composer	Librettist	Number of Acts
		DUKE OR DEVIL (farcical opera)		
Dec. 16, 1909	Manchester	Nicholas Gatty	I. Gatty	1

*A VILLAGE ROMEO AND JULIET
(first English performance of ROMEO UND JULIA AUF DEM DORFE, 1907)

Feb. 22, 1910	Covent Garden	F. Delius	Jelka Delius	Pr., 3
		EITHNE		
May 16, 1910	Dublin	O'Dwyer	O'Ceallaigh (O'Kelly) (E.)	2
		*A SUMMER NIGHT		
July 23, 1910	His Majesty's	Clutsam	Clutsam	1
		* NOËL		
Dec. 28, 1910	Paris, Opéra Comique	d'Erlanger	J. and P. Ferrier (Fr.)	3
		* LES TROIS MASQUES		
Feb. 24, 1912	Marseilles	de Lara	Méré (Fr.)	4
		* NAÏL		
April 22, 1912	Paris, Gaîté	de Lara	Bois (Fr.)	3

* THE CHILDREN OF DON
(PART I of THE CAULDRON OF ANNWEN)

| June 15, 1912 | London Opera House | Holbrooke | Ellis | Pr., 3 |

* WESTWARD HO!

| Dec. 4, 1913 | Lyceum | Napier Miles | E. F. Benson | Pr., 3 |

THE CRICKET ON THE HEARTH

| June 6, 1914 | Royal Academy of Music | Mackenzie | Sturgis, after Dickens | 3 |

* DYLAN, SON OF THE WAVE
(PART II of THE CAULDRON OF ANNWEN)

| July 4, 1914 | Drury Lane | Holbrooke | Ellis | 3 |

Date of Production	Place and Theatre	Composer	Librettist	Number of Acts
		* THE IMMORTAL HOUR		
Aug. 26, 1914	Glastonbury	Rutland Boughton	Sharp, after Fiona MacLeod	2
		* OITHONA		
Aug. 11, 1915	Glastonbury	Edgar L. Bainton	Bainton, after Ossian	1
		* BETHLEHEM		
Dec. 28, 1915	Street	Boughton	Coventry Nativity Play	2
		* ROMEO AND JULIET		
Jan. 7, 1916	Middlesbrough	Barkworth	Barkworth, after Shakespeare	4
		THE CRITIC, OR, AN OPERA REHEARSED		
Jan. 14, 1916	Shaftesbury Theatre	Stanford	James, after Sheridan	2
		THE BOATSWAIN'S MATE		
Jan. 28, 1916	Shaftesbury Theatre	Smyth	Smyth, after W. W. Jacobs	2 Sc.
		* THE ROUND TABLE		
Aug. 14, 1916	Glastonbury	Boughton	R. Buckley and Boughton	3
		THE SUMIDA RIVER		
Aug. 15, 1916	Glastonbury	Clarence Raybould	Japanese Nō play, trans. Marie Stopes	1
		* SAVITRI		
Nov. 5, 1916	Wellington Hall	Holst	Holst, after the Malabharata	1
		* LES TROIS MASQUES (first performance in English of LES TROIS MASQUES, 1912)		
June 27, 1919	Greenock	de Lara	Méré, trans. Anon.	4

Date of Production	Place and Theatre	Composer	Librettist	Number of Acts

* NAÏL
(first performance in English of NAÏL, 1912)

| July 18, 1919 | Covent Garden | de Lara | Bois, trans. E. Evans | 3 |

* FENNIMORE UND GERDA

| Oct. 21, 1919 | *Frankfurt* | *Delius* | *Delius, after Jacobsen* (G.) | 9 Sc. |

* PRINCE FERELON,
OR, THE PRINCESS'S SUITORS (a musical extravaganza)

| Nov. 27, 1919 | Florence Ettlinger Opera School | Gatty | Gatty | 1 |

QUENTIN DURWARD
(written and published in 1894)

| Jan. 13, 1920 | Newcastle-upon-Tyne | MacLean | Ross, after Scott | 3 |

* THE TEMPEST

| April 17, 1920 | Surrey Theatre | Nicholas Gatty | R. Gatty, after Shakespeare | 3 |

AMY ROBSART
(first production in English of AMY ROBSART, 1893)

| May 14, 1920 | Grand Theatre, Croydon | de Lara | Harris | 3 |

THE BEGGAR'S OPERA (1728)

| June 5, 1920 | Lyric, Hammersmith | arr. F. Austin | Gay | 3 |

* THE BIRTH OF ARTHUR

| Aug. 16, 1920 | Glastonbury | Boughton | Boughton and Buckley | 2 |

DAVID GARRICK

| Dec. 9, 1920 | Covent Garden | Somerville | Somerville | 3 |

* LES TROIS MOUSQUETAIRES

| March 3, 1921 | *Cannes* | *de Lara* | *Cain and Payen, after Dumas* (Fr.) | 6 Sc. |

Date of Production	Place and Theatre	Composer	Librettist	Number of Acts
	ALL FOOLS' DAY (a fantasy)			
Aug. 29, 1921	Glastonbury	Clive Carey	T. M. Baretti	I
	THAÏS AND TALMAAE			
Sept. 13, 1921	Manchester	Campbell	Bourne, after Anatole France	I
	★ THE TWO SISTERS			
Feb. 14, 1922	Cambridge	Rootham	Fausset	3
	★THE SHEPHERDS OF THE DELECTABLE MOUNTAINS[1] (a pastoral episode)			
July 11, 1922	Royal College of Music	Ralph Vaughan Williams	after Bunyan	I
	★ALKESTIS			
Aug. 26, 1922	Glastonbury	Boughton	Gilbert Murray, after Euripides	2
	POLLY (1777)			
Dec. 30, 1922	Kingsway	arr. F. Austin	Gay, adapt. by Clifford Bax	3
	★THE PERFECT FOOL			
May 14, 1923	Covent Garden	Holst	Holst	I
	FÊTE GALANTE (a dance-dream)			
June 4, 1923	Birmingham	Smyth	Shanks, after Baring	I
	SRUTH NA MAOILE (THE SEA OF MOYLE)			
July 25, 1923	Dublin	Palmer	O'Ceallaigh (O'Kelly) (E.)	
	BUBBLES			
Nov. 26, 1923	Belfast	Bath	after Lady Gregory	I

[1] This was afterwards incorporated in Vaughan Williams's opera *The Pilgrim's Progress*, 1951.

Date of Production	Place and Theatre	Composer	Librettist	Number of Acts

THE BLUE PETER (comic opera)

Dec. 11, 1923	Royal College of Music	C. Armstrong Gibbs	A. P. Herbert	1

*ST. JOHN'S EVE

April 16, 1924	Liverpool	Mackenzie	Farjeon	1

*LE CARROSSE DU SAINT-SACREMENT

April 24, 1924	*Paris, Théâtre des Champs-Elysées*	Berners	*after Mérimée* (Fr.)	1

*LES TROIS MOUSQUETAIRES
(first performance in English of LES TROIS MOUSQUETAIRES, 1921)

May 2, 1924	Newcastle-upon-Tyne	de Lara	trans. A. Kalisch	

MIDSUMMER MADNESS (comic opera)

July 3, 1924	Lyric, Hammersmith	Armstrong Gibbs	Clifford Bax	3

*HUGH THE DROVER,
OR, LOVE IN THE STOCKS (a romantic ballad opera)

July 4, 1924	Royal College of Music	Vaughan Williams	Child	2

* THE QUEEN OF CORNWALL

Aug. 21, 1924	Glastonbury	Boughton	Thomas Hardy	2

* THE SEAL WOMAN

Sept. 27, 1924	Birmingham	Bantock	Fraser	2

*MARKHEIM (dramatic sketch)

Oct. 13, 1924	Clifton, Bristol	Napier Miles	after Stevenson	1

*FIRE FLIES (comedy of masques)

Oct. 13, 1924	Clifton, Bristol	Napier Miles	Sturgis	1

Date of Production	Place and Theatre	Composer	Librettist	Number of Acts
		THE DUENNA (1775)		
Oct. 23, 1924	Lyric, Hammersmith	Alfred Reynolds, after Linley	Sheridan	3
		*AT THE BOAR'S HEAD		
April 3, 1925	Manchester	Holst	Holst, after Shakespeare	1
		*THE TRAVELLING COMPANION		
April 30, 1925	Liverpool	Stanford	Newbolt, after Andersen	4
		*DER ALCHIMIST		
May 28, 1925	Essen	Cyril Scott	Cyril Scott, trans. Andreae (G.)	3 Sc.
		ENTENTE CORDIALE (a post-war comedy)		
July 22, 1925	Royal College of Music	Smyth	Smyth	1
		MR. PEPYS (ballad opera)		
Feb. 11, 1926	Everyman, Hampstead	Martin Shaw	Clifford Bax	3
		*THE POLICEMAN'S SERENADE[1] (comic opera)		
April 10, 1926	Lyric, Hammersmith	Reynolds	A. P. Herbert	1
		THE LEPER'S FLUTE		
Oct. 15, 1926	Glasgow	Bryson	Colvin	4
		* FIORELLA (first performance in English of FIORELLA, 1905)		
March 6, 1928	Royal College of Music	Webber	Sardou and Gheusi	1

[1] This one-act opera, together with Arne's *Thomas and Sally* (1760), formed part of the revue *Riverside Nights*.

Date of Production	Place and Theatre	Composer	Librettist	Number of Acts
	WATERLOO LEAVE (ballad opera)			
Nov. 12, 1928	Maddermarket, Norwich	Martin Shaw	Clifford Bax	2
	★ BRONWEN (PART III of THE CAULDRON OF ANNWEN)			
Feb. 1, 1929	Huddersfield	Holbrooke	Ellis	3
	★ SIR JOHN IN LOVE			
March 21, 1929	Royal College of Music	Vaughan Williams	after Shakespeare	4
	★ AT THE SIGN OF THE STAR			
Dec. 6, 1929	Royal Albert Hall	Martin Shaw	Barclay Baron	1
	★ JUDITH			
June 25, 1929	Covent Garden	Eugene Goossens	Arnold Bennett	1
	THE VILLAGE OPERA (1729)			
1929(?)	Oxted, Barn Theatre	arr. Michael Tippett	after Johnson	
	★SAMUEL PEPYS			
Dec. 21, 1929	Munich	Albert Coates	Drury and Price, trans. Meyerfeld (G.)	1
	★MESSALINE (first performance in English of MESSALINE, 1899)			
Jan. 22, 1930	King's, Hammersmith	de Lara	trans. Blackburn	4
	KING ALFRED AND THE CAKES			
Dec. 10, 1930	Royal College of Music	Nicholas Gatty	Reginald Gatty	1
	★ TANTIVY TOWERS (comic opera)			
Jan. 6, 1931	Lyric, Hammersmith	Dunhill	A. P. Herbert	3

Date of Production	Place and Theatre	Composer	Librettist	Number of Acts

* THE THORN OF AVALON

| June 6, 1931 | Crystal Palace | Martin Shaw | Barclay Baron | 3 |

THE PRIDE OF THE REGIMENT, OR, CASHIERED FOR HIS COUNTRY (comic opera)

| Sept. 19, 1931 | Midhurst | Walter Leigh | V. C. Clinton-Baddeley and Scobie Mackenzie | 2 |

* THE DEVIL TAKE HER

| Dec. 1, 1931 | Royal College of Music | Arthur Benjamin | Alan Collard | Pr., 1 |

DERBY DAY (comic opera)

| Feb. 24, 1932 | Lyric, Hammersmith | Reynolds | A. P. Herbert | 3 |

* THE BRIDE OF DIONYSUS

| April 25, 1932 | Edinburgh | D. Tovey | R. C. Trevelyan | 3 |

THE JOLLY ROGER, OR, THE ADMIRAL'S DAUGHTER (comic opera)

| Feb. 13, 1933 | Manchester Opera House | Walter Leigh | Mackenzie and Clinton-Baddeley | 3 |

* THE WANDERING SCHOLAR (opera di camera)

| Jan. 31, 1934 | Liverpool, David Lewis Theatre | Holst | Clifford Bax | 1 |

* MACBETH

| April 12, 1934 | Sadler's Wells | Lawrance Collingwood | L. Collingwood, after Shakespeare | 3 |

* THE LILY MAID

| Sept. 10, 1934 | Stroud | Boughton | Boughton | 3 |

Date of Production	Place and Theatre	Composer	Librettist	Number of Acts
		* IERNIN		
Nov. 6, 1934	Penzance	G. Lloyd	W. Lloyd	3
		* THE EVER YOUNG		
Sept. 9, 1935	Bath, The Pavilion	Boughton	Boughton	3
		* KOANGA		
	(first performance in English of KOANGA, 1904)			
Sept. 23, 1935	Covent Garden	Delius	C. F. Keary, after Cable	Pr., 3, Ep.
	THE POISONED KISS,			
	OR, THE EMPRESS AND THE NECROMANCER (a romantic extravaganza)			
May 12, 1936	Cambridge, Arts Theatre	Vaughan Williams	Evelyn Sharp	3
		* MASTER VALIANT		
June, 1936	Crystal Palace	Martin Shaw	Barclay Baron	3
		* PICKWICK		
Nov. 20, 1936	Covent Garden	Coates	Coates, after Dickens	3
		* THE WEIRD OF COLBAR		
March 22, 1937	Glasgow, Theatre Royal	W. B. Moonie	G. M. Reith	3
		* DON JUAN DE MAÑARA		
June 24, 1937	Covent Garden	Goossens	Bennett	4
		* RIDERS TO THE SEA		
Nov. 30, 1937	Royal College of Music	Vaughan Williams	J. M. Synge	1
		* THE SERF		
Oct. 20, 1938	Covent Garden	G. Lloyd	W. Lloyd	3

Date of Production	Place and Theatre	Composer	Librettist	Number of Acts
	PAUL BUNYAN			
1941	New York, Columbia University	Benjamin Britten	W. H. Auden	
	* THE PEARL TREE			
May 20, 1944	Sydney, N.S.W., State Conservatorium of Music	Bainton	R. C. Trevelyan	2
	THE BEGGAR'S OPERA (1728)			
May 22, 1944	Birmingham, The Big Top	arr. E. J. Dent	Gay	3
	* PETER GRIMES			
June 7, 1945	Sadler's Wells	Britten	M. Slater, after Pr. Crabbe	3
	* THE PARTISANS			
May 28, 1946	St. Pancras Town Hall	Inglis Gundry	Inglis Gundry	2 Sc.
	* THE RAPE OF LUCRETIA			
July 12, 1946	Glyndebourne Opera House	Britten	R. Duncan, after Obey	Pr., 2, Ep.
	* ALBERT HERRING			
June 20, 1947	Glyndebourne Opera House	Britten	Eric Crozier, after de Maupassant	3
	* LADY ROHESIA (an operatic frolic)			
March 17, 1948	Sadler's Wells	Antony Hopkins	after Barham	1
	THE BEGGAR'S OPERA (1728)			
March 24, 1948	Cambridge, Arts Theatre	arr. Britten	Gay	3
	* PRIMADONNA			
Feb. 23, 1949	Fortune	Benjamin	Cedric Cliffe	1

s

274 APPENDICES

Date of Production	Place and Theatre	Composer	Librettist	Number of Acts
★ AVON				
April 11, 1949	Scala	Gundry	Gundry	3
THE LITTLE SWEEP *being the third act of an entertainment for young people entitled* LET'S MAKE AN OPERA!				
June 14, 1949	Aldeburgh, Jubilee Hall	Britten	Crozier	1
★ THE OLYMPIANS				
Sept. 29, 1949	Covent Garden	Arthur Bliss	J. B. Priestley	3
★ THE CORN KING (a ritual opera)				
Nov 21, 1950	Paddington Hall Theatre	Brian Easdale	Naomi Mitchison	Pr., 2
★ JOHN SOCMAN[1]				
April, 1951	Glasgow	G. Lloyd	W. Lloyd	3
★ THE PILGRIM'S PROGRESS (a morality with music)				
April 26, 1951	Covent Garden	Vaughan Williams	after John Bunyan	Pr., 4, Ep.
★ THE SLEEPING CHILDREN[1]				
July 9, 1951	Cheltenham	Easdale	Tyrone Guthrie	2
★ A TRIP TO ITALY[1]				
1951	Canterbury	Hopkins	Christopher Hassall	2
★ BILLY BUDD[1]				
Oct., 1951	Covent Garden	Britten	E. M. Forster and E. Crozier	Pr., 4, Ep.

[1] At the time of going to press the first performances of these new English operas had been announced, but without precise indications of date, etc.

A Short List of First Performances in Great Britain of Operas by Gluck, Mozart, Beethoven, Weber, Rossini, Wagner, Verdi, Puccini and Richard Strauss

C. W. GLUCK, 1714–1787

LA CADUTA DE' GIGANTI (pasticcio)
(1746)

Jan. 18, 1746	King's, Hay-market	1st performance (in Italian)

ARTAMÈNE (pasticcio)
(1746)

March 15, 1746	King's, Hay-market	1st performance (in Italian)

PIRAMO E TISBE (pasticcio)
(1746)

	King's, Hay-market	1st performance (in Italian)

CYTHÈRE ASSIÉGÉE
(1759)

July 19, 1950	Falmouth, Cornwall	in English, translated by the Misses M. and E. Radford as *Love's Citadel Besieged*

L'YVROGNE CORRIGÉ
(1760)

March 12, 1931	Birkbeck College	in English as *The Devil's Wedding*, translated by Geoffrey Dunn

LE CADI DUPÉ
(1761)

April 22, 1893	Manchester	amateur performance in German

ORFEO ED EURIDICE
(1762)

April 7, 1770	King's, Hay-market	in Italian as 'an Opera in the Grecian taste', with additional music by J. C. Bach, P. Guglielmi and Guadagni
Jan. 3, 1784	Dublin, Smock Alley	in English, translated by F. Gentleman, music adapted by F. Tenducci
Jan. 18, 1934	Old Vic	in English, translated by E. J. Dent[1]

LA RENCONTRE IMPRÉVUE
(1764)

| July 21, 1939 | Loughton, Essex | in English, translated by Geoffrey Dunn as *The Pilgrims of Mecca* |

ALCESTE
(1767)

| April 30, 1795 | King's, Hay-market | in Italian for Brigitta Banti's Benefit. (An Italian selection from this opera had been given at a fête at the King's Theatre, April 10, 1780.) |
| Dec. 2, 1904 | His Majesty's | in English, translated by J. Troutbeck |

IPHIGÉNIE EN AULIDE
(1774)

| June, 1906 | Birmingham and Midland Institute School of Music | in English, translated by J. Troutbeck |

ARMIDE
(1777)

| July 6, 1906 | Covent Garden | in French |
| Nov. 24, 1936 | Falmouth | in English, translated by M. and E. Radford |

IPHIGÉNIE EN TAURIDE
(1779)

| April 7, 1796 | King's, Hay-market | in Italian |
| July 9, 1840 | Prince's | in German |

[1] In view of the importance of Edward J. Dent's opera libretto translations, separate entries are included for the first performances of these.

April,	The Guildhall	in English, translated by J. Troutbeck
1908	School of Music	
	and Drama	

There is no record of performances in Great Britain of the following:

Artaserse (1741)
Demetrio (1742)
Demofoonte (1742)
Il Tigrane (1743)
La Sofonisba (1744)
Ipermestra (1744)
Poro (1744)
Ippolito (1745)
Le Nozze d'Ercole e d'Ebe (1747)
Semiramide Riconosciuta (1748)
La Contesa dei Numi (1749)
Ezio (1750)
Issipile (1752)
La Clemenza di Tito (1752)
Le Cinesi (1754)

L'Innocenza Giustificata (1755)
La Danza (1755)
Antigono (1756)
Il Re Pastore (1756)
L'Ile de Merlin (1758)
La Fausse Esclave (1758)
L'Arbre Enchanté (1759)
Tetide (1760)
Il Trionfo di Clelia (1763)
Il Telemaco (1765)
Il Parnasso Confuso (1765)
Prologo (1767)
Le Feste d'Apollo (1769)
Paride ed Elena (1770)
Echo et Narcisse (1779)

W. A. MOZART, 1756–1791

BASTIEN UND BASTIENNE
(1768)

Dec. 26,	Daly's	in English, translated by Constance
1894		Bache
May 2,	Covent Garden	in German
1907		

LA FINTA GIARDINIERA
(1775)

Jan. 7,	Scala	in English, translated by H. Dowd
1930		

IDOMENEO
(1781)

March 12,	Glasgow	in English, translated by M. and E.
1934		Radford. (Parts of the music were used in an English pasticcio, The Casket, by M. R. Lacy, produced at Drury Lane, March 10, 1829.)

DIE ENTFÜHRUNG AUS DEM SERAIL
(1782)

Nov. 24, 1827	Covent Garden	in English as *The Seraglio* translated by W. Dimond
June 23, 1841	Drury Lane	in German

L'OCA DEL CAIRO
(1783)

May 12, 1870	Drury Lane	(Victor Wieder version), in Italian, translated by G. Zaffira, with recitatives by Bottesini
May 30, 1940	Sadler's Wells	(Hans F. Redlich version), in Italian

DER SCHAUSPIELDIREKTOR
(1786)

May 30, 1857	St. James's	in French, translated by L. Battu and L. Halevy
Sept. 14, 1877	Crystal Palace	in English as *The Manager*, translated by W. Grist

LE NOZZE DI FIGARO
(1786)

June 18, 1812	King's, Haymarket	in Italian
March 6, 1819	Covent Garden	in English, adapted by T. Holcroft, music arranged by Bishop[1]
Jan. 15, 1920	Old Vic	in English, translated by E. J. Dent

IL DISSOLUTO PUNITO,
OSSIA, IL DON GIOVANNI
(1787)

April 12, 1817	King's, Haymarket	in Italian
May 30, 1817	Covent Garden	in English as *The Libertine*, translated by I. Pocock, music adapted by Bishop
Nov. 24, 1921	Old Vic	in English, translated by E. J. Dent

[1] Cf. p. 87.

COSÌ FAN TUTTE,

OSSIA, LA SCUOLA DEGLI AMANTI
(1790)

May 9, 1811	King's, Hay-market	in Italian
July 29, 1828	Lyceum	in English as *Tit for Tat, or, The Tables Turned*, translated by S. J. Arnold, music arranged by W. Hawes

LA CLEMENZA DI TITO
(1791)

March 27, 1806	King's, Hay-market	in Italian
Nov. 12, 1930	Falmouth	in English, translated by M. and E. Radford

DIE ZAUBERFLÖTE
(1791)

June 6, 1811	King's, Hay-market	in Italian, translated by G. de Gamerra
May 27, 1833	Covent Garden	in German
March 10, 1838	Drury Lane	in English, adapted by J. R. Planché
Dec. 1, 1911	Cambridge, New Theatre	in English, translated by E. J. Dent

There is no record of performances in Great Britain of the following:

Apollo et Hyacinthus (1767)   *Il Sogno di Scipione* (1772)
La Finta Semplice (1769)   *Lucio Silla* (1772)
Mitridate, Re di Ponto (1770)   *Il Re Pastore* (1775)
Ascanio in Alba (1771)   *Zaïde* (1779)

LUDWIG VAN BEETHOVEN, 1770–1827

FIDELIO
(1805)

May 18, 1832	King's, Hay-market	in German
June 12, 1835	Covent Garden	in English, translated by W. McGregor Logan

| May 20, 1851 | Her Majesty's | in Italian, translated by S. M. Maggioni, with recitatives by Balfe |
| Nov. 3, 1937 | Sadler's Wells | in English, translated by E. J. Dent |

C. M. VON WEBER, 1786–1826

SILVANA
(1810)
a new version of Das Waldmädchen (1800)

| Sept. 2, 1828 | Surrey Theatre | in English, translated by C. A. Somerset |

ABU HASSAN
(1811)

| April 4, 1825 | Drury Lane | in English, translated by W. Dimond, music adapted by T. S. Cooke |

PRECIOSA
(1821)

| April 28, 1825 | Covent Garden | in English, translated by G. Soane or W. Ball, music arranged by W. Hawes |
| July 8, 1853 | St. James's | in German |

DER FREISCHÜTZ
(1821)

July 22, 1824	English Opera House (Lyceum)	in English, translated by W. McGregor Logan, music adapted by W. Hawes
May 9, 1832	King's, Haymarket	in German
March 16, 1850	Covent Garden	in Italian as Il franco Arciere, with recitatives by Costa
March 2, 1950	Fettes College, Edinburgh	in English, translated by E. J. Dent

EURYANTHE
(1823)

| June 29, 1833 | Covent Garden | in German |
| Oct. 30, 1900 | Daly's | in English, translated by W. Thornthwaite |

OBERON
(1826)

April 12, 1826	Covent Garden	first performance (in English)
April 19, 1841	Drury Lane	in German
July 3, 1860	Her Majesty's	in Italian, translated by S. M. Maggioni, with recitatives by Benedict

There is no record of performances in Great Britain of the following:

Das Waldmädchen (1800)   *Die Drei Pintos* (1821)
Peter Schmoll und Seine Nachbarn (1803)

GIOACCHINO ROSSINI, 1792–1868

L'INGANNO FELICE
(1812)

July 1, 1819	in Italian

CIRO IN BABILONIA,
OSSIA, LA CADUTA DI BALDASSARE
(1812)

Jan. 30, 1823	Drury Lane	in Italian (in concert form)

L'OCCASIONE FA IL LADRO
(1812)

Jan. 14, 1929	Little	in English (by marionettes)

TANCREDI
(1813)

May 4, 1820		in Italian
April 17, 1843	Princess's	in English

L'ITALIANA IN ALGERI
(1813)

Jan. 26, 1819	King's, Haymarket	in Italian
Dec. 30, 1894	Princess's	in English

AURELIANO IN PALMIRA
(1813)

June 22, 1826	King's, Hay-market	in Italian

IL TURCO IN ITALIA
(1814)

May 19, 1821	King's, Hay-market	in Italian
May 1, 1827	Drury Lane	in English, as *The Turkish Lovers*, adapted by M. R. Lacy

ELISABETTA REGINA D'INGHILTERRA
(1815)

April 30, 1818	in Italian

IL BARBIERE DI SEVIGLIA
(1816)

March 10, 1818	King's, Hay-market	in Italian
Oct. 13, 1818	Covent Garden	in English, translated by J. Fawcett and D. Terry, music arranged by Bishop

OTELLO,
OSSIA, IL MORO DI VENEZIA
(1816)

May 16, 1822	King's, Hay-market	in Italian
March 21, 1844	Princess's	in English, translated by G. Soane

LA CENERENTOLA,
OSSIA, LA BONTA IN TRIONFO
(1817)

Jan. 8, 1820	King's, Hay-market	in Italian
April 13, 1830	Covent Garden	in English, as *Cinderella, or, The Fairy Queen and the Glass Slipper*, adapted by M. R. Lacy

LA GAZZA LADRA
(1817)

March 10, 1821	King's, Haymarket	in Italian
Feb. 4, 1830	Covent Garden	in English, translated by Fitzball as *Ninetta, or, The Maid of Palaiseau*, music adapted by Bishop

MOSÈ IN EGITTO
(1818)

April 23, 1822	King's, Haymarket	(first version) in Italian, as *Pietro l'Eremita*
Feb. 22, 1833	Covent Garden	(pasticcio) in English by M. R. Lacy, entitled *The Israelites in Egypt, or, The Passage of the Red Sea*, based partly on Rossini's opera and partly on Handel's oratorio *Israel in Egypt*
April 20, 1850	Covent Garden	as *Zora* after the second version of the opera, *Moise* (1827)

RICCIARDO E ZORAIDE
(1818)

June 5, 1823	King's, Haymarket	in Italian

LA DONNA DEL LAGO
(1819)

Feb. 18, 1823	King's, Haymarket	in Italian
Jan. 4, .?7	Drury Lane	in English

LE SIÈGE DE CORINTHE
(1820)

June 5, 1834	King's, Haymarket	in Italian
Nov. 8, 1836	Drury Lane	in English, translated by Planché, music arranged by T. S. Cooke

MATILDE DI SHABRAN,
OSSIA, BELLEZZA E CUOR DI FERRO
(1821)

July 3, 1823	King's, Haymarket	in Italian

ZELMIRA
(1822)

| Jan. 24, 1824 | King's, Hay-market | in Italian |

SEMIRAMIDE
(1823)

| July 15, 1824 | King's, Hay-market | in Italian |
| Oct. 1, 1842 | Covent Garden | in English, translated by T. H. Reynoldson |

IVANHOE
(1826)

| March 7, 1829 | Covent Garden | (pasticcio) in English, translated by M. R. Lacy as *The Maid of Judah, or, The Knight Templars* |

LE COMTE ORY
(1826)

| Feb. 28, 1829 | King's, Hay-market | in Italian, translator anon. |
| June 20, 1849 | St. James's | in French |

GUILLAUME TELL
(1829)

May 1, 1830	Drury Lane	in English, translated by Planché as *Hofer, or, The Tell of the Tyrol*, music arranged by Bishop
July 11, 1839	Her Majesty's	in Italian, translator anon.
June 6, 1845	Covent Garden	in French

There is no record of performances in Great Britain of the following:

La Cambiale di Matrimonio (1810)
L'Equivoco Stravagante (1811)
La Scala di Seta (1812)
La Pietra del Paragone (1812)
Il Signor Bruschino, ossia, Il Figlio per Azzardo (1813)
Sigismondo (1814)
Torvaldo e Dorliska (1815)
La Gazzetta (1816)

Armida (1817)
Adelaide di Borgogna (1817)
Adina (1818)
Ermione (1819)
Eduardo e Cristina (1819)
Bianca e Falliero, ossia, Il Consiglio dei Tre (1819)
Il Viaggio a Reims, ossia, L'Albergo del Giglio d'Oro, (1825)

RICHARD WAGNER, 1813–1883

COLA RIENZI, DER ·LETZTE DER TRIBUNEN
(1842)

Jan. 27,   Her Majesty's   in English, translated by J. P. Jackson
1879

DER FLIEGENDE HOLLÄNDER
(1843)

July 23,   Drury Lane   in Italian as *L'Olandese Dannato*, trans-
1870   lated by S. de Castrone, Marchese
                           della Rajata

Oct. 3,   Lyceum   in English, translated by J. P. Jackson
1876

May 20,   Drury Lane   in German
1882

TANNHÄUSER UND DER SÄNGERKRIEG AUF WARTBURG
(1845)

May 6,   Covent Garden   in Italian
1876

Feb. 14,   Her Majesty's   in English, translated by J. P. Jackson
1882

May 23,   Drury Lane   in German
1882

May 27,   Covent Garden   in French, translated by E. Roche,
1896   R. Lindau and C. Nuitter with
                              alterations and additions

LOHENGRIN
(1850)

May 8,   Covent Garden   in Italian
1875

Feb. 7,   Her Majesty's   in English, translated by J. P. Jackson
1880

May 18,   Drury Lane   in German
1882

TRISTAN UND ISOLDE
(1865)

June 20,   Drury Lane   in German
1882

April 15,   Liverpool   in English
1898

DIE MEISTERSINGER VON NÜRNBERG
(1868)

May 30, 1882	Drury Lane	in German
July 13, 1889	Covent Garden	in Italian, translated by G. A. Mazzu-cato
April 16, 1896	Manchester	in English

DIE WALKÜRE
(1870)

Oct. 16, 1895	Covent Garden	in English, translated by H. and F. Corder[1]
May 13, 1896	Covent Garden	in French

SIEGFRIED
(1876)

Oct. 18, 1901	Manchester	in English, translated by H. and F. Corder

DER RING DES NIBELUNGEN
(1876)

May 5–9, 1882	Her Majesty's	in German by Angelo Neumann's touring 'Richard-Wagner-Theater'
Jan. 27–Feb. 1, 1908	Covent Garden	in English, translated by F. Jameson

PARSIFAL
(1882)

Nov. 10, 1884	Royal Albert Hall	Concert performance under J. Barnby
Feb. 2, 1914	Covent Garden	in German
Nov. 17, 1919	Covent Garden	in English

There is no record of performances in Great Britain of the following:

Das Liebesverbot, or, *Die Novize von Palermo* (1836)
Das Rheingold (1869), (apart from *Der Ring des Nibelungen*)
Götterdämmerung (1876), (apart from *Der Ring des Nibelungen*)
Die Feen (1888) (composed 1833).

[1] Loewenberg records an earlier performance in English in Mexico (April 14, 1891).

GIUSEPPE VERDI, 1813-1901

NABUCODONOSOR
(1842)

March 3, 1846	Her Majesty's	in Italian as *Nino*
May 30, 1850	Covent Garden	as *Anato*

ERNANI
(1844)

March 8, 1845	Her Majesty's	in Italian
Nov. 1, 1851	Surrey Theatre	in English, translated by J. W. Mould

I DUE FOSCARI
(1844)

April 10, 1847	Covent Garden	in Italian

ATTILA
(1846)

March 14, 1848	Her Majesty's	in Italian

MACBETH
(1847)

March 30, 1859	Dublin	in Italian
May 21, 1938	Glyndebourne	in Italian

I MASNADIERI
(1847)

July 22, 1847	Her Majesty's	first performance (the only opera Verdi wrote for London)

LUISA MILLER
(1849)

June 8, 1858	Her Majesty's	in Italian
June 3, 1858	Sadler's Wells	in English, translated by C. Jefferys

RIGOLETTO
(1851)

May 14, 1853	Covent Garden	in Italian
Nov. 25, 1886	Her Majesty's	in French
Oct. 20, 1909	Covent Garden	in English, translated by N. Macfarren
April 10, 1912	People's	in Yiddish, translated by S. Alman
Feb. 24, 1937	Sadler's Wells	in English, translated by E. J. Dent

IL TROVATORE
(1853)

May 10, 1855	Covent Garden	in Italian
March 24, 1856	Drury Lane	for the first time in English as *The Gipsy's Vengeance*, translated by C. Jefferys
Jan. 25, 1939	Sadler's Wells	in English, translated by E. J. Dent

LA TRAVIATA
(1853)

May 24, 1856	Her Majesty's	in Italian
June 8, 1857	Surrey Theatre	in English, translated by T. H. Reynoldson
April 6, 1948	Covent Garden	in English, translated by E. J. Dent

LES VÊPRES SICILIENNES
(1855)

July 27, 1859	Drury Lane	in Italian

SIMONE BOCCANEGRA
(1857, revised in 1881)

Oct. 27, 1948	Sadler's Wells	1881 version in English, translated by Norman Tucker

UN BALLO IN MASCHERA
(1859)

June 15, 1861	Lyceum	in Italian

LA FORZA DEL DESTINO
(1862)

June 22, 1867	Her Majesty's	in Italian
Nov. 25, 1909	Manchester	in English, translated by P. E. Pinkerton

DON CARLOS
(1867)

June 4, 1867	Covent Garden	in Italian, translated by A. de Lauzières
Dec. 6, 1938	Sadler's Wells	in English, translated by S. Austin

AÏDA
(1871)

June 22, 1876	Covent Garden	in Italian
Feb. 19, 1880	Her Majesty's	in English, translated by H. Hersée

OTELLO
(1887)

July 15, 1889	Lyceum	in Italian
Oct. 8, 1892	Manchester	in English, translated by F. Hueffer

FALSTAFF
(1893)

May 19, 1894	Covent Garden	in Italian
Dec. 11, 1896	Lyceum	in English, translated by W. B. Kingston, revised by F. Hart (Royal College of Music performance)

There is no record of performances in Great Britain of the following:

Oberto, Conte di S. Bonifacio (1839)
Un Giorno di Regno, ossia, Il Finto Stanislao (1840)
I Lombardi alla Prima Crociata (1843)
Giovanna d'Arco, (1845)
Alzira (1845)
Il Corsaro (1848)
La Battaglia di Legnano (1849)
Stiffelio (1850)

T

GIACOMO PUCCINI, 1858-1924

LE VILLI
(1884)

Sept. 24, 1897	Manchester	in English, translated by P. E. Pinkerton

MANON LESCAUT
(1893)

May 14, 1894	Covent Garden	in Italian
Feb. 15, 1916	Shaftesbury	in English, translated by M. Marras

LA BOHÈME
(1896)

April 22, 1897	Manchester	in English, translated by W. Grist and P. E. Pinkerton
July 1, 1899	Covent Garden	in Italian

TOSCA
(1900)

July 12, 1900	Covent Garden	in Italian
Oct. 20, 1915	Shaftesbury Theatre	in English

MADAM BUTTERFLY
(1904)

July 10, 1905	Covent Garden	in Italian
Aug. 16, 1907	Lyric	in English

LA FANCIULLA DEL WEST
(1910)

May 29, 1911	Covent Garden	in Italian
May 31, 1917	Drury Lane	in English, as *The Girl of the Golden West*

TRITTICO
(1918)

June 18, 1920	Covent Garden	in Italian
July 13, 1937	Royal Academy of Music	in English

IL TABARRO
(1918)

Oct. 23, 1935	Sadler's Wells	in English, translated by H. Withers

SUOR ANGELICA
(1918)

Jan. 30, 1931	Royal Manchester College of Music	in English, translated by H. Withers

GIANNI SCHICCHI
(1918)

Jan. 15, 1924	Covent Garden	in English, translated by P. Pitt

TURANDOT
(1926)

June 7, 1927	Covent Garden	in Italian
Sept. 27, 1929	Halifax	in English, translated by R. H. Elkin

There is no record of performances in Great Britain of:

Edgar (1889), or *La Rondine* (1917), with the exception of a broadcast of the latter from London, June 24, 1929, in an English version by D. M. Craig.

RICHARD STRAUSS, 1864–1949

FEUERSNOT
(1901)

July 9, 1910	His Majesty's	in English, translated by W. Wallace

SALOME
(1905)

| Dec. 8, 1910 | Covent Garden | in German, translated from the French of Oscar Wilde by Hedwig Lachmann |
| Nov. 11, 1949 | Covent Garden | in English, translated by Lord Alfred Douglas |

ELEKTRA
(1909)

| Feb. 9, 1910 | Covent Garden | in German |
| Feb. 28, 1912 | Hull | in English, translated by A. Kalisch |

DER ROSENKAVALIER
(1911)

Jan. 1, 1913	Covent Garden	in German
Sept. 29, 1913	Birmingham	in English, translated by A. Kalisch
March 8, 1939	Sadler's Wells	in English

ARIADNE AUF NAXOS
(first version, 1912)

| May 27, 1913 | His Majesty's | in German |

(second version, 1916)

| May 27, 1924 | Covent Garden | in German |

ARABELLA
(1933)

| May 17, 1934 | Covent Garden | in German |

There is no record of performances in Great Britain of the following:

Guntram (1894)
Die Frau Ohne Schatten (1919)
Intermezzo (1924)
Die Ägyptische Helena (first version, 1928; second version, 1933)
Die Schweigsame Frau (1935)
Friedenstag (1938)
Daphne (1938)
Die Liebe der Danae (1944)
Capriccio (1942)

APPENDIX C

A List of Foreign Operas Produced in English for the First Time by the Carl Rosa, the Sadler's Wells and the Covent Garden Opera Companies

THE CARL ROSA OPERA COMPANY
(founded 1873)[1]

Date	Theatre	Composer	Translator
		THE PORTER OF HAVRE (1871)	
Sept. 15, 1875	Princess's	Cagnoni	J. Oxenford
		THE WATER CARRIER[2] (1800)	
Oct. 27, 1875	Princess's	Cherubini	A. Baildon
		GIRALDA (1850)	
Sept. 21, 1876	Lyceum	Adam	A. Baildon
		THE FLYING DUTCHMAN (1843)	
Oct. 3, 1876	Lyceum	Wagner	J. P. Jackson
		JOCONDE (1814)	
Oct. 25, 1876	Lyceum	Isouard	C. Santley
		THE MERRY WIVES OF WINDSOR (1849)	
Oct. 10, 1877	Aberdeen	Nicolai	H. Hersée

[1] Although the company first appeared in Great Britain in 1873, 1875 (the year when it first performed in London) is usually taken as its foundation year.
[2] The Carl Rosa Company can legitimately claim this as the first English production of The Water Carrier, since the earlier version of it given at Covent Garden on October 14, 1801, under the title The Escapes was a musical entertainment composed by Thomas Attwood, in which the original score was drastically altered, only two or three of Cherubini's themes being actually used.

294 APPENDICES

Date	Theatre	Composer	Translator
		THE GOLDEN CROSS (1875)	
March 2, 1878	Adelphi	Brüll	J. P. Jackson
		PICCOLINO (1876)	
Jan. 4, 1879	Dublin	Guiraud	S. Samuel
		RIENZI (1842)	
Jan. 27, 1879	Her Majesty's	Wagner	J. P. Jackson
		CARMEN (1875)	
Feb. 2, 1879	Her Majesty's	Bizet	H. Hersée
		MIGNON (1866)	
Aug. 18, 1879	Dublin	A. Thomas	A. Matthison
		THE TAMING OF THE SHREW (1874)	
Jan. 20, 1880	Her Majesty's	Goetz	J. Troutbeck
		LOHENGRIN (1850)	
Feb. 7, 1880	Her Majesty's	Wagner	J. P. Jackson
		AÏDA (1871)	
Feb. 19, 1880	Her Majesty's	Verdi	H. Hersée
		I PROMESSI SPOSI (1856)	
March 23, 1881	Edinburgh	Ponchielli	H. Hersée
		TANNHÄUSER (1845)	
Feb. 14, 1882	Her Majesty's	Wagner	J. P. Jackson

Date	Theatre	Composer	Translator

MEFISTOFELE
(1868)

| Aug. 21, 1884 | Dublin | Boito | T. Marzials |

MANON
(1884)

| Jan. 17, 1885 | Liverpool | Massenet | J. Bennett |

FADETTE
(an adaptation of LES DRAGONS DE VILLARS,[1] 1856)

| Jan. 18, 1886 | Liverpool | Maillart | W. Grist |

RUY BLAS
(1869)

| Feb. 4, 1886 | Liverpool | Marchetti | W. Grist |

GALATEA
(1852)

| Oct. 8, 1887 | Bristol | Massé | F. A. Schwab |

ROMEO AND JULIET
(1867)

| Jan. 15, 1890 | Liverpool, Royal Court | Gounod | H. B. Farnie |

THE STAR OF THE NORTH
(1854)

| April 17, 1890 | Drury Lane | Meyerbeer | |

RUSTIC CHIVALRY
(CAVALLERIA RUSTICANA)
(1890)

| Jan. 14, 1892 | Liverpool, Royal Court | Mascagni | F. E. Weatherley |

L'AMICO FRITZ
(1891)

| Aug., 1892 | Dublin | Mascagni | F. E. Weatherley |

[1] An earlier English adaptation by H. Hersée, called *The Dragoons*, was given at the Folly Theatre, London, on April 14, 1879.

Date	Theatre	Composer	Translator

DJAMILEH
(1872)

| Sept. 10, 1892 | Dublin | Bizet | J. Bennett |

OTHELLO
(1887)

| Oct. 8, 1892 | Manchester | Verdi | F. Hueffer |

PAGLIACCI
(1892)

| Aug. 23, 1893 | Dublin | Leoncavallo | F. E. Weatherley |

I RANTZAU
(1892)

| Oct., 1893 | Birmingham | Mascagni | F. E. Weatherley |

THE DAMNATION OF FAUST[1]

| Feb. 3, 1894 | Liverpool | Berlioz | T. H. Friend |

AT SANTA LUCIA
(1892)

| Oct. 1, 1894 | Manchester | Tasca | W. Grist |

BASTIEN AND BASTIENNE
(1768)

| Dec. 26, 1894 | Daly's | Mozart | Anon. |

HANSEL AND GRETEL
(1893)

| Dec. 26, 1894 | Daly's | Humperdinck | C. Bache |

LA VIVANDIÈRE
(1895)

| March 10, 1896 | Liverpool | Godard | G. Whyte |

THE MASTERSINGERS
(1868)

| April 16, 1896 | Manchester | Wagner | |

[1] First performed as a cantata in 1846 and as an opera in 1893.

Date	Theatre	Composer	Translator
		LA BOHÈME (THE BOHEMIANS) (1896)	
April 22, 1897	Manchester	Puccini	W. Grist and P. E. Pinkerton
		TRISTAN AND ISOLDE (1865)	
April 15, 1898	Liverpool	Wagner	F. Jameson
		PICCOLO HAYDN	
March 17, 1900	Brighton	Cipollini	
		A BASSO PORTO (1894)	
March 17, 1900	Brighton	Spinelli	P. E. Pinkerton
		THE CRICKET ON THE HEARTH (1896)	
Sept. 23, 1900	Brixton	Goldmark	P. E. Pinkerton
		CINQ-MARS (1877)	
Oct. 26, 1900	Leeds	Gounod	W. Van Noorden and S. J. A. Fitz-Gerald
		SIEGFRIED (1876)	
Oct. 18, 1901	Manchester	Wagner	H. and F. Corder
		ANDRÉ CHENIER (1896)	
Feb. 2, 1903	Manchester	Giordano	P. E. Pinkerton
		GIOCONDA (1876)	
May 6, 1903	Kennington	Ponchielli	H. Hersée
		LA FORZA DEL DESTINO (1862)	
Nov. 25, 1909	Manchester	Verdi	P. E. Pinkerton

Date	Theatre	Composer	Translator
	THE QUEEN OF SHEBA		
	(1875)		
April 12, 1910	Manchester	Goldmark	J. H. Cornell
	THE JEWELS OF THE MADONNA		
	(1911)		
Feb. 28, 1913	Glasgow	Wolf-Ferrari	C. Aveling
	L'ATTAQUE DU MOULIN		
	(1893)		
Oct. 15, 1915	Birmingham	Bruneau	F. E. Weatherley
	LAKME		
	(1883)		
March 8, 1918	Liverpool	Delibes	C. Aveling
	STELLA MARIS		
	(1910)		
April 15, 1919	Liverpool	de Keyser	
	THE DEPARTURE		
	(1898)		
Sept. 3, 1925	King's, Hammersmith	d'Albert	M. Bond and A. Skalski
	THE KISS		
	(1876)		
Oct. 15, 1948	King's, Hammersmith	Smetana	M. and J. Knap

(2) The Sadler's Wells Opera Company
(founded 1931)

	BORIS GODUNOV		
	(original version, 1868–9)		
Sept. 30, 1935	Sadler's Wells	Mussorgsky	M. D. Calvoco-ressi
	IL TABARRO		
	(1918)		
Oct. 23, 1935	Sadler's Wells	Puccini	H. Withers

Date	Theatre	Composer	Translator

THE BARTERED BRIDE
(1866)

| Nov. 21, 1935 | Sadler's Wells | Smetana | R. Newmarch |

DON CARLOS
(1867)

| Dec. 6, 1938 | Sadler's Wells | Verdi | S. Austin |

DER ROSENKAVALIER
(1911)

| March 8, 1939 | Sadler's Wells | R. Strauss | A. Kalisch, revised by Clive Carey |

SCHOOL FOR FATHERS
(I QUATTRO RUSTEGHI, 1906)

| June 7, 1946 | Sadler's Wells | Wolf-Ferrari | E. J. Dent |

SIMONE BOCCANEGRA
(revised version, 1881)

| Oct. 27, 1948 | Sadler's Wells | Verdi | Norman Tucker |

SCHWANDA THE BAGPIPER
(1927)

| Dec. 15, 1948 | Sadler's Wells | Weinberger | Dennis Arundell |

(3) The Covent Garden Opera Company
(founded 1946)

SALOME
(1905)

| Nov. 11, 1949 | Covent Garden | R. Strauss | Lord Alfred Douglas |

THE QUEEN OF SPADES
(1890)

| Dec. 21, 1950 | Covent Garden | Chaikovsky | R. Newmarch |

APPENDIX D

Sample Lists of Operas, etc., Performed in London in 1732, 1791, 1851, 1891 and 1948

Some idea of the change in operatic taste of audiences in this country can be obtained by comparing London's operatic fare at various periods. For this purpose, five different years have been arbitrarily chosen at intervals of roughly half a century. The term 'opera' has been interpreted more loosely than in Appendix A, and a number of farces, burlettas and musical comedies have been included in order to reflect the full range of London's musical entertainments in general.

These lists also give a good idea of the theatres engaged in opera production.

The 1732 list has been compiled from Allardyce Nicoll's *XVIII Century Drama: 1700–1750*. The other four lists are literally quoted from contemporary advertisements in the London press; and their (often inaccurate) spelling and wording have been left untouched.

1732

There is Italian opera at the King's Theatre and English opera at Drury Lane and elsewhere. This is the year in which Covent Garden opened. Handel is still at the height of his operatic career and famous as a composer, not only of Italian operas, but also of a masque (or serenata) that was adapted for the stage as an English pastoral opera. The enormous vogue for ballad opera that followed the success of *The Beggar's Opera* four years previously is evident from the spate of imitations that flood the theatres; and *The Beggar's Opera* itself is still being played in every London theatre of note, except the Italian Opera House.

Theatre Royal, Drury Lane

THE BEGGAR'S OPERA

THE BEGGAR'S WEDDING

BETTY, or, THE COUNTRY BUMP-
KINS N.P.

A COMICAL REVENGE, or, A DOCTOR
IN SPIGHT OF HIS TEETH

DAMON AND PHILLIDA, or, THE
LOVER RECLAIM'D

THE DEVIL OF A DUKE

THE EPHESIAN MATRON

THE JOVIAL CREW

THE LOTTERY

THE LOVER'S OPERA

THE MOCK DOCTOR

THE WEDDING

King's Theatre, Haymarket

ACIS AND GALATEA
ADMETO, RE DI TESSAGLIA
ALESSANDRO
CAIUS MARIUS CORIOLANUS
CATONE
EZIO
FLAVIO, RE DE' LONGOBARDI
GIULIO CESARE IN EGITTO
LUCIO PAPIRIO DITTATORE
SOSARME, RE DI MEDIA

Lincoln's Inn Fields Theatre

THE BEGGAR'S OPERA
FLORA
THE MAGGOT
A SEQUEL TO THE OPERA OF FLORA
TELEMACHUS
TERAMINTA

Theatre Royal, Covent Garden

THE BEGGAR'S OPERA

Little Theatre, Haymarket

ACIS AND GALATEA
AMELIA
THE BEGGAR'S OPERA
BRITANNIA
DAMON AND PHILLIDA, or, THE LOVER RECLAIM'D
THE DISAPPOINTMENT
THE WANTON JESUIT, or, INNOCENCE SEDUCED

Goodman's Fields Theatre

THE BEGGAR'S OPERA
DAMON AND PHILLIDA, or, THE LOVER RECLAIM'D
FATHER GIRARD THE SORCERER, or, THE AMOURS OF HARLEQUIN AND MISS CADIERE
FLORA
THE FOOTMAN
THE LOVER'S OPERA
PHEBE, or, THE BEGGAR'S WEDDING
THE SAILOR'S WEDDING, or, THE HUMOURS OF WAPPING
THE STAGE-COACH OPERA

1791

English opera is in the doldrums. Many of the theatrical entertainments are comic operas, musical pieces, or burlettas. Among the more serious contemporary English composers Storace, recently returned to London from Vienna, has no fewer than four of his light operas running. There is no sign as yet of Mozart, though this is the year of the first performances of *La Clemenza di Tito* and *Die Zauberflöte* in Vienna.

The theatrical position in London is complicated by the fact that the King's Theatre was burned down in 1789. (Arson was suspected.) While it was being rebuilt the company played at the Little Theatre in the Haymarket. By 1791 it was ready to reopen; but the Earl of

Mount Edgcumbe describes[1] how, when the public expected it to be opened, 'fresh and unforeseen difficulties arose, another theatre having been prepared for operas, under other managers, who had not only secured the Lord Chamberlain's licence, but even got the sanction of the King to call it *his* theatre. This was the Pantheon, in its original state the largest and most beautiful room in London, and a very model of fine architecture. . . . Here the regular opera was successfully carried on, with two very good companies and ballets.' As for the rebuilt King's Theatre, 'it was with difficulty they at length succeeded in getting leave to open the theatre with *music* and dancing; but the permission not extending to dramatic performances, no opera could be acted'. The following year the Pantheon was burnt down; and the King's Theatre ultimately got back its opera licence in 1793.

Meanwhile, old Drury Lane closed down on June 4, 1791, and the 117-year-old building was forthwith demolished.

Theatre Royal, Drury Lane

THE SIEGE OF BELGRADE
THE DEVIL TO PAY
NO SONG, NO SUPPER
THE HAUNTED TOWER (comic
    opera)
ACIS AND GALATEA
THE TEMPEST, or, THE ENCHANTED
    ISLAND
THE CAVE OF TROPHONIUS (comic
    opera)

King's Theatre, Haymarket
H.M. Company from the Theatre Royal, Drury Lane

THE CAVE OF TROPHONIUS (comic
    opera)
NO SONG, NO SUPPER
THE HAUNTED TOWER (comic
    opera)
THE SIEGE OF BELGRADE
SHE WOU'D AND SHE WOU'D NOT
INKLE AND JARICO
THE DOCTOR AND THE APOTHECARY
    (musical entertainment)
ARTAXERXES
CYMON (musical entertainment)

Theatre Royal, Covent Garden

THE WOODMAN (comic opera)
THE POOR SOLDIER (comic opera)
HOB IN THE WELL (ballad farce)
A FAVOURITE OPERA
LOVE AND WAR (comic opera)
THE FARMER (comic opera)
PRIMROSE GREEN, or, LOVE IN A
    GARDEN (2-act opera)
THE COTTAGE MAID (musical enter-
    tainment)
FONTAINEBLEAU, or, OUR WAY IN
    FRANCE (comic opera)

[1] *op. cit.*

ROBIN HOOD, or, SHERWOOD FOREST (comic opera)
INKLE AND JARICO
THE JOVIAL CREW (comic opera)
ROSE AND COLIN (musical piece)
LOVE IN A CAMP, or, PATRICK IN PRISON (comic opera)

TOM THUMB (burletta)
CYMON (musical entertainment)
THE BEGGAR'S OPERA
THE CASTLE OF ANDALUSIA (comic opera)
LOVE IN A VILLAGE
ARTAXERXES

Theatre Royal, Haymarket

THE SPANISH BARBER (comic opera)
INKLE AND JARICO
THE AGREEABLE SURPRISE (comic opera)
GRETNA GREEN (musical farce)
THE SON-IN-LAW (musical farce)
THE PADLOCK (comic opera)

THE BEGGAR'S OPERA
THE SURRENDER OF CALAIS
THE CAVE OF TROPHONIUS (comic opera)
THE GENTLE SHEPHERD (Scots musical pastoral comedy)

Theatre Royal, Richmond

INKLE AND JARICO
ROBIN HOOD, or, SHERWOOD FOREST (comic opera)

THE HIGHLAND REEL (comic opera)
THE PADLOCK (comic opera)

King's Theatre, Pantheon

ARMIDA (grand serious opera)
LA BELLA PESCATRICE (comic opera)
IDALIDE (grand serious opera)
LA MULINARELLA (comic opera)

QUINTUS FABIUS (grand serious opera)
LE LOCCANDA (comic opera)
LA PASTORELLA NOBILE (comic opera)

Theatre of Variétés Amusantes, (Fantoccini) 10 Saville Row

LES PETITES AFFICHES (musical comedy)
LES DEUX JUMEAUX (musical farce)
LES DEUX CHASSEURS ET LA LAITIÈRE (comic opera)

LE DEVIN DU VILLAGE (musical piece)
L'AMORE DISCADE (musical piece)
LA BUONA FIGLIULA (opera)
THE WIDOW IN TEARS (burletta)
LE ROY ET LE FERMIER (comic opera)

Lyceum

THE ODDITIES, or, DAME NATURE IN A FROLICK (an entertainment)
THE WAGS, or, THE CAMP OF PLEASURE

Royal Grove, Astley's Amphitheatre, Westminster Bridge

THE KING AND THE COBLER (musical piece)

THE WITTY WIFE, or, A LESSON FOR CUCKOLD-MAKERS (musical piece)

THE TEMPLE OF PLUTUS, or, THE MISER REFORM'D (comic musical piece)

THE BLUNT TAR, or, TRUE LOVE REWARDED (musical piece)

THE TINKER (musical piece)

THE MILLINER'S SHOP (musical piece)

THE TYTHE SHEAF, or, THE WITTY OUTWITTED (musical piece)

Sadler's Wells

THE BROOM (musical piece)

HOOLY AND FAIRLY, or, THE HIGHLAND DADDIE (musical piece)

1851

During this year, the year of the Great Exhibition, English romantic operas by Balfe, Benedict and Macfarren are given at several London theatres, especially the Royal Surrey; but the greater part of London's operatic activities consists of Italian opera at Covent Garden and Her Majesty's, now under the management of Mr. Frederick Gye and Mr. Benjamin Lumley respectively. The chief operas of Mozart, Rossini, Donizetti, Bellini, Meyerbeer and Auber are well represented. Beethoven's *Fidelio* is done with specially composed recitatives by Balfe. One of Verdi's operas is given, together with a single act from a second one. Mendelssohn's operetta, *Son and Stranger*, receives one of its very few performances. It will be noted that *The Beggar's Opera* is produced at more than one London theatre, despite the fact that George Hogarth in his *Memoirs of the Opera* (published this year) says 'it may be presumed that the time is come, or at least approaching, when its licentiousness will banish it from the stage, notwithstanding its wit and the beauty of its music'.

Theatre Royal, Drury Lane

THE CADI'S DAUGHTER (operetta)

AZAEL THE PRODIGAL (operatic spectacle after Auber's *L'Enfant Prodigue*)

Her Majesty's

LUCIA DI LAMMERMOOR

GUSTAVE III, OU, LE BAL MASQUÉ

MUTA DI PORTICI (MASANIELLO)

IL PRODIGO

LES METAMORPHOSES (first act)

LA PROVA D'UN OPERA SERIA

LA SONNAMBULA
I DUE FOSCARI (last act)
L'ELISIR D'AMORE
LUCREZIA BORGIA
LE TRE NOZZE
IL MATRIMONIO SEGRETO (selection from)
LA FIGLIA DEL REGGIMENTO
DON GIOVANNI
IL BARBIERE DI SIVIGLIA
FIDELIO
NORMA
DON PASQUALE

FLORINDA, or, THE MOORS IN SPAIN
LE NOZZE DI FIGARO
LA CENERENTOLA
ERNANI
ZERLINA, ou, LA CORBEILLES D' ORANGES
I QUATTRO FRATELLI (LES QUATRE FILS AYMON)
LINDA DI CHAMOUNI
LA GAZZA LADRA
ANNA BOLENA
BOHEMIAN GIRL (excerpts)
DER FREISCHÜTZ (selection from)
OTELLO (last act)

Royal Italian Opera, Covent Garden

SEMIRAMIDE
MASANIELLO
ROBERTO IL DIAVOLO
LES HUGUENOTS
LA DAMA DEL LAGO
LUCREZIA BORGIA
DER FREISCHÜTZ
FIDELIO
DON GIOVANNI
NORMA

LA FAVORITA
LE PROPHÈTE
IL FLAUTO MAGICO
I PURITANI
L'ELISIR D'AMORE
LA PROVA D'UN OPERA SERIA (comic scene)
LA GAZZA LADRA
SAFFO
OTELLO

Theatre Royal, Haymarket

THE CROWN DIAMONDS
GOOD NIGHT, SIR, PLEASANT DREAMS (comic opera)
THE CADI, OR, AMOURS AMONG MOORS (2 act)
SON AND STRANGER (operetta)

THE QUEEN OF A DAY (comic opera)
LA SONNAMBULA
HIS FIRST CHAMPAGNE (burletta)
KING CHARLES THE SECOND
THE BEGGAR'S OPERA

Theatre Royal, Richmond

THE SULTANA (burletta)

Royal Surrey Theatre

DON GIOVANNI
THE ENCHANTRESS
THE BOHEMIAN GIRL
MIDAS

THE MOUNTAIN SYLPH
LUCIA DI LAMMERMOOR
LA SONNAMBULA
THE DAUGHTER OF THE REGIMENT

U

THE FAVOURITE   THE HUGUENOTS
DER FREISCHÜTZ   THE BEGGAR'S OPERA
FRA DIAVOLO   LINDA DI CHAMOUNI
MASANIELLO   NORMA
MARITANA   ERNANI

Theatre Royal, Adelphi

O'FLANNIGAN AND THE FAIRIES, OR,   GOOD NIGHT SIGNOR PANTALON
  A MIDSUMMER NIGHT'S DREAM   (1 act comic opera)
  (a musical, historical, pastoral,   TAMING A TARTAR (grand operatic,
  comical fairy drama)   romantic, terpsichorean, semi-
    burlesque burletta)

Theatre Royal, Marylebone, and London English Opera[1]

THE VAMPIRE   THE WATERMAN

Royal Marylebone Theatre

LA SONNAMBULA   LUCIA DI LAMMERMOOR

Sadler's Wells

THE WATERMAN

Strand Theatre

THE VILLAGE NIGHTINGALE (burletta)

Hanover Square Rooms

MARAVILLA (grand Spanish opera, 3 act) (rehearsal)

1891

This year marks the virtual end of the Gilbert and Sullivan partner-ship. *The Gondoliers* finishes its two years' run at the Savoy Theatre, while early in the year *Ivanhoe*, Sir Arthur Sullivan's only attempt at a grand opera (so called), opens at the ill-fated Royal English Opera House in Cambridge Circus. At Covent Garden, now under the management of Sir Arthur Harris, Verdi has become one of the most popular composers in the country, and his supremacy is rivalled only by Wagner and Gounod. Meanwhile, the works of the earlier Italian opera composers—Rossini, Bellini and Donizetti—are receding into the background and the English romantic operas have completely dis-appeared. Bizet's *Carmen* is perhaps the most successful of the novelties

---

[1] This opera season was advertised in advance to begin on February 10, but no adver-tisements appeared of actual performances.

of the last fifteen years. As a sign of the growing interest in the work of
earlier centuries, it should be noticed that there are three different
revivals of Gluck's *Orfeo*. During this year Bernard Shaw acts as music
critic to *The World*; and his weekly notices (reprinted in *Music in
London*, 1890–94) provide a brilliant conspectus of the operatic field.

Theatre Royal, Drury Lane

CARMEN

Royal Italian Opera, Covent Garden

ORFEO
FAUST (later called FAUST E MARG-
  HERITA) (also given in French)
CARMEN
LOHENGRIN
ROMÉO ET JULIETTE
TANNHÄUSER
LA TRAVIATA
LE PROPHÈTE
MEFISTOFELE
DON GIOVANNI
MANON (in French)
LES HUGUENOTS
DIE MEISTERSINGER

RIGOLETTO
LUCIA DI LAMMERMOOR
MARTA
MIREILLE (in French)
OTELLO
FIDELIO
AÏDA
IL TROVATORE
ROBERTO IL DIAVOLO
LA GIOCONDA
NORMA
L'ETOILE DU NORD
PHILÉMON ET BAUCIS (in French)
LE RÊVE (in French)

Royal English Opera, Cambridge Circus

IVANHOE
LA BASOCHE

Shaftesbury Theatre
Signor Lago's Royal Italian Opera

LA CENERENTOLA
CRISPINO E LA CANARE[1]
CAVALLERIA RUSTICANA
ERNANI
IL BARBIERE DI SIVIGLIA

IL VASCELLO FANTASMA (THE FLYING
  DUTCHMAN)
ORFEO
IL MATRIMONIO SEGRETO
L'ELISIR D'AMORE
JOAN OF ARC (burlesque)

Savoy

THE GONDOLIERS, OR, THE KING
  OF BARATARIA

THE NAUTCH GIRL, OR, THE RAJAH
  OF CHUTNEYPORE (Indian comic
  opera)

[1] Misprint for *Crispino e la Camare*.

308

APPENDICES

Prince of Wales

MAID MARIAN (comic opera)

L'ENFANT PRODIGUE (musical play without words)

CAPT. THERESE (comic opera) (Carl Rosa Light Opera Company)

MISS DECIMA (operatic comedy)

Crystal Palace Theatre

ORFEO

FAUST

PAUL JONES

THE MOCK DOCTOR

THE MIKADO

Lyric Opera House, Hammersmith

FALKA (comic opera)

Gaiety

CARMEN UP TO DATE (burlesque)

JOAN OF ARC (burlesque)

CINDER-ELLEN, OR, UP TOO LATE (burlesque)

Opéra Comique

JOAN OF ARC (burlesque)

Lyric

LA CIGALE (opéra comique, 3 act)

Criterion

MISS DECIMA (operatic comedy)

Avenue Theatre

YVETTE (musical play without words)

THE TWO BLIND (operetta)

Royalty

HIS LAST CHANCE (operetta)

FAUVETTE (comic opera)

Olympia

VENICE, THE BRIDE OF THE SEA (operatic spectacular drama)

1948

This has been chosen as a representative year after the Second World War. The Covent Garden Opera Company, established at the end of 1946, has already built up a repertory of opera in English (including one English opera) that enables it to play in the Royal Opera House

for about nine months in the year to an audience that now averages
eighty-three per cent of capacity. The Sadler's Wells Company plays
for about eight months in the year at Sadler's Wells Theatre and repairs
ninety years' neglect by performing Verdi's *Simone Boccanegra* for the
first time in this country. In May an uninterrupted two years' season
of Italian opera sung in Italian comes to an end at the Cambridge
Theatre. The English Opera Group, now in the third year of its
existence, brings Benjamin Britten's new adaptation of *The Beggar's
Opera* to Sadler's Wells and the People's Palace, and revives his comic
opera, *Albert Herring*. A visiting American Company presents two
short operas by Gian-Carlo Menotti at the Aldwych Theatre.

Theatre Royal, Drury Lane

OKLAHOMA

Royal Opera House, Covent Garden

PETER GRIMES	THE VALKYRIE (in English and also
IL TROVATORE	in German)
TURANDOT	LA TRAVIATA
RIGOLETTO	BORIS GODUNOV
CARMEN	AIDA
ROSENKAVALIER	LA BOHÈME
THE MASTERSINGERS	SIEGFRIED (in German)
THE MAGIC FLUTE	FIDELIO
TRISTAN UND ISOLDE (in German)	

Sadler's Wells

MARRIAGE OF FIGARO	FAUST
LA BOHÈME	RIGOLETTO
SNOW-MAIDEN	COSÌ FAN TUTTE
CAVALLERIA RUSTICANA	BARBER OF SEVILLE
I PAGLIACCI	IL TROVATORE
HANSEL AND GRETEL	IL TABARRO
DIE FLEDERMAUS	LADY ROHESIA
MADAM BUTTERFLY	SCHWANDA THE BAGPIPER
SCHOOL FOR FATHERS	SIMONE BOCCANEGRA
THE BARTERED BRIDE	SHEPHERDS OF THE DELECTABLE
TOSCA	MOUNTAINS

The English Opera Group

THE BEGGAR'S OPERA	ALBERT HERRING

D'Oyly Carte Opera Company

THE GONDOLIERS
MIKADO
IOLANTHE
TRIAL BY JURY
PIRATES OF PENZANCE

YEOMEN OF THE GUARD
PATIENCE
COX AND BOX
PINAFORE

Cambridge Theatre
New London Opera Company

DON GIOVANNI
RIGOLETTO
BARBER OF SEVILLE
DON PASQUALE

TOSCA
LA BOHÈME
FALSTAFF

Aldwych

THE MEDIUM

THE TELEPHONE

King's, Hammersmith
Carl Rosa Opera Company

THE BARBER OF SEVILLE
LA BOHÈME
CARMEN
LA TOSCA

LA TRAVIATA
IL TROVATORE
THE KISS
MADAM BUTTERFLY

People's Palace

THE BEGGAR'S OPERA
ALBERT HERRING

THE QUAKER GIRL
SONG OF NORWAY

Adelphi

BLESS THE BRIDE

Coliseum

ANNIE GET YOUR GUN

Palace

CARISSIMA

SONG OF NORWAY

Mercury
Intimate Opera Company

Hippodrome
HIGH BUTTON SHOES (American musical comedy)

The Contribution by Amateurs and Students to English Opera in the Twentieth Century

During the first half of the twentieth century the amateur contribution to English opera and to opera in English has been outstanding. Amateurs have helped to nourish a real love of opera, sometimes in places that never receive visits from professional companies; and the intelligence and initiative shown in the choice of operas have been remarkable. Only a small number of these amateur operatic societies can here be mentioned, and a small proportion of their productions. Even so, this abbreviated record is most impressive.

Foremost among these societies is the Glasgow Grand Opera Society, which was founded as a result of the special appeal for increased public support for opera made in 1906 by Charles Manners of the Moody Manners Opera Company. To it belongs the honour of having given the first performances in Great Britain of Mozart's *Idomeneo* (1934)[1] and both parts of Berlioz's *The Trojans* (1935). It has departed from the beaten track in reviving such operas as Goldmark's *The Queen of Sheba* (1921), Verdi's *Ernani* (1930), Ponchielli's *Gioconda* (1931), Berlioz's *Beatrice and Benedict* and *Benvenuto Cellini* (1936), Chaikovsky's *Eugen Onegin* (1948) and Bizet's *The Pearl Fishers* (1950). Of English operas, it has revived Goring Thomas's *Esmeralda* (1920) and *Nadeshda* (1927), Wallace's *Maritana* (1923) and MacCunn's *Jeanie Deans* (1951), and given the first performance of W. B. Moonie's *The Weird of Colbar* (1937).

Remarkable enthusiasm was shown in the 1920's in Liverpool, where for several consecutive seasons the Liverpool Repertory Opera, a company of amateurs stiffened by the addition of professionals, gave occasional performances of opera in the David Lewis Theatre. Low admission prices were charged, and a decided preference shown for English works. Revivals included Stanford's *Shamus O'Brien*, Holbrooke's *The Stranger* and *Dylan*, Boughton's *The Immortal Hour* and *The Queen of Cornwall*, Ethel Smyth's *The Boatswain's Mate*, Vaughan Williams's *Hugh the Drover*, Bantock's *The Seal Woman* and Napier Miles's *Markheim*. But this company's most outstanding achievements were the first performance of Stanford's *The Travelling Companion* in 1925, just a year after his death, and a special operatic production of Sir Edward Elgar's cantata, *Caractacus*, on January 13, 1928.

[1] Cf. Appendix B.

The Falmouth Operatic Society, founded by the Misses M. and E. Radford in 1924, has a most distinguished record. It has been responsible for the first performances in English of Gluck's *Armide* (1936) and *Cythère Assiégée* (1950) and Mozart's *La Clemenza di Tito* (1930) in translations specially made by the Misses Radford themselves.[1] English operas performed have included Purcell's *King Arthur* (1924), Gatty's *Prince Ferelon* (1924), Vaughan Williams's *The Shepherds of the Delectable Mountains* (1928 and 1950), Stanford's *The Travelling Companion* (1934) and Holst's *Savitri*. The Falmouth Society has also followed the Cambridge example of experimenting with dramatised versions of some of Handel's oratorios.

Since its foundation in 1930 the Swindon Musical Society has concentrated almost exclusively on Russian opera. It has staged two ambitious revivals of Borodin's *Prince Igor* (1935 and 1946); but in the main it has concentrated on Rimsky-Korsakov, producing no fewer than five of his operas—*Snow Maiden* (1930 and 1938), *Tsar Saltan* (1932), *Sadko* (1934), *Mlada* (1936 and 1947), and *Ivan the Terrible* (1937).

It is impossible to survey the work of all the other amateur operatic societies, but special mention should be made of the Penzance Operatic Society, which first produced George Lloyd's *Iernin* (1934) a year before London saw it at the Lyceum; the Birmingham Clarion Singers, who gave the first performance of Dent's version of *The Beggar's Opera* (1944); the Wilderness Opera Company, which has presented a number of the operas of Ethel Smyth, Holst, Boughton and Vaughan Williams's; the Workers' Music Association which commissioned and produced Inglis Gundry's *The Partisans* (1946) and gave the first performance in Great Britain of Dvorak's *The Jacobin* (1947); and the John Lewis Partnership Music Society, which also gave the first performance of a Dvorak opera in this country—*Rusalka* (1950) in a translation by Christopher Hassall.

Similar initiative has been shown in student productions at the universities.

The Cambridge production of *Orfeo ed Euridice* in 1890 led to a revival of interest in Gluck's operas throughout the country; and to Cambridge too belongs the honour of having revived Mozart's *The Magic Flute* (1911) in the first of Dent's brilliant opera libretto translations. Their production of Purcell's *The Fairy Queen* in 1920 was that opera's first stage appearance since 1692; and *King Arthur* was given in 1928. Through the initiative of Dennis Arundell various experiments have been made in dramatising some of Handel's oratorios: *Semele, Samson, Jephtha, Saul, Susanna, Solomon* and *The Choice of Hercules*. First performances of native operas include Rootham's *The Two*

[1] Cf. Appendix B.

Sisters (1922) and Vaughan Williams's comic opera, *The Poisoned Kiss* (1936). In 1949, about three and a half centuries after its original production in Rome, Cavaliere's musical morality, *Rappresentazione di Anima e di Corpo*, was produced by the Girton College Musical Society.

The Oxford performances of *Fidelio* (1910) and *Der Freischütz* (1912) deserve mention; and of special importance were their revivals of *Orfeo* (1925) and *The Coronation of Poppea* (1927), which focused considerable interest in this country on Monteverdi as an opera composer. In 1931 Oxford performed Rimsky-Korsakov's *May Night* for the first time in English and the following year gave the first performance in this country of Dvorak's *The Devil and Kate*. Stanford's *Much Ado About Nothing* was revived in 1949.

Liverpool students took part in the first performance of Holst's chamber opera, *The Wandering Scholar*, in 1934.

The Royal Colleges have naturally played an important part with their student performances and public rehearsals.

The Royal College of Music had a particularly distinguished record when its productions were under Stanford's direction. It was responsible for the first performances in English of Schumann's *Genoveva* (1893), Delibes's *Le Roi l'a Dit* (1894), Weber's *Euryanthe* (1900) and Goetz's *Francesca* (1908); and the English operas it has produced include Ethel Smyth's *Entente Cordiale* (1925), Vaughan Williams's *The Shepherds of the Delectable Mountains* (1922), *Hugh the Drover* (1924), *Sir John in Love* (1929) and *Riders to the Sea* (1937), and Arthur Benjamin's *The Devil Take Her* (1931)—all first performances—and revivals of Purcell's *Dido and Aeneas* (1895), Stanford's *Much Ado About Nothing* (1901) and *Shamus O'Brien* (1906 and 1925), Mackenzie's *Colomba* (1912), Holst's *Savitri* (1921) and Delius's *A Village Romeo and Juliet* (1934).

The Royal Academy of Music gave the first performance of Mackenzie's *The Cricket on the Hearth* in 1914 and repeated it in 1936. It was responsible for the first performances in English of Pergolesi's *Livietta and Tracollo* (1933), Wolf's *Der Corregidor* (1934), and Puccini's complete *Trittico* (1937), and for revivals of a number of English operas including Blow's *Venus and Adonis* (1926), part of Sullivan's *Ivanhoe* (1932), Purcell's *Dido and Aeneas* (1933), Dibdin's *The Ephesian Matron* (1933), and Britten's *Albert Herring* (1950).

The Royal Manchester College of Music gave regular opera performances in the Lesser Free Trade Hall between 1928 and 1935, including the first performance in English of Puccini's *Suor Angelica* (1931). Since the destruction of the hall by bombing, in 1940, it has not been able to find alternative accommodation.

As regards the Royal Scottish Academy of Music, Glasgow, student performances were given between 1901 and 1910 by its predecessor, the Atheneum School of Music, and between 1931 and 1940 by the Scottish National Academy of Music. Massé's *Les Noces de Jeannette* was produced in 1910; and English operas have included Sullivan's *Haddon Hall* (1901), selections from *The Bohemian Girl* (1904), *Dido and Aeneas* (1932 and 1940), scenes from *King Arthur* (1932 and 1936), Holst's *Savitri* (1935), Dibdin's *The Ephesian Matron* (1936), Vaughan Williams's *The Shepherds of the Delectable Mountains* (1936) and also Arne's masque of *Comus* (1938).

The Guildhall School of Music, London, concentrated for a period on Gounod, producing his *Faust* (1893), *Philemon and Baucis* (1893), *Romeo and Juliet* (1895), *Mock Doctor* (1899), *Mirella* (1899) and *Irène* (1909). Other revivals of foreign operas in English included Mendelssohn's *Son and Stranger* (1882 and 1896), Gluck's *Orpheus* (1894), Hérold's *Le Pré aux Clercs* (1909), and the first English performance of Gluck's *Iphigenia in Tauris* (1908).[1] There was a period during which the School concentrated on light opera—particularly Sullivan and German—but at other times the following English operas have been revived: Wallace's *Maritana* (1890), Wallworth's *Kevin's Choice* (1891), Balfe's *The Bohemian Girl* (1891), Goring Thomas's *Esmeralda* (1896), Waldo Warner's *Royal Vagrants* (1900), Barnett's *The Mountain Sylph* (1906), Purcell's *Dido and Aeneas* (1910) and Stanford's *Shamus O'Brien* (1936). Weber's *Oberon* was given in 1910.

Of the various operas staged by the students of Trinity College of Music, perhaps the most interesting was the revival of *The Village Coquettes* of Hullah and Dickens in 1924, with incidental music consisting partly of numbers by Hullah and partly of old English airs arranged by Sir Frederick Bridge.

Early in the century the Birmingham and Midland Institute School of Music gave three important Gluck revivals under the direction of Granville Bantock: *Orpheus* (1904), *Iphigenia in Tauris* (1909), and the first performance in Great Britain of *Iphigenia in Aulis* (1906).[2] Later revivals included the following English operas: Stanford's *The Critic* (1933) and *Shamus O'Brien* (1938), Boughton's *Bethlehem* (1934) and *Alkestis* (1947) Bantock's *The Seal Woman* (1936) and Mackenzie's *St. John's Eve* (1938).

This record of the initiative and devotion of amateurs and students would be incomplete if no mention was made of opera in schools. Britten's *Let's Make an Opera!* has shown a wide public how effective an opera can be in which children play specially written parts. But that they can also tackle certain adult operas was demonstrated with success by C. T. Smith shortly after the first World War, when he produced *Faust* and *The Magic Flute* with the children of dock-labourers in the Isle of Dogs, and also (to choose more recent examples) by the Fettes

[1] Cf. Appendix B.   [2] *Ibid.*

College, Edinburgh, productions of *The Bartered Bride* and *Der Freischütz*, and the Leighton Park School, Reading, production of *The Quaker's Opera* (1950). In the words of Edward J. Dent,[1] such productions have an educational value from the standpoint of 'training in music, acting, speaking, movement and dance, co-operation—including boys' or girls' work in designing and painting scenery and dresses, lighting, property-making, handicrafts, etc. and all the communal and collective work with its moral training in team work. And on top of that, the intensive study of a classical opera.' In such an atmosphere Purcell's *Dido and Aeneas* was written and produced; and it is to be hoped that the interest shown by schools will lead to the creation of new works in the future.

[1] From an unpublished letter to E. W. White, dated September 23, 1950.

APPENDIX F

Select Bibliography

COUNT ALGAROTTI, F.R.S., F.S.A., etc., *An Essay on the Opera*. R. Urie, Glasgow, 1768.

LUIGI ARDITI, *My Reminiscences*. Edited and compiled with Introduction and Notes by the Baroness von Zedlitz. Skeffington & Son, London, 1896.

FRANK AUSTIN, *A National School of Opera for England*. W. Reeves, London, 1882.

HENRY C. BANISTER, *George Alexander Macfarren: his Life Works and Influence*. George Bell & Sons, London, 1891.

WILLIAM ALEXANDER BARRETT, *Balfe: his Life and Work*. William Reeves, London (n.d.).

C. R. BASKERVILL, *The Elizabethan Jig*. University of Chicago Press, 1929.

SIR THOMAS BEECHAM, BART., *A Mingled Chime: Leaves from an Autobiography*. Hutchinson & Co., Ltd., London, 1944.

SIR JULIUS BENEDICT, *Carl Maria von Weber* (1786–1826). Sampson Low, Marston & Co., Ltd., London (n.d.).

ERIC BLOM, *Stepchildren of Music*. G. T. Foulis & Co. Ltd., London (n.d.). (Contains essays on *The Dragon of Wantley* and *Fennimore und Gerda*.)

Music in England. Penguin, London, 1942.

RUTLAND BOUGHTON and REGINALD R. BUCKLEY, *Music-Drama of the Future*. William Reeves, London, 1911.

RUTLAND BOUGHTON, *A National Music Drama*. A Lecture delivered to the Royal Musical Association in 1917.

The Glastonbury Festival Movement. Somerset Press Reprints No. 03 (reprinted from *Somerset and the Drama*). Somerset Folk Press, London, 1922.

ALFRED BUNN, *The Stage: both before and behind the Curtain from 'Observations taken on the Spot'*. 3 vols. Richard Bentley, London, 1840.

DR. CHARLES BURNEY, *A General History of Music from the Earliest Ages to the Present Period*. Vols. iii and iv. London, 1789.

An Account of the Musical Performances in Westminster Abbey and the Pantheon, May 26th, 27th, 29th; and June the 3rd, and 5th, 1784 in Commemoration of Handel. London, 1785.

JEREMY COLLIER, *A Short View of the Immorality and Profaneness of the English Stage: together with the Sense of Antiquity Upon this Argument*. S. Keble and R. Sare, London, 1698.

EDWARD J. DENT, *Foundations of English Opera:* A Study of Musical Drama in England during the Seventeenth Century. Cambridge University Press, 1928.

Handel. Great Lives Series. Duckworth, London, 1934.

Opera. Penguin, London. First edition, 1940; revised edition, 1949. (This contains three chapters on Opera in England.)

A Theatre for Everybody: The Story of the Old Vic and Sadler's Wells. T. V. Boardman & Co., Ltd., London. First edition, 1945; second edition (enlarged), 1946.

(See also *Purcell's 'The Fairy Queen'*, Loewenberg's *Annals of Opera*, Royal Musical Association and Streatfeild's *The Opera.*)

(CHARLES DIBDIN), *The Musical Tour of Mr. Dibdin; in which—previous to his Embarkation for India—He Finished his Career as a Public Character.* J. Gales, Sheffield, 1788.

(THOMAS DIBDIN), *The Reminiscences of Thomas Dibdin of the Theatres Royal, Covent Garden, Drury Lane, Haymarket, &c.* 2 vols. Henry Colburn, London, 1827.

J. DOWNES, *Roscius Anglicanus, or, an Historical Review of the Stage after it had been Suppres'd by means of the late Unhappy Civil War, begun in 1641, till the time of Charles the II's restoration in May 1660.* H. Playford, London, 1708.

JOHN DRYDEN, Prefaces and Dedications to *The Conquest of Granada* (1668), *The State of Innocence* (1677), *Albion and Albanius* (1685), *Amphitryon* (1690), and *King Arthur* (1691).

JOHN EBERS, *Seven Years of the King's Theatre.* William Harrison Ainsworth, London, 1828.

H. SUTHERLAND EDWARDS, *The Lyrical Drama: Essays on Subjects, Composers, and Executants of Modern Opera.* 2 vols. W. H. Allen and Co., London, 1881.

English Masques, selected and with an introduction by Herbert Arthur Evans, M.A. Blackie & Son, Ltd., London (n.d.).

EDWARD FITZBALL, *Thirty-Five Years of a Dramatic Author's Life.* 2 vols. T. C. Newby, London, 1859.

CECIL FORSYTH, *Music and Nationalism:* A Study of English Opera. Macmillan, London, 1911. (This book contains a very valuable bibliography of English Opera.)

W. JOHNSON GALLOWAY, *The Operatic Problem.* John Long, London, 1902.

WILHELM GANZ, *Memories of a Musician: Reminiscences of Seventy Years of Musical Life.* John Murray, London, 1913.

JAMES M. GLOVER, *Jimmy Glover His Book.* Methuen & Co. Ltd., London, 1911.

JOSEPH GODDARD, *The Rise and Development of Opera: Embracing Comparative View of the Art in Italy, Germany, France and England—*

Showing the Cause of the Falling Back of the English School in the Modern Period and the Compensation which that Falling Back Involved. William Reeves, London, 1911.

HARRY PLUNKET GREENE, *Charles Villiers Stanford.* Edward Arnold, London, 1935.

Hinrichsen's Musical Year Book. Hinrichsen Edition Ltd., London. (This frequently contains articles of interest on opera, such as 'English Opera and Opera in English', by Edward J. Dent, in Vol. II, 1945–6, and 'The Royal Carl Rosa Opera Company', by J. C. Handby, in Vol. VI, 1949–50.)

GEORGE HOGARTH, *Memoirs of the Musical Drama.* 2 vols. London, 1838. *Memoirs of the Opera in Italy, France, Germany, and England:* a new edition of the 'Musical Drama'. 2 vols. Richard Bentley, London, 1851.

FRANK HOWES and PHILIP HOPE-WALLACE, *A Key to Opera.* Blackie and Son, Ltd., London, 1939. (Chapter VIII is devoted to English Opera.)

ARTHUR HUTCHINGS, *Delius.* Macmillan & Co., Ltd., London, 1948.

(MICHAEL KELLY), *Reminiscences of Michael Kelly of the King's Theatre and Theatre Royal, Drury Lane, including a period of nearly half a century; with original anecdotes of many distinguished persons, political, literary and musical.* 2 vols. Henry Colburn, London, 1826.

KENNEY, *Memoir of Balfe.*

HERMAN KLEIN, *The Golden Age of Opera.* George Routledge & Sons, Ltd., London, 1933. *Thirty Years of Musical Life in London.* Heinemann, London, 1903.

HUBERT LANGLEY, *Doctor Arne.* Cambridge University Press, 1938.

E. MARKHAM LEE, *The Story of Opera.* Walter Scott Publishing Co. Ltd., London, 1909.

JOHN MEWBURN LEVISON, *Six Sovereigns of Song.* Novello, London (n.d.). (This book contains separate lectures on John Braham and Sir Charles Santley.)

ALFRED LOEWENBERG, *Annals of Opera* (1597–1940). With an introduction by Edward J. Dent. Heffer & Sons, Ltd., Cambridge, 1943.

(JOHN MAINWARING), *Memoirs of the Life of the late George Frederic Handel. To which is added a Catalogue of his Works and Observations upon them.* R. & J. Dodsley, London, 1760.

The Mapleson Memoirs. 2 vols. Remington & Co., London, 1888.

(*Masques: cf. English Masques.*)

JOHANN MATTHESON, *Grundlagen einer Ehren-Pforte, worin der tüchtigsten Capellmeister, Componisten, Musikgelehrten, Tonkünstler usw. Leben, Wercke, Verdienste usw. erschienen sollen.* Hamburg, 1740. (This contains an account of Handel in Hamburg. In 1761, Mattheson published a German translation of Mainwaring's *Memoirs of the Life of Handel* with important notes.)

THE EARL OF MOUNT EDGCUMBE, *Musical Reminiscences of an old Amateur chiefly respecting the Italian Opera in England for fifty years from 1773 to 1823*. John Andrews, London. First edition, 1827. Fourth edition under the title, *Musical Reminiscences, containing an Account of the Italian Opera in England from 1773 continued to the present time and including the Festival in Westminster Abbey*, 1834. (Section VIII contains observations on English Music.)

Music: A Report on Musical Life in England sponsored by the Dartington Hall Trustees. PEP, London, 1949. (This contains a chapter on Opera and a section on Amateur Opera.)

Opera in English by Tyrone Guthrie, Edwin Evans, Joan Cross, Edward J. Dent, Ninette de Valois. (Sadler's Wells Opera Books, No. 1.) The Bodley Head, London, 1945.

Peter Grimes: essays by Benjamin Britten, E. M. Forster, Montagu Slater and Edward Sackville-West. (Sadler's Wells Opera Books, No. 3.) The Bodley Head, London, 1945.

(J. R. PLANCHÉ), *The Recollections and Reflections of J. R. Planché (Somerset Herald): A Professional Autobiography*. 2 vols. Tinsley Bros., London, 1872.

NIGEL PLAYFAIR, *The Story of the Lyric Theatre, Hammersmith*. Chatto & Windus, London, 1925.

Purcell's 'The Fairy Queen' as presented by the Sadler's Wells Ballet and the Covent Garden Opera: a photographic record·by Edward Mandinian with the Preface to the Original Text, a Preface by Prof. E. J. Dent, and articles by Constant Lambert and Michael Ayrton. John Lehmann, London, 1948.

The Rape of Lucretia: a symposium by Benjamin Britten, Ronald Duncan, John Piper, Henry Boys, Eric Crozier, Angus McBean. The Bodley Head, London, 1948.

ROYAL MUSICAL ASSOCIATION, PROCEEDINGS OF:

J. SIMS REEVES, *My Jubilee, or, Fifty Years of Artistic Life*. The London Music Publishing Co. Ltd., London, 1889.

CHARLES RICE, *The London Theatre in the Eighteen-Thirties*. The Society for Theatre Research, London, 1950. (Contains contemporary notices of *The Mountain Sylph, The Maid of Artois* and *Catherine Gray*.)

ARUNDELL, DENNIS, *Operatic Ignorance*, 1925 (LI, 73).

BOUGHTON, RUTLAND, *A National Music Drama*, 1917 (XLIV, 19).

CUMMINGS, W. H., *The Lord Chamberlain and Opera in London 1700-1740*, 1914 (XL, 37).

DENT, E. J., *English Opera*, 1926 (LII, 71). *The Translation of Operas*, 1935 (LXI, 81).

CHARLES SANTLEY, *Reminiscences of My Life*. Sir Isaac Pitman & Sons, Ltd., London, 1909.

Student and Singer. Edward Arnold, London, 1892.

PERCY A. SCHOLES, *The Mirror of Music* (1844–1944): *A Century of Musical Life in Britain as reflected in the pages of the Musical Times*. 2 vols. Novello & Co., Ltd. and Oxford University Press, 1947.

BERNARD SHAW, *London Music in* 1888–89 *as heard by Corno di Bassetto*. Constable, London, 1937. (Contains reviews of revivals of *Robin Hood* and *Lurline*.)

Music in London 1890–94. 3 vols. Constable, London, 1932. (Contains reviews of the first performances of *Ivanhoe*, *The Mountebanks*, *The Light of Asia*, *Haddon Hall*, *Caedmar*, *The Magic Opal*, *The Golden Web*, *Utopia* (*Limited*), *Signa*.)

C. J. SISSON, *Lost Plays of Shakespeare's Age*. Cambridge University Press, 1936. (Mentions two hitherto unpublished jigs.)

ETHEL SMYTH, *Impressions that Remained*. 2 vols. Longmans, Green & Co., London, 1919.

Beecham and Pharaoh. Chapman & Hall, Ltd., London, 1935.

As Time Went On. Longmans, Green & Co., London, 1937.

What Happened Next. Longmans, Green & Co., London, 1940.

C. V. STANFORD, *Studies and Memories*. Constable, London, 1908. (This contains Stanford's paper 'The Case for National Opera'.)

Pages from an Unwritten Diary. Edward Arnold, London, 1914.

R. A. STREATFEILD, *The Opera: A Sketch of the Development of Opera with full Descriptions of all Works in the Modern Repertory*. Routledge & Kegan Paul Ltd., London, 1896. Fifth Edition, revised and enlarged by Edward J. Dent, 1925. (Chapter XVI is devoted to English Opera.)

J. A. WESTRUP, *Purcell*. J. M. Dent & Sons, Ltd., London, 1937.

ERIC WALTER WHITE, *Benjamin Britten: a sketch of his life and works*. Boosey & Hawkes, London, 1948.

H. SAXE WYNDHAM, *The Annals of Covent Garden*. 2 vols. Chatto and Windus, London, 1906.

INDEX

1. All references to English operas in the text and in Appendix E are indexed—
also the greater part of the material in Appendix A. English opera entries are followed
by the year of first performance, which enables reference to be made to the details of
each particular opera in Appendix A. Where an English opera has not been performed,
the composer's name is added between brackets.

2. References to foreign operas in the text and in Appendices B, C and E are
indexed. Foreign opera entries are followed by the composer's name.

3. References to opera houses and theatres are indexed under the names of the
towns in which they are situated. For instance, the Royal Opera House, Covent Garden,
is to be found under the general heading "London Theatres, Opera Houses," etc.

A BASSO PORTO (Spinelli),
297
à Beckett, Gilbert, 194, 257
ABROAD AND AT HOME
(1796), 238
ABU HASSAN (Weber), 280
ACHILLES (1733), 225
ACHILLES IN PETTICOATS
(1773), 231
ACIS AND GALATEA (1732),
59, 146, 186, 224
Act of 1916, Finance, 162
Act of 1737, Licensing, 108
Act of 1948, Local Govern-
ment, 165
Act of 1843 for Regulating
Theatres, 108, 109, 159
Adam, Adolphe Charles,
293
Addison, Joseph, 47, 48, 49,
60, 219, 225
ADMETO (1727), 58, 221
ADVENTURE OF DON QUIXOTE
AN (1846), 90, 100, 250
AETHIOP, THE (1812), 90, 242
AGRIPPINA (1709), 53, 219
AÏDA (Verdi), 120, 169, 208,
289, 294
ALADDIN (1826), 90-1, 244
ALARBAS (Anon), 48
Albeniz, Isaac, 259
ALBERT HERRING (1947), 115,
155, 156, 171, 189, 201,
273, 313
ALBION AND ALBANIUS
(1685), 37, 38-40, 47,
50, 191, 216
ALCESTE (Gluck), 62, 276
ALCHIMIST, DER (1925), 137,
269
ALCINA (1735), 226
Aldeburgh, 156
Festival, 156, 171, 172, 204
Jubilee Hall, 156, 274

ALESSANDRO (1726), 221
Algarotti, Count, 62, 63,
188
ALGONAH (1802), 240
ALKESTIS (1922), 145, 149,
150-1, 267, 314
ALL FOOL'S DAY (1921), 151,
153, 267
ALLAN OF ABERFELDY (Mac-
farren), 100 n.
ALMAHIDE (G. Bononcini),
49
ALMENA (1764), 70, 77,
229
ALMIRA (1705), 52, 218
AMADIGI DI GAULA (1715),
55, 220
AMBER WITCH, THE (1861),
111, 189, 253
AMELIA (1732), 59, 224
AMERICANS, THE (1811),
242
AMICO FRITZ, L' (Mascagni),
295
AMILIE (1837), 93, 247
AMY ROBSART (1893), 86,
259, 266
Andersen, Hans Christian,
85
ANDRÉ CHENIER (Giordano),
297
ANDROMÈDE (Dassoucy), 35
ANGELINA (Bishop), 87
ANGELUS, THE (1909), 263
ANNO ED UN GIORNO, UN
(1836), 90, 246
APOLLO AND HYACINTH
(Mozart), 14
Appia, Adolphe, 190
ARABELLA (R. Strauss), 292
Arditi, Luigi, 105
Argyll, Duke of, 119
ARIADNE IN CRETE (1734),
225

ARIADNE AUF NAXOS (R.
Strauss), 144, 292
ARIANE (Cambert), 37
ARIODANTE (1735), 226
Ariosti, Attilio, 55
ARMIDE (Gluck), 276, 312
ARMINIO (1737), 226
ARMOURER OF NANTES, THE
(1863), 253
Arne, Michael, 70, 229, 231,
233
Arne, Thomas Augustine,
59-61, 70, 71, 74, 225-
32
Arnold, Samuel, 70, 71,
229-39, 279
ARSINOE (1705), 48, 219
ARTAMENE (Gluck), 275
ARTAXERXES (1762), 61, 74,
79, 87, 92, 186, 228
ARTIFICE, THE (1780), 233
Arts Council of Great
Britain, The, 164-5,
168, 169, 206, 207, 208
ASTIANATTE (Bononcini), 55
AT THE BOAR'S HEAD (1925),
145, 183, 269
AT SANTA LUCIA (Tasca), 296
AT THE SIGN OF THE STAR
(1929), 270
ATALANTA (1736), 226
ATTAQUE DU MOULIN, L'
(Bruneau), 298
ATTILA (Verdi), 287
ATTOWELL'S JIG (1595), 214
Attwood, Thomas, 87, 237,
239, 243
Auber, Daniel, 85, 87, 103
Auden, W. H., 167, 213,
273
AULD ROBIN GRAY (Arnold,
1794), 238
(Lee, 1828), 244
(Mackinlay, 1858), 252